Douglas MacArthur

THE PHILIPPINE YEARS

Douglas MacArthur

THE PHILIPPINE YEARS

Carol Morris Petillo

INDIANA UNIVERSITY PRESS BLOOMINGTON

To
Jay, Chris,
Anna, and Joe

Library of Congress Cataloging in Publication Data

Petillo, Carol Morris, 1940–
  Douglas MacArthur, the Philippine years.

  Bibliography: p.
  Includes index.
  1. MacArthur, Douglas, 1880–1964. 2. United States—
History, Military—20th century.   3. Philippines—History, Military.   4. Generals—United States—Biography.
5. United States.   Army—Biography.   I. Title.
E745.M3P43   959.9'03'0924 [B]   81–47166
ISBN 0–253–11248–6   AACR2
1 2 3 4 5 85 84 83 82 81

Contents

Introduction

MORE THAN ONE QUARTER of Douglas MacArthur's professional career was spent in the Philippine Islands. There, in 1903 and 1904, he served his first tour after graduation from West Point. There, nearly forty years later, he faced what he for a time believed would be his last battle. In the years between, he returned to the archipelago again and again in positions of increasing power. Just as he became more and more important to the Islands, the Philippines took on a more significant role for MacArthur. His first vision, shaped through the medium of his father's experience there during and shortly after the Spanish-American War, gave to the beautiful Islands a particularly personal definition. With each return, the support, friendship, and security that he found there took on added weight within the boundaries of his view of the world. There he could prove himself in ways unavailable elsewhere. There, also, he could find solace and support when failure on other fronts seemed imminent. For forty years, the Philippine Islands provided both safe haven and appropriate center stage for Douglas MacArthur. The development of this complex relationship between the man and the country is the focus of this study.

From the outset, this project has been shaped by two concerns. The first was an attempt to delineate MacArthur's Philippine experience. The second evolved from my longstanding conviction that analysis of the public activities of world leaders cannot stand alone. While certainly easier to define, public life nonetheless represents only the tip of the iceberg, and it is often impossible to understand unless an assessment of the private concerns, motivating factors, and patterns of adaptation of the individual is made. Needless to say, this is almost always much more difficult. The sources necessary for this type of analysis have usually never existed or been overlooked and discarded as unimportant. In many cases, the private documentation in the form of personal letters and diaries is deliberately destroyed in an attempt to hide motives which have been considered by previous generations as at best private and at worst dishonorable. All of these difficulties face the MacArthur scholar and insure that any attempt at personality analysis will be, at best, sketchy and speculative. Nonetheless, since most readers in the post-Freudian age infer some psychological interpretation into any supposedly "objective" analysis, this interpretation and its foundations will be as explicit as possible.

The first goal, to tell the story, was reasonably easy to achieve. Although tracing MacArthur's years in the Philippines involved thousands of miles of travel and months of sifting through sources, there was, nonetheless, more than enough material to be found. In the diaries, letters, memoirs, and transcribed interviews of many American veterans who had served in the Islands and later left their records to the United States Army Military History Institute, I was able to find details specifically relevant to MacArthur's Philippine experience as well as learn the more general characteristics of this American military adventure in the Pacific. In the personal and public papers of Manuel Quezon, Sergio Osmeña, Manuel Roxas, and Jorge Vargas in Manila, I obtained a Philippine perspective for my study. The papers of Leonard Wood, Henry Stimson, and Harold Ickes, to mention only a few, provided new insights into these years when one looked specifically for that information. Finally, and of particular interest, were the recently opened papers of General Richard K. Sutherland, MacArthur's chief of staff during World War II.

My second task, to understand MacArthur's personal motivation and lifelong behavioral patterns as they applied to the Philippine years, was much more difficult. Intent upon obscuring any visions which conflicted with the carefully nurtured public image that he himself wished to convey, the General seems to have made certain that many of the sources which would be helpful in this regard would not be available. In addition, the fact that most of his personal papers from the first sixty years were left behind in Manila in 1941 and thereafter destroyed by both the Japanese and American onslaughts which followed made the search even more difficult. Nonetheless, some of the letters and private writings found, or analyzed here for the first time, provide new insights in this direction. Most helpful in this regard were the letters of MacArthur's mother, and his maternal grandmother and grandfather. Other letters, written by the General at the time of his mother's death, were found in the papers of John Callan O'Laughlin, another source previously unexamined by MacArthur scholars. Poetry written by MacArthur in the period around 1908 was also helpful to this study. Finally, interviews with relatives and acquaintances of Isabel Cooper provided new insight into a particularly hidden and personal aspect of the General's life. These sources, largely overlooked in previous studies, provide much of the basis for the personality study. If the admittedly scant and highly speculative analysis, which grows out of these records, is not as easily verifiable as are the battle plans and political mechanisms usually studied by the historian, they nonetheless complement previous understanding of the man. It must be clearly understood, however, that this psychological interpretation is by no means an attempt to explain all of MacArthur's experience—or to provide a complete psychological portrait—only to add one more new dimension to the existing scholarship.

In combination with these sparse but intriguing new sources, certain interpretive models have informed my analysis. Foremost among these are the theories of Sigmund Freud, Erik Erikson, and George Vaillant. The advantage of any theory is not that it provides an all-inclusive answer to the historical "why," but that it offers suggestions for further empirical research, and new perspectives from which to evaluate data. The theoretical assumptions of these three men certainly follow this prescription, and although the work of each is subject to certain criticisms, together they form helpful ways of discerning personality.

Most psychoanalytic perspectives have a core of Freudian, or id-directed explanation, arguing that infantile, four-phase sexual integration (polymorphous, oral, anal, and genital), or the failure thereof, is the determining factor in personality. Although it is often criticized as particularly culture-bound, Freudian theory nonetheless provides one valuable level of insight into the life of a man like MacArthur, who was as much a product of Victorian repressions and beliefs as was Freud himself. The General's personality development was, I believe, shaped very much by the physiological and culturally imposed sexual repressions to which Freud directed his inquiries.

There were, however, many other developmental influences in MacArthur's life. If people are partly shaped by the success or failure of their sexual integration, much more is also involved. Reality factors such as class, time, inheritance, and opportunity must not be overlooked. In an attempt to include these other considerations, the neo-Freudians, led by Erik Erikson, offer an explanation which incorporates both conscious choice and external happenings. Building upon his acceptance of the essential validity of the Freudian insights, Erikson has developed a model which, although certainly not all-inclusive, attempts to explain the interaction among these unconscious impulses, conscious choices, and the cultural and social influences which shape them. The model, which Erikson has called "the eight ages of man," provides one framework through which human development may be observed. This view also encourages more than the simple diagnosis of pathology so long the hindrance of early "psychobiographies," and instead emphasizes standard psychic activity. In other words, Erikson believes that within specific cultural boundaries, all individuals are faced with growth tasks that they must successfully accomplish at certain ages, insofar as their capacities will allow at the moment. If these efforts are successful, the individual is free to move onto more complex developmental phases, each of which incorporates and subsumes all those which have gone before. If for some reason one phase cannot be successfully integrated within the individual, then that person's continued development is contingent upon the successful resolution of this situation at some later stage or a practical adaptation to the continuing crisis evoked by this lack of resolution. If an integration is not achieved, the personality structure of the individual takes on specific dimensions subject to the contours of this unresolved task.

It is important to emphasize that within the Eriksonian model no phase stands alone. All developmental tasks continually reassert themselves in the face of more complex experience. Successful resolution at one stage, however, encourages continued adjustment as the individual matures. Just as important, the various degrees of integration achieved are not meant to imply attached value judgments. The eight stages as outlined by Erikson include: trust vs. mistrust; autonomy vs. shame, doubt; initiative vs. guilt; industry vs. inferiority; identity vs. identity confusion; intimacy vs. isolation; generativity vs. stagnation; and integrity vs. despair. In their entirety, they are meant to cover the normal human life span. In his work of the last twenty-five years, particularly in *Childhood and Society, Young Man Luther,* and *Gandhi's Truth,* the Eriksonian model and its importance to the biographical process have become increasingly clear.

The Eriksonian approach, however, while very helpful for studies which involve childhood and adolescence, diminishes in vision for the mature years. Since leadership analyses almost invariably focus on the adulthood of the individuals involved, this poses a serious problem. Nonetheless, more recent analysts, continuing to build on the work of Freud and Erikson, have begun to remedy the situation. In the work of George Vaillant, in particular, this problem becomes somewhat easier to solve. Vaillant, although firmly in the Eriksonian camp, has been

forced by his role in the Grant Study, a longitudinal study of
Harvard undergraduates undertaken in 1937 and still continuing, to examine developmental experiences and patterns of adaptation in mature individuals. His findings, strengthened by
empirical studies of more than forty years, are clearly explained
in his recently published *Adaptation to Life.* Although his study
and analysis deal with men somewhat younger than Douglas
MacArthur, they focus most helpfully on individuals who in
many cases became leaders and, as did MacArthur, achieved
success and a reasonable amount of adjustment according to the
values of their society. Vaillant, while not denying the importance of the Freudian vision nor the Eriksonian adaptation
thereof, argues convincingly that longstanding relationships
and adaptive patterns, which develop over many years, are just
as influential in explaining personality as are childhood sexual
adjustments and adolescent identity formation processes. It is a
point of view which is, I believe, firmly substantiated by MacArthur's experience.

While this examination of Douglas MacArthur has been informed by the insights of these three men, as well as many
others in their field, I have in no way felt constrained to follow
their explanations rigidly. On the contrary, the psychological
aspect of this interpretation should be regarded as only one tool
employed in the overall analysis of MacArthur's years in the
Philippines; the psychological explanations, when offered,
should be considered as only possible ways to more completely
understand occurrences which were also shaped by economic,
social, and historical realities outside the realm of the psyche.
This approach, while providing additional insight, has forced
certain structural difficulties on the study.

As a consequence, this study of Douglas MacArthur's Philippine years is really an examination of Douglas MacArthur's life
through the end of World War II, with an emphasis on the time
spent in the Philippines. The psychological explanation could
not stand without a thorough examination of the childhood
experience. The four separate tours in the Islands made no
sense unless placed in the context of the rest of his life. To

facilitate these two requirements within the space of this study, I have attempted to summarize the non-Philippine years briefly. Only occasionally, in instances when the work of other scholars did not offer enough information, have I developed new documentation for those periods. For the summaries which connect the Philippine years, I have relied heavily on the many previous studies of Douglas MacArthur's life.

Aside from the popular, mythic, and episodic treatments of MacArthur which began to surface in the thirties and reached mammoth proportions in 1942, the literature surrounding the General's life can be divided into three categories. The first category, which includes at least one complete biography, several partial studies, and the memoirs of the General and several of his close associates, is, on the whole, seriously flawed. In the main, MacArthur tended to encourage only those studies which would favor his public image. As a consequence, the works of Frazier Hunt, and of Clark Lee and Richard Henschel, to name only the most comprehensive, were intriguing in their use of information never thereafter available to other scholars, but weakened by their attempts to justify all of MacArthur's activities as sound, honorable, and disinterested. The memoirs which began to appear during the fifties and sixties were largely written by the "Bataan Gang," and were almost exclusively efforts to persuade the public that MacArthur was indeed an almost superhuman leader, and that, more importantly, all the activities of the General and his advisers after the beginning of World War II were the result of unselfishness, immense foresight, and totally honorable goals. When failure could not be hidden, it was attributed to a conspiracy in Washington. Foremost among these accounts was the work of Courtney Whitney. Others, somewhat less biased and more reasonable, include the stories of Sidney Huff, Charles Willoughby, and Carlos Romulo. General MacArthur himself contributed to this genre when, just before his death, he finally published his long-awaited *Reminiscences.* This work, often mistaken in detail, and in large part an attempt to justify the controversial incidents of his last twenty-four years, additionally encouraged the myth and obscured the reality of MacArthur. It is, nonetheless, a valuable source for the historian interested in the inner workings of the General's mind and memory.

The second category of MacArthur literature includes studies of the General as soldier and as a world leader. Without exception, these works examined the World War II years and, less often, Korea. They study questions of strategy, tactics, and the mechanics of leadership and unfortunately often assume that individual public action is largely disconnected from private motivation or experiences. On the whole these efforts were scholarly, objective, and vital to an understanding of what actually happened at times when historical reality complicated and made difficult any rational understanding of events. Particularly helpful examples of this type of study were the efforts of Louis Morton, Richard Rovere, Arthur M. Schlesinger, John Jacob Beck, and Gavin Long.

Finally, and most important to this effort, are the two major biographies of the General. William Manchester's recently published *American Caesar* is a popular, one-volume account of the General's life. With its skillful use of language and understanding of the importance of dramatic emphasis, Manchester's work provides a manageable, easily readable, and exciting account of the General's career. There are, however, few new insights, and for the serious scholar, little helpful direction. Those truly interested in the overall definition of MacArthur's life must rely, as did Manchester, on the enterprise of D. Clayton James.

Devoting what will, in the end, total nearly two decades to the project, Professor James has already produced two volumes of a projected three-volume life-and-times study entitled *The Years of MacArthur.* Since the publication of the first volume in 1970, all future MacArthur scholars have found within its covers a wealth of information, detail, clues to further research, and a reasoned and even interpretation of the public man. Without this source, the enormity of research projects into the General's long and heavily documented life would undoubtedly daunt even the most valiant historian. Nonetheless, James also spends most of his energies on the years after 1941. In fact, two of the three volumes deal with only one quarter of the General's long life. The other sixty years are relegated to the first and shortest volume. There are practical reasons for this decision. First, the last twenty-four years of MacArthur's life contain more of importance to the broader picture of modern American experience. Second, they are much easier to document. As the General entered the mainstream of American leadership during those years, nearly everyone who came into contact with him kept records of his public activities. In fact, the major problem with the sources from this period is that there are too many rather than too few. The earlier years create the opposite problem and, as a consequence, are much more difficult to discuss with certainty.

Professor James, nonetheless, does touch on the issues of these first sixty years with precision and care. As he himself points out, however, certain aspects of those years require more detailed research and interpretation. Among these are the Philippine years which have been obscured by distance, disinterest, and the difficulty of incorporating the perspective of a developing nation into our view of MacArthur. Although James carefully develops the years leading up to World War II in the Islands, the other three tours of duty which MacArthur spent in the Philippines are only briefly described. Unable to visit Manila, James was largely limited to records maintained in the Army files from the period, the few remnants from these years which have found their way into the MacArthur Archives, and contemporary newspaper accounts. With rare exception, he did not examine the newest Philippine-American scholarship. In addition, certain recently opened sources were not available at the time Professor James was conducting his research on this period. Therefore, because James did not deal as effectively with the Philippine years as with the later years, and because I believe that the Philippine years provided the understanding and impetus which later shaped and explained MacArthur's activities in the other areas of his life, I have felt justified in separating these periods out for special emphasis.

Douglas MacArthur's first glimpse of the Philippine Islands was secondhand. His father, serving there at the turn of the century both as military commander and first military governor, conveyed to his son an assessment of the Pacific and its importance to the United States that Douglas would hold all the rest of his life. In addition, Arthur MacArthur's unusual appreciation of the Filipinos and their national interest encouraged a parallel sympathy and understanding in his son.

In 1903, as a young engineer fresh out of West Point, MacArthur first visited the Islands. Stationed both in the provinces and in the capital, he experienced the excitement of still-uncontained postrevolutionary activity as well as the cosmopolitan life of Manila. His individual successes during this period coupled with the romance and sanctuary offered by the archipelago always thereafter encouraged MacArthur to return. Further, the tour of the Orient with his parents during 1905–1906 confirmed many of the insights he had drawn from his first Philippine tour.

Eighteen years separated MacArthur's first and second visits to the Islands. When he returned in 1922, he had seen service throughout the world, and achieved the rank of brigadier general for his leadership in World War I and later at West Point. His vision and perceptions had certainly changed in nearly two decades, but once again the Philippines offered a special haven. Here, somehow protected from the attacks and disloyalty of the military establishment in Washington to which he and his family had always felt prey, he was free to grow within the confines of command responsibilities, professional and personal friendships, and familial pressures. During these three years, he flourished professionally and strengthened many of the relationships which would later be so important to him.

In 1928 he once again found himself in Manila—this time as Commander of the Philippine Department. With the failure of his first marriage and the onset of his middle years, MacArthur this time sought even more from the Islands. Perhaps they could provide another outlet for his overriding ambitions. Certainly, for a time, he believed that one of their most beautiful women could help him adjust to the increased insecurities of his personal life. This time, as he later recalled, he wanted very much to stay in the Philippines.

Finally, in 1935, after a five-year period as Chief of Staff of the Army in Washington, the General found his chance. He would return to Manila to serve as Military Adviser to the newly established Philippine Commonwealth Government. Had world affairs not intervened, there are some indications that he would have lived out the rest of his life in the Islands. There his mother died, and there he found a new and remarkably suitable wife. There his only child was born.

Douglas MacArthur was born at one Army post, raised at several others, and spent fifty more years in makeshift quarters around the world. After his retirement, he chose to spend the rest of his days in a hotel. He changed his legal residence from Wisconsin to Virginia for simple convenience. He lived only briefly in Wisconsin, and never in Virginia. In one sense, the General had no home. And yet, on another level, one place fulfilled these needs. He both began and ended his career in the Pacific, and within that realm, the Philippine Islands were of special importance. Their beauty and the friendship nurtured there sustained Douglas MacArthur as no other place had ever done. If their hopes sometimes encouraged his capacity for vast misjudgment, their sacrifice inspired his greatest successes. For Douglas MacArthur, the Philippines were home. For this reason, their influence on the man deserves consideration.

This work was made possible with the help of many people. Foremost of these were three friends at Rutgers University, Lloyd Gardner, Philip Greven, and Richard Kohn. Without their guidance, advice, confidence, and patience, these pages would never have been written. Their professional wisdom, and, more importantly, their friendship, made the time necessary for this study well spent. In addition, I am also particularly grateful to the United States Army Center of Military History, Washington, D.C., the Eleanor Roosevelt Institute, Hyde Park, N.Y., and the Philippine National Library, Manila, P.I., for the funds and technical support which underwrote my research.

In addition to their formal support of my research, the people in the Center of Military History served as an informal support system during my months in Washington, and my thanks go to everyone there, especially to Robert Ross Smith, Detmar Finke, and William Strobridge. Archivists in the many repositories that I visited frequently offered advice and assistance far beyond reasonable expectations. This is particularly true of John E. Taylor, George Challou, Edward Reese, and Timothy Nenninger of the National Archives, Richard I. Sommers at the U.S. Army Military History Institute, Adoracion M. Bolos of the Philippine National Library, and Mauro Garcia of the Vargas Foundation. Many scholars in the fields of both Philippine and American history have offered comments and encouragement, and I am grateful to Peter W. Stanley, Forrest C. Pogue, Edward M. Coffman, Henry I. Tragle, Vicente Pacis, Richard Immerman, Keith Nelson, D. Clayton James, and Robert Sherrod for their advice and criticism. Any errors of fact or interpretation are, of course, my own.

During my travels, many more people smoothed the way than I could ever thank individually. Certain of these, however, deserve special mention: Lewis Gleeck, Jr., Tom Carter and Mercedes Sotelo, Harry A. Edelstein, Mr. & Mrs. Ray B. Liberato, Bonifacio Salamanca, the Antonio Quirino family, and B. B. Figueroa in the Philippines, as well as Donald P. Shaw, Allen Cooper, William W. Jenna, Jr., and my many friends in the history departments at Rutgers University and Boston College here in the United States. Virginia Grogan's assistance, as well as her patience and good cheer, contributed greatly to the final production of the manuscript.

I am particularly indebted to Wayne Cooper for his helpful advice and steadfast support throughout this long project, and to my parents, AnnaBelle and Carroll Morris, who have always been especially patient and encouraging of my efforts. Finally, to my children, Jay, Chris, Anna, and Joe, to whom this work is dedicated, I owe a very special debt which only they and I can understand.

(1)

The Early Years

Whenever I perform a mission and think
I have done it well, I feel that I can stand
up squarely to my dad and say, "Governor, how about it?"

Douglas MacArthur
Tokyo, late 1940s[1]

DOUGLAS MACARTHUR was past sixty-five when he uttered
these words, and the "Governor" had been dead for more than
thirty years. Yet the patterns of adaptation that the son developed during his long life clearly supported his remark. To an
unusual degree, Douglas MacArthur's values, fears, strengths,
and weaknesses stemmed from his first years of family experience. No understanding of the man can be complete without a
close investigation of the lives of his austere and upright father,
his determined mother, and the brothers whom he lost. Only
then do the sources of the energy which impelled MacArthur to
his greatest victories as well as to his subsequent defeats
emerge.

Arthur MacArthur, Jr., was the son of an immigrant barrister
who achieved national prominence in the late nineteenth century.[2] The MacArthurs of Wisconsin were linked by tradition to
the MacArtairs of Scotland, a warrior clan of medieval fame, and
a source of great pride for their descendants.[3] As he grew up in
Milwaukee, Arthur, Jr., heard of their adventures, and both he
and his father, Judge Arthur MacArthur, Sr., impressed upon
young Douglas the importance of carrying on the worthy traditions of this heritage.

From all accounts, Arthur, Jr.'s childhood was secure and
uneventful. This changed when he decided to join the Union
Army at the outset of the Civil War. His father (Douglas's grand-

father), recently elected judge of Wisconsin's second judicial circuit, disagreed with this decision and arranged for the young patriot to spend a year in a private military school. When this did not dissuade the boy from his goal, the Judge sought an appointment to West Point for his son. The young, would-be soldier was taken to visit President Abraham Lincoln by a family friend serving in Congress, but an immediate appointment to the academy could not be arranged. Although a nomination was promised for the next year, young Arthur could wait no longer. In a surge of youthful independence, encouraged by tales of military adventure he had devoured as a boy, he volunteered for duty with the 24th Wisconsin Infantry and in late summer, 1862, was commissioned first lieutenant of volunteers. He was only seventeen, and although later he would make a halfhearted attempt to train for the legal profession—his father's first choice for him—he believed already that he had been called to the glory and the romance of military life. Wisely, the Judge chose not to pursue the conflict further, and the possibility of a family rift was averted.

Throughout the rest of his life, Arthur, Jr., felt that his Civil War adventures were the most significant in his long military career. Certainly, they were the most exciting. In the fall of 1862, the young Lieutenant, serving in Philip A. Sheridan's division in the Army of the Ohio, performed bravely in the battle of Perryville (Kentucky) and was promoted to brevet captain. By midwinter, Captain MacArthur had helped to occupy Nashville and had distinguished himself once again, this time in the Battle of Stone's River, where according to one observer, "by his ringing orders and perfect coolness [he checked] the impending panic, restored confidence, rallied and held the regiment in line."[4] In a young man who had not yet celebrated his eighteenth birthday, this bravery and presence of mind were indeed impressive.

The high point of Arthur MacArthur, Jr.'s Civil War career occurred on November 25, 1863, at the Battle of Missionary Ridge. As the first phase of an effort to dislodge General Braxton Bragg's Confederate troops from their stronghold around

Chattanooga, General Ulysses S. Grant, commanding the newly strengthened Union forces, ordered General George H. Thomas's Army of the Cumberland to capture the Confederate rifle pits at the foot of the ridge. The Union troops, with the 24th Wisconsin positioned in the center of the line, succeeded beyond all expectations. When the smoke of battle cleared, they had achieved not only the limited objective assigned to them, but, contrary to orders, mounted a frenzied charge up the ridge, routed Bragg's troops entrenched on the crest, and won the position for the Union. According to some accounts, young Arthur's part in this valiant movement was vital to its success, and later earned him a Congressional Medal of Honor. His son best conveyed its glory in these words:

> No one seems to know just what orders may have been given, but suddenly the flag of the 24th Wisconsin started forward. With it was the color sergeant, the color guard of two corporals, and the adjutant [Captain MacArthur]. . . . Down went the color bearer. One of the corporals seized the colors as they fell, but was bayoneted before he could move. A shell took off the head of the other corporal, but the adjutant grasped the flag and kept on. . . . A Confederate colonel thrust viciously at his throat, but even as he lunged a bullet struck and the deflected blade just ripped a shoulder strap. No movement yet from the Union lines. And then, above the roar of battle, sounded the adjutant's voice: "On, Wisconsin!"
>
> They come then; they come with a rush and a roar, a blue tide of courage, a whole division of them. Shouting, cursing, struggling foot by foot, heads bent as in a gale! Gasping breath from tortured lungs! . . . Men tumble over like tenpins! The charge is losing momentum! They falter! Officers are down! Sergeants now lead! And then, suddenly, on the crest—the flag! Once again that cry: "On, Wisconsin!" Silhouetted against the sky, the adjutant stands on the parapet waving the colors where the whole regiment can see him! Through the ragged blue line, from one end of the division to the other, comes an ugly roar, like the growl of a wounded bear! They race those last few steps, eyes blazing, lips snarling, bayonets plunging! And Missionary Ridge is won.[5]

The accuracy of this account may be questioned. More important, however, was the mythic weight the story was given in the MacArthur family tradition. Seen as the most glorious moment of his career, the father, Arthur, Jr., often repeated the account to his young son Douglas. For the son, it became an icon, an image of valor after which he would pattern his own behavior whenever circumstances allowed. The young Adjutant, forever silhouetted in his mind's eye, served Douglas always as his most significant hero and, in less confident moments, as his most formidable competitor as well. The young man who became his father taught Douglas to be brave in the face of great danger, and he taught him one thing more. As his father emphasized in each retelling, and as Douglas later recounted to at least one future biographer, sometimes one had to decide for oneself the relevancy of orders.[6] Had not his own defiance achieved more in this battle, and more for his career, than all the long dutiful years which followed on the frontier? It was a lesson the son took seriously.

Shortly after the Battle of Missionary Ridge, Arthur Mac-Arthur, Jr., was advanced to major and put in command of the 24th Wisconsin. During the rest of the war, he served valiantly in Tennessee and Georgia, and displayed unusual leadership potential during a reconnaisance at the beginning of the Battle of Kenesaw Mountain. His last combat experience, at Franklin, Tennessee, in December 1864, resulted in serious wounds which forced him to retire from active duty. For this engagement, he was commended for "gallant and Meritorious service."[7] In June 1865 he was discharged from the army with the permanent volunteer rank of lieutenant colonel.

Back in Milwaukee, the young man faced a difficult choice. Across the country, the cities and towns of the victorious North feted their brave veterans. Milwaukee was no exception. His outstanding military successes, as well as his father's political position, assured that Arthur, Jr., would be the center of many of these celebrations, and he enjoyed them as only one who has just turned twenty can. But the plaudits soon faded, and it was time to think about what he would do with the rest of his life.

In the late 1860s, the reestablished Union, increasingly nationalized and with a strong sense of the opportunities made possible by its recent victory, stood on the brink of a period of great expansion. While the problems of Reconstruction demanded the attention of federal leaders, the rest of the country restlessly sought to take advantage of Republican war legislation, which encouraged westward movement, a national transportation system, rapid industrial development, and increased educational opportunity. A sense of new beginning filled the air, and the MacArthurs, representative of many of their class and place at this time, were not immune to its persuasion.

For the family, it was a time of personal readjustment as well. When his wife died in 1864, the Judge was forced to face the sole responsibility of raising his eleven-year-old son, Frank. The older son's return lightened this burden, and the Judge renewed his attempt to convince his namesake to join him in the practice of law. Arthur, Sr., anticipated wider political horizons for himself and believed he could ease his elder son's reentry into civilian life and on to success in an honorable profession. Young Arthur reluctantly acquiesced and for the next few months he read law under his father's tutelage. By early 1866, however, he abandoned this hesitant attempt and chose, instead, to accept a commission as second lieutenant in the Regular Army. He would leave the opportunity to carry on the family's legal tradition to his brother Frank.[8]

From a practical standpoint, Arthur, Jr.'s decision was surprising. While chances for civilian success expanded impressively during these years, a military career offered no comparable opportunities. Following longstanding American tradition, Congress immediately began to cut back military appropriations at war's end. The generally accepted opinion held that the nation need make only a limited commitment to an army which would serve, at most, as a constabulary force. Recalcitrant Southerners and headstrong Indians would be its chief concern, and neither had the capacity to offer much resistance.[9] Consequent reductions in the strength of the officer corps meant that advancement would be slow and painful. Second Lieutenant MacArthur's commission, despite entreaties from his father's friends and many of his own recent commanding officers, reflected this reality. What, then, impelled him to this decision? One can never be certain, but at an age when self-definition often required rejection of roles which seemed safe, the young man was drawn inexorably to a career of risk and romance. He had always loved tales of military adventure, and his recent martial experience only served to reinforce this predilection. If the Civil War had not occurred when it did, he might have been content to contain his military enthusiasm in fantasy. If he had not succeeded so completely and performed so brilliantly in the war, the attraction might have waned. But social reality, coupled with personal needs and adequate reinforcement, provided many reasons for his decision. Others might seek advancement in the opportunity offered by what has come to be known as the "age of big business," but for Arthur MacArthur, Jr., the parapet called. The borders of his identity were defined by what he would *not* do. His self-image needed a broader canvas than that provided by an urban legal career. He would wait nearly twenty years before this inner choice was validated by external events.

The years between 1866 and 1874 provided ample opportunity for the young man to develop expertise in his chosen field. Although chance for promotion ended shortly after his reentry —when he achieved the rank of captain—sources of new experience were everywhere. After brief stints with the 17th and 26th Infantry regiments, he was assigned to the 36th Infantry, duty he held until mid-1870. Although most of this period was spent in the territories of Nebraska, Colorado, Dakota, and Wyoming, twice he was given the opportunity to contrast these arid vistas with the complexities of life in New York City. On the second assignment to the city, as a recruiting officer, he was reassigned once again, this time to the 13th Infantry, one of the oldest and proudest regiments in the United States Army.[10] The association lasted nineteen years. Weakened by the postwar Army retrenchment, the 13th (with Captain MacArthur commanding Company "K") was, predictably, assigned to frontier duty. From

1870 to 1874 the regiment served in the Utah and Wyoming territories, where its commanding officer, Colonel Philippe Régis de Trobriand, faced Mormons and Sioux alike with equanimity.[11] Diplomacy and guard duty more frequently involved the regiment than did the necessity for military engagement. Nevertheless, those eight years provided much that was new for the developing young officer, and on the surface, those years seemed to provide interest and satisfaction. Closer examination of the record, however, suggests that seeds of discontent, nurtured by the frustration of slow advancement, already had begun to grow within the maturing soldier.

From the very beginning of his military career, Arthur MacArthur, Jr., had been encouraged to seek special notice through the auspices of his father's influential political and military acquaintances. Although these attempts met with little success during the war years, both the Judge and the young soldier were not discouraged, and when he reentered the Army in 1866, Arthur, Jr., almost immediately began to use these channels again. Although not unique, the intensity of these efforts reflected early disenchantment with the progress of his career and, more significantly, a sense of frustration at what he saw as his unrecognized potential. In October 1866, only eight months after accepting his commission, he began his campaign for this recognition with a letter to Postmaster General S.W. Randall. In this letter, Arthur, Jr., explained to Randall that he had recently received orders to move to Texas with the 26th Infantry. At the same time, Judge MacArthur had told him about his forthcoming promotion to captain in the 36th Infantry. Arguing that the promotion would cancel the transfer, he asked Randall to bring this to the attention of the Secretary of War. The request, although reasonable, certainly disregarded ordinary military channels of communication. Even more revealing, however, was the concluding paragraph: "This fortunate promotion, now, my [*sic*] decide my life. The undeveloped events of the future may place it in my power to reciprocate."[12] Already he was predicting his future greatness, and was certainly willing to use whatever means were at hand to assure its arrival.

The ploy worked. He joined the 36th Infantry in New York, but real advancement still eluded him. His efforts increased, and during the next eight years, both he and his father wrote letter after letter requesting propitious transfers, reevaluation of his enlistment dates, and consequent adjustment of his lineal rank. They even argued that a clerical mistake had occurred at the time of his Civil War enlistment and caused the present lower ranking of his file.[13] He was transferred, but not promoted, and when, in October 1874, the 13th Infantry was relieved from its frontier responsibilities and reassigned to Reconstruction duties in Louisiana, Captain MacArthur took solace in the hope that the new locale would provide another vantage point from which to manipulate the system which frustrated his ambitions. Although promotion still escaped him, the move to New Orleans nonetheless proved to be a turning point in his life, for it was here that he would meet Mary Pinckney Hardy, the young southern belle who became his wife.

Mary Hardy, or "Pinkie" as she was known to her family, was born in 1852 somewhere in the middle of a family which would eventually number fourteen children. Her father, Thomas A. Hardy, whose ancestral roots lay buried in the seventeenth- and eighteenth-century history of North Carolina, migrated to Norfolk, Virginia, in the late 1820s. There he established a wholesale cotton business, and by the mid-1840s succeeded to the extent that he was able to buy a comfortable home for his expanding family. The house, located on the Elizabeth River, was known, appropriately, as "Riveredge." Here the family spent its winters. During the summers, Mrs. Hardy and several of the children often went to "Burnside," the family farm near Henderson, North Carolina.[14]

While not among Norfolk's elite, the Hardys were well on their way up the social and economic ladder, due in part to the unparalleled rise in the price of cotton in the world market during those years. Two of the elder boys joined Thomas in the business. Other brothers enrolled at the Virginia Military Institute in Lexington. Pinkie and her sisters prepared for their entry into southern society by learning the skills and arts suitable for young women of their class. This comfortable life collapsed in early 1861 with the first shots fired at Fort Sumter. The occupation of Norfolk by the union Army soon thereafter forced the Hardys to retire to Burnside, where Mr. and Mrs. Hardy and the younger children anxiously awaited news from the six sons who fought with the Confederate Army.[15] They saw the actual conflict only from a distance until the early spring of 1865, when General W.T. Sherman, en route from Savannah, Georgia, to Petersburg, Virginia, encamped one night in the fields at Burnside. This "occupation," coupled with the subsequent reduction of the family fortunes in the years following the war, left an indelible imprint of bitterness on the Hardys.

During the two years between the end of the war and the time when Thomas Hardy finally took the oath of allegiance necessary to recover his southern properties, the family lived in Baltimore, where young Pinkie, now in her mid-teens, graduated from Mount de Sales Academy. The Hardy men established a short-lived mercantile firm in Baltimore, but decided, in 1867, to attempt to recapture their fortune by returning to Norfolk. Riveredge, which had been used as a Union hospital during the war, required renovation, but was once again comfortable by the early 1870s. The reestablished family business never again equaled its prewar successes, but at his death in 1876, Thomas Hardy still owned much of his original real estate, which he divided among his wife and nine surviving children. Aware that the depression, which swept the country in the 1870s, had diminished its immediate value, he urged that his heirs try to retain it intact until the return of better times. In the years immediately preceding and following his death, the effort to maintain the family heritage often caused hardship for the family and conflict among his children.[16]

Pinkie, now a vivacious and attractive young woman, escaped the turmoil of life at home by frequent travel. She had enjoyed her schooling in Baltimore, and after returning to Norfolk, acquainted herself with other northern cities through visits to schoolmates and to her sister, Elizabeth, now married and living in Northampton, Massachusetts. Although frequently accompanied on these trips by other family members, Pinkie also traveled alone at times, and developed, during these years, the independence of spirit which characterized her throughout her life. The large family and postwar hardship which drove her mother to retreat into depression and spiritualism persuaded Pinkie to extend these carefree years as long as possible. When on a visit to New Orleans, in the winter of 1874, she finally met and fell in love with Captain Arthur MacArthur, Jr., she undoubtedly also recognized that his profession offered an opportunity for adventure and travel as well. Quite deliberately, she chose to marry a representative of the dynamic North rather than a member of the available southern gentry of her heritage. As had her future husband, she abandoned the security of the known for the potential of the unknown. These two always shared a strength of will, which neither their original families nor the family they would produce together could change.

After a whirlwind courtship enhanced by the romance and excitement of Mardi Gras, Pinkie returned to Riveredge to break the news to her family. The young couple corresponded after her return, and in May 1875 Captain MacArthur obtained a three-month leave of absence and journeyed to Norfolk. There they were married on May 19, 1875. Although her parents seem to have accepted the former Union hero with equanimity, several of her brothers could not bring themselves to attend the wedding. Influenced by her schooling, Pinkie chose to be married in a Catholic ceremony, although the MacArthurs would maintain a nominal allegiance to the Episcopal Church throughout their lives together. Despite her characteristic determination to marry the man she chose, in the way she chose, the family ties remained relatively firm, and the young couple visited Riveredge frequently until Pinkie's mother died in 1881.

With Arthur on interim assignment as a member of examining and retiring boards in Washington, D.C., the MacArthurs' first months of married life fulfilled their dual expectations far better than would most of the next fifteen years. In 1870 Judge

MacArthur, Arthur's father, had been appointed associate justice of the supreme court of the District of Columbia by President Grant. In 1872 the Judge remarried, and he and his new wife helped to introduce the young couple to Washington society. Pinkie thrived in the cosmopolitan atmosphere of the capital, and was undoubtedly disappointed when her husband was ordered to return to Louisiana at the end of the year. Already pregnant with her first child, however, she soon returned to the East and spent most of the spring at home in Norfolk, where Arthur II was born on June 1, 1876. During the next three years, her husband commanded Company "K" of the 13th Infantry in Louisiana during the waning years of Reconstruction, with one temporary assignment to Pennsylvania to deal with labor unrest in the mining areas in 1877.

Pinkie took every opportunity to be with her family, and was again with the Hardys on vacation in New England, in October 1878, when a second son, Malcolm, was born. At twenty-six, with two sons under the age of two, she showed promise of duplicating her mother's fecundity. Since her mother's experience had clearly not been rewarding, it was a prospect that she did not relish.[17] Nonetheless, when her husband's regiment was transferred to Fort Dodge, in what is now part of Little Rock, Arkansas, in July 1879, she was once again pregnant. Again she planned to return to Norfolk for the birth of this third child, but he arrived prematurely on January 26, 1880. He was christened Douglas, and with his birth, the MacArthur family was complete. Although his early arrival caused some family concern, the baby flourished, and by July, when his father was ordered to Fort Wingate, in the New Mexico Territory, Douglas was considered strong enough to undertake the long journey.

The common crucible shared by all men and women is the experience of childhood. The drama enacted at the domestic hearth becomes life's major drama, its chief characters, the paradigms after which the tiny observers model their own role, as well as their understanding of the roles played by others. While individual characteristics are shaped by biological proclivities, as well as the personal and cultural variations of day-to-day occurrences, each person's early years provide the setting within which he or she will make conscious and unconscious assessments concerning the world into which they have come. Because these variations are often subtle, and frequently obscured by later memories, they are difficult to recreate, and even harder to document. Nevertheless, if we are to understand the adult, we must attempt to know the child. In other words, we must examine the first years of Douglas MacArthur's experiences in order to understand why certain patterns of adaptation developed, how they were reinforced by his social reality, and how, then, he reworked and redirected these patterns into the fabric of his maturity.

When the young MacArthur family began its journey to Fort Wingate, in the northwest corner of the New Mexico Territory, their three boys ranged in age from four years to six months. Arthur II, already four, could be trusted to his father's care, but the two infants, Malcolm (nineteen months), and Douglas (six months), required the constant attention of their mother. The baby could still be nourished from his mother's breast, but young Malcolm, prematurely weaned by the necessities of his mother's unplanned third pregnancy, still required some special food. Well into his second year, he may also have exhibited the desire to explore, a characteristic of that age, with its consequent risk. The trip from Little Rock, by train and coach, required at least a week, and all the courage and forbearance that Mrs. MacArthur could muster.

Once settled in the new surroundings, Pinkie faced a different set of problems. Already well aware that her husband's advancement in part depended upon her own social skills, she immediately set about the business of establishing a comfortable home in one of the small adobe buildings allotted as officer's quarters. It was a difficult task. The dust and heat of July in New Mexico, coupled with the constant necessity to keep an eye on her sons, taxed her considerable ingenuity to its limit.[18] She succeeded to a remarkable degree, and was remembered by an acquaintance from that period for her vivacity and energy.[19]

Her husband's responsibilities included policing the Navajo reservation to the north, guarding the Kansas and Stockton Express route nearby, and protecting the workmen involved in laying track for the Atchison, Topeka and Santa Fe Railway. He was frequently away, and although the red and white desperados who peopled the area seem never to have caused immediate danger to the fort, the ever-present threat added one more source of tension. The care and upbringing of the boys often fell to Pinkie alone, and the impact of her presence was foremost in their experience during these early years.

Although only in his mid-thirties during this period, Captain MacArthur had already begun to assume the austerity of manner which was to characterize him for the rest of his life. His relationship to the troops of his command was friendly, yet formal. When not involved in actual company responsibilities, he studied history, law, and political science, often preparing papers on topics of interest. He was interested in the newly established school at Fort Wingate, and followed his eldest son's progress there with care. The Captain seldom participated in the informal social affairs of the post, leaving this aspect of their life to his wife. If his retreat from social contact caused conflict within the family, there is no record of the ways in which it manifested itself. Although undoubtedly dissatisfied with the assignment, both of the adult MacArthurs were still confident that their exile was to be temporary.[20]

For the boys, the Wingate years were not so oppressive. Although Douglas and Malcolm were still usually confined to play areas near the house, Arthur II could participate in many of the opportunities offered by the post. He played soldier, learned to ride, and often accompanied the men of his father's command on short supply trips. Separated by the enormous distances of childhood from his younger brothers' nursery, he enjoyed the special privileges often allowed the eldest child, and undoubtedly assumed the responsibilities of that position with a seriousness patterned after his father. His position in the family encouraged a certain independence of decision evident throughout his later life.[21] Douglas and Malcolm looked up to their older brother, but the constant companionship imposed

on them by their unusual closeness in age provided the land-
scape within which each would form their first patterns of social
interaction. Malcolm was probably Douglas's first friend, the
bigger brother who could walk and talk, and who had developed
capacities for achievement to which the baby Douglas could only
aspire. If, however, their relationship contained the usual elements of sibling rivalry, Malcolm was also the prime competitor
for their mother's attention, and in this area, the object of the
unmanageable rage to which Douglas, as all infants, may have
occasionally fallen prey. If they were like most young children
their age, they would have generally enjoyed each other's company, however, and relied upon each other for stimulation and
comfort at the basic level demanded by this stage of their development. On the other hand, they would also have been rivals for
the most valuable object in their world: their mother. This rivalry, coupled with Douglas's inarticulate need to be able to do
what Malcolm could already do, might have provided the basis
for the ambivalence present in all sibling relationships.

After a little more than two years at Fort Wingate, Captain
MacArthur was granted a leave of absence and the family returned to Norfolk. Pinkie's mother had died the year before and
settlement of the estate may have caused the return. The trip
probably included visits to Judge MacArthur in Washington, but
most of the leave, which eventually extended to eight months,
was spent in Virginia. There, in April 1883, disaster struck. All
three MacArthur children developed serious cases of measles,[22]
and on April 12, Malcolm died at the age of four and a half. He
was buried in the Hardy family plot in Cedar Grove Cemetery
in Norfolk. In the hope that a change of assignment would aid
his family in its recovery from this tragedy, Captain MacArthur
requested transfer to China, where he hoped to serve as military
attaché. Although his father's friend, former President Grant,
looked favorably upon this idea, he was unable to offer much
help. The request denied, the disheartened and disturbed family
returned to Fort Wingate in June 1883.

The impact of Malcolm's death on the development of
young Douglas was undoubtedly immense.[23] Just three when he

suffered this loss, Douglas probably had begun to attain comfortably the skills which would allow him to gain a measure of independence over his environment. He might now move about easily and with this increased agility, his active participation in the control of objects and persons of importance to him would have met with more success. In all likelihood, his parallel mental development now included imaginative prowess. The new independence which resulted from these increased skills would often have been frightening, however. His physical competence could prove inadequate for the problems which developed if he attempted too much. The extent of his fantasies may have frightened the little boy. When this happened, he, like other children at the same age, probably relied upon the safe haven provided by mother. She usually could extricate him from whatever precarious position he had achieved. If the imaginary figures of his daydreams threatened to overpower him, her arms and lap probably offered reassurance that reality was secure. The developmental task he faced at this time was that of defining his own capacities for independent action. If he succeeded in his assessments most of the time, a sense of initiative would become incorporated into his personality, allowing him the freedom to broaden his horizons as he continued to grow. If his attempts at independent exploration failed too frequently, the guilt engendered both by his own need to continue struggling and by the restrictions placed upon his activity by those who controlled his world would overpower his as yet weak belief in his own ability to assess risk.[24] Under usual circumstances, this phase of his development probably would have proceeded uneventfully. Malcolm's sudden death, and the fact of Douglas's survival, almost certainly interrupted the steady process, and made this normal phase of growth one that he was doomed to repeat again and again.

Douglas's faltering attempt at independence at this time, typical of all three year olds, was complicated, of course, by the responses of other family members to the tragedy. His father, although apparently able to grieve openly in the privacy of his home, was required by duty and by social convention to mourn only briefly and then to take up once again the responsibilities of his profession. The emotional energy, which resulted from his response to his son's death, could be directed toward the broader necessities of his life and work outside the home. He had little time to impose his reactions on his youngest son.

Arthur II, while probably experiencing the certain amount of guilt always associated with the death of a sibling, was seven at the time and perhaps involved in a less intense phase of development. His more developed understanding helped him to accept the explanations offered concerning Malcolm's death. He could return to the distractions of the fort and the responsibilities of school. His age, and less intimate relationship to Douglas, prevented his grief from becoming too important an influence on the younger boy. But Pinkie was buffeted from all sides by family tragedy and the mental chaos it brought on. When her husband and older son left in the morning, she and young Douglas were left alone to deal with their grief and the powerful emotional reactions it inspired.

Although the death of a child was not uncommon in the late nineteenth century, this reality did nothing to mitigate the personal grief involved. Coming, as it did, on the heels of her mother's death, the tragedy may even have had a more vital effect on Pinkie's immediate response. If, as so frequently happens, she dealt with the first loss by incorporating some of the dimensions of her mother's personality into her own outlook,[25] Malcolm's death might have resulted in an even more intense guilt than usual. In her last years, Pinkie's mother had retreated into a maternal pessimism unrelieved by the comfort of her religion or the attention of her children. Malcolm's death, therefore, occurring as it did in Pinkie's childhood home, may have stirred and intensified the feelings of remorse which always accompany the death of a close family member. In addition, Pinkie's third pregnancy, so soon after Malcolm's birth, required his early weaning. Douglas's birth and the hardships of the assignment to Fort Wingate may have caused her to react impatiently to her second son on occasion. Although this behavior was perfectly human, her memories of this shortness of temper may have intensified her contrition after his death. But whatever the reality of her feelings during this period, they certainly influenced her responses to the young child who remained hers. Her behavior, coupled with his probable confusion and incomplete understanding of what had occurred, may have instilled fears and uncertainties in his mind from which he could never escape. Certainly, many of his future patterns of behavior are more easily understood in this light.

At three and a half, Douglas undoubtedly returned to Fort Wingate in confusion. All of the people important to him had gone to a strange place; he and his brothers had suddenly sickened; Malcolm went away (apparently forever); and now, somehow, his world was no longer secure. His mother, and to a lesser degree probably his father as well, now seemed to fear for his safety. He had also been sick but did not die. He could not know whether this meant that he had survived through a special providence, or that, perhaps, the next sickness would result in his own death. Perhaps his mother or father or brother would also go away. His response may have been, quite naturally, to retreat to a more infantile dependence upon those who had previously offered protection. But the success of this ploy depended upon his ability to convince himself that those he needed would remain available to him. They must be as omnipotent in his mind as they had been to him in his infancy. To allay his enormous insecurity, both he and his loved ones must assume an invulnerability to the risks of life which had become so suddenly obvious. For the moment, his earlier efforts to achieve the independence natural to a three year old probably diminished. He needed to be cautious, and the fears and concern evident in his parents' warnings to him must be carefully obeyed.

An alternative and contradictory response may also have taken root at this time. Douglas had twice survived events which could have literally destroyed him: once at his premature birth; again in his bout with the measles, which killed his brother. To both the young child and his family, these occurrences may have seemed providential. Perhaps this child, increasingly precious after the events of 1883, was meant to prevail over the vicissitudes of childhood for a special purpose.[26] Pinkie, whose ambitions for her husband and children later became very obvious, may even have conveyed this message to Douglas in one way or another. If so, this idea may have combined with his intense sense of vulnerability in the immediate period following Malcolm's death, transforming his terror into a reassuring belief in his destiny. If he was specially chosen, then he once again could attempt independent action. The very real fears he experienced provided the psychic energy which impelled him to otherwise inexplainable risks in later life. Each time the fears became conscious, the response became a necessity. In the framework of his relationship with his parents, and particularly his mother, he needed always to carefully follow their advice. In other arenas, however, acts which often appeared heroic, but frequently bordered on actual indiscretion, allowed the release of tension inspired by his early fears. If this arena was the battlefield, it enjoyed the additional sanction of parental approval.

In the months following Malcolm's death, the MacArthur family gradually recovered its equilibrium. In February 1884, Captain MacArthur was assigned to command Fort Selden, farther south in the New Mexico Territory, along the Rio Grande. The transfer involved a grueling 300-mile journey, by wagon and foot, through the dusty wastelands of the Southwest. The hot intemperate days contrasted with the cold chilling winds at night. The Chiricahua Apache, led by the revengeful Geronimo, at that time were preparing one last assault from their reservation immediately to the west. The trip, which must have required at least two weeks, entailed very real dangers which were intensified, for Mrs. MacArthur, by her still exaggerated concerns for her family. Nevertheless, the necessity of preparing for the move provided her with a welcome distraction from her grief, and by May 1884, she could write to her sister in Massachusetts, that she "lik[ed] Selden very much." This letter, the only surviving one from this period, revealed much of Pinkie's outlook and adjustment at the time.

Writing to console her sister, Elizabeth, in her recent widowhood, Pinkie's grief for Malcolm was still fresh in her mind. Poignantly, she explained, "sometimes I nearly go crazy over my loss," and yet she was able to take comfort in the hope that her son and Elizabeth's husband were joined "before Jesus, ... pleading for us." Her loss had only intensified her devotion to her two remaining sons, and reconfirmed her decision to have no more children.[27] That she was well on the way to recovery from her grief was reflected in her characteristic statement that while "it [Fort Selden] is a lonely place, ... Arthur is in command and I can do just as I want. I have only three rooms and a small kitchen, but it is enough with my family."[28]

Significantly, Douglas later recalled that this trip to Selden was his first conscious memory. The trip, fraught with excitement and adventure, quite naturally contained much that a young boy, now past four, would relish. Nevertheless, the fact that it undoubtedly provided distraction from the intense emotions which had engulfed the family in the past few months, made it doubly important. Douglas and his family could now selectively "forget" those feelings which had disrupted the domestic arrangements, and move on, with a reassured inner security nurtured by time, to the next phases of their development. At another level, however, he always remembered the crisis, and at the end of his life could still accurately assess its importance: "Malcolm's loss was a terrible blow to my mother, but it seemed only to increase her devotion to Arthur and myself. This tie was to become one of the dominant factors of my life."[29] Not unpredictably, the MacArthurs, and particularly young Douglas, survived and incorporated this tragedy into their collective past. Douglas went on to develop in many of the usual ways of young men in his time period. In the depths of his inner life, however, the conflicts engendered by this threat to his growing sense of independence were never totally resolved. They would return at crisis points in his later youth, and throughout his life, to haunt the image of himself as a brave warrior which he needed to keep foremost in his mind.[30]

The years at Fort Selden always retained a place of warmth in Douglas MacArthur's memory. "It was here I learned to ride and shoot even before I could read or write—indeed, almost before I could walk and talk."[31] This obvious overstatement reflected one of the important aspects of the two years that he spent there. He "trudged . . . at the head of the column" on the way to his new home, and clearly identified with the roughened foot soldiers of his father's command. Although Captain MacArthur did not participate in the Indian engagements of 1885, which occurred nearby, tales of these adventures provided much to excite the young boys. Douglas met cowboys and Indians, and never heard enough of the earlier adventures of the infantrymen who had served in the more active phases of the settlement of the western frontier. For the five year old, such stories were easily incorporated into the fantasies that he spun for himself in lazy afternoons under the hot New Mexico sun. Now Buffalo Bill, now Dead-eye Dick, young Douglas could become anybody he wanted to be in these dreams. These fantasies allowed him to see himself as hero—unafraid as he could not be in his real life—and perhaps dressed in manly gear, which, at this point, Pinkie would not allow.

Until the age of five, at least, Douglas was frequently dressed in skirts, long and full blouses, and bows. His hair was carefully curled and hung to his shoulders.[32] Certainly this attire, while not unique for young men of this period, would have complicated the rough-and-tumble play that he later chose to remember from these years. In addition, it may have confused his developing sexual identity. Dressed like his mother, he was increasingly expected, at least on one level, to act like his father. These contradictory signals may have added still another facet to MacArthur's ambivalent nature in later life.

Whatever the effect of his clothes on his developing self-image, his identification with the adventurers of the Old West helped to support his vision of himself throughout his entire life. He always chose to recall the western aspects of his childhood, selected clothes and accessories which supported this image of himself, and saw the world in the simple outlines of his cowboy heroes. Indeed, the fantasies themselves may have continued for the rest of his life. But for now, he could not always escape into daydreams; his outdoor diversions were often interrupted by the attempts his mother and, to a lesser extent, his father made toward educating their sons. This post, smaller than Wingate, did not offer a regular school. Along with the basic rudiments, Pinkie stressed "above all else, a sense of obligation" to the boys.[33] The military ceremonies his father directed, coupled with his mother's emphasis on the importance of love of one's country, instilled in young Douglas a romantic response to flag and bugle that he would carry with him all the rest of his life.

The middle years of Douglas MacArthur's childhood coincided with the beginnings of change in his family's status within the military establishment. In the fall of 1886, after the long, frustrating years in the Southwest, Captain MacArthur's company was transferred to Fort Leavenworth, Kansas, where he taught in the advanced school for infantry officers. It was an opportunity which exactly suited his scholarly bent, and offered the advantages of better schooling for the boys, and better housing for them all. The school commandant, Major General Alexander M. McCook, remembered the Captain's earlier bravery during the Civil War, and encouraged and supported his efforts to achieve still further advancement.

For Douglas this was a period of broader horizons, but the definitions of those horizons remained essentially the same. All things military fascinated him. He had reached the age when he could imagine himself in the adult world, and he now wanted to perfect the skills which would prepare him for the future. He was drawn to the more involved ceremonies of a larger post, and particularly enjoyed those afternoon parades his father commanded. The new school which he and his brother attended was more challenging than any he had known previously, but, although he enjoyed the "competition between classmates,"[34] he remained a poor student. At this point, he still believed that physical activity and experience were really more relevant if he was to succeed as the soldier he and his family agreed he should become. In an age when increased emphasis on efficiency and technical knowhow encouraged more prolonged career preparation, often of an academic nature, he would soon have to reevaluate this assessment.[35] But for a little boy between the ages of six and nine at the time, these concerns were still far away. He could ride, play soldier, and dream of western adventure. When Captain MacArthur was temporarily assigned to serve in the Oklahoma Territory, Douglas pleaded to go along. Reminding him that his studies must come first, his father denied the request. Disappointed, he stayed home with mother, tried to study a little harder, and waited, perhaps less than patiently, for the day when he, too, could command the troops.

In July 1889, the longstanding efforts of Captain MacArthur and his father in Washington finally paid off. A flurry of letters changed hands between the War Department, MacArthur's superiors at Leavenworth, and his father's friends in Washington. The result was that the now mature infantry Captain was promoted to major, transferred to Washington, and appointed assistant adjutant general. After twenty-three years, his talents (and his connections) at last had been recognized. Major and Mrs. MacArthur and the two boys, now nine and thirteen, set off to the capital. The assignment provided them with the opportunity to renew their ties with the senior MacArthurs, and, more importantly for Pinkie, to make acquaintances and cement relationships which would help her family reap the rewards she believed should be theirs.

For Douglas, it was a time of contrasts. Washington offered him his first chance to really know city life, and he later remembered that he "found it no substitute for the color and excitement of the frontier West."[36] While later experiences would change this opinion, it probably accurately reflected his view at the time. Again he enrolled in a new school, and again his performance in the last years of grade school was only average. His later tendency to link the concept of competition with these early school years is revealing. At this time, his brother, Arthur, was seriously preparing for a hoped-for appointment to the Naval Academy. Certainly the accomplishments appropriate to the older boy's age were beyond the abilities of the younger Douglas, and he may have felt this deficiency keenly. Arthur's success at school may or may not have impeded Douglas's progress, but it is perhaps significant that the vistas of intellectual achievement did not open for Douglas until after his brother, whom he described as "an excellent scholar,"[37] left home.

The MacArthurs stayed in Washington a little over three years. For each separately, and for the family as a whole, this assignment provided opportunities heretofore unavailable to them. Young Arthur used the years to choose and prepare for a career, which significantly was both patterned after and different from that of his father. Major MacArthur spent his time in the War Department demonstrating to his superiors his attention to duty. Although only one of sixteen assistant adjutant generals, he was particularly suited to the aspects of record keeping which were his main responsibility, and he impressed his superior, Brigadier General J.S. Kelton, as thorough and conscientious.[38] At this time he was finally able to obtain the Medal of Honor for his bravery on Missionary Ridge. Most importantly, he made contacts which would later aid his progress up the chain of command at the end of the century.

While her husband attended to his professional duties, Pinkie put down roots in the city which would be her home for many years later in her life. The social graces that she had learned in the antebellum South were finally put to good use. She entertained, visited, and made every effort to promote her husband's career. In the future, whenever she deemed it necessary, she did not hesitate to contact the acquaintances in high places whom she had met during these years.

For Douglas, despite his rejection of urban life, it was a time of reprieve from the intense emotions of his earlier years. The attention of his parents was at times focused on other concerns. He had time to enjoy his grandfather's companionship and while in Washington imbibed the older man's wisdom and skill at games. With less parental direction, he relaxed and grew, only occasionally bothered by his academic shortcomings. Without knowing it, he was gathering strength for his next developmental surge.

In the fall of 1893, Major MacArthur was again transferred, this time to Fort Sam Houston in San Antonio, Texas. Although the Major and his wife may not have been overjoyed at leaving the centers of power, their younger son was delighted. Once again he would be right in the middle of the military activity he loved so much. Arthur II, now establishing a brilliant career at Annapolis, remained behind, while the three other MacArthurs settled into their quarters and into the social and professional activities of the base.

On the brink of a new phase of growth, the thirteen-year-old Douglas again was in an environment which would reinforce those elements of his self-image which would eventually predominate. The little-boy fantasies of military prowess now developed further, encouraged and enhanced by almost everything he saw at the large fort. Bigger guns, more troops, and vast ceremony nurtured these dreams. Best of all, a new school, the West Texas Military Academy, provided him with an academic context which supported his military ambitions, while advancing the intellectual efforts which had remained dormant thus far.

The school, located on grounds adjoining the military reservation, opened its doors just two weeks before the MacArthurs arrived in San Antonio.[39] As soon as possible, Douglas was enrolled in the fourth form (ninth grade), outfitted in a uniform of cadet gray, and incorporated into a student body of forty-nine. The curriculum was heavily classical, but was balanced by a military regime to which he easily adapted. For Douglas, the school provided an atmosphere that was particularly salutary. He could live at home, thereby postponing the anxieties separation would later bring. The nearby fort and the military training he received fed his martial ambitions. As he relaxed into the school setting, he gradually began to participate in the wide range of extracurricular activities the school offered. Finally, and to an amazing extent, the Rector A.L. Burleson and his faculty of ten succeeded in inspiring the young cadet after everyone else had failed. As he remembered years later, "there came a desire to know, a seeking for the reason why, a search for the truth. . . . My studies enveloped me. . . ."[40] This intellectual awakening was only one of the many changes occurring in Douglas during these early teenage years.

By the 1890s, the idea of a specific developmental phase known as adolescence was incorporated into the outlook of many of the middle class in western Europe and America.[41] While certainly not yet psychologically aware, knowledgeable and concerned parents attempted during this period in their children's development to provide models and influences which would turn the young people's inclinations in the direction their parents thought they should go. Like many of their predecessors, parents in the late nineteenth century recognized the value of childhood training as one important determinant for mature success. They differed only in that they believed the period of this training should last longer than ever before. Their children, too, saw this time as a period of decision, and reacted to the stresses engendered by the importance of the decision in significant ways.

The cultural stresses on the young adolescent were heightened by the personal tensions to which puberty gave rise. A larger and constantly changing body, coupled with the forces of increased sexuality, encouraged a new desire for independence. These same physical realities were often frightening. Now brave and forceful, the teenager was just as likely, the next minute, to scurry back into the security of an earlier stage of childhood. The early teenage years were, then, a time when both external and inner needs demanded that the young person reincorporate all conscious and unconscious prior choices into a new self-image which, if developed in the usual way, would contain in its still shadowy outlines the patterns of the mature adult. It was a formidable task made more difficult by the unpredictable physical changes which accompanied it. Douglas MacArthur, alone now with his parents in Texas, was not immune to the pressures of this process. With one exception, he succeeded in surmounting its difficulties, and established patterns of adaptation which did not conflict with his personal needs or the demands of his immediate or extended cultures.

Although telescoped in his memory, the impressive changes in Douglas's outlook and achievement which occurred at West Texas apparently did not happen all at once.[42] His intellectual interest was almost immediately engaged, and by the end of his first year he attained an academic average of 96.3 percent. According to his own account, everything was new and wonderful: "Abstruse mathematics began to appear as a challenge to analysis, dull Latin and Greek seemed a gateway to the moving words of the leaders of the past, laborious historical data led to the nerve-tingling battlefields of the great captains. Biblical lessons began to open the spiritual portals of a growing faith, literature to lay bare the souls of men."[43]

He worked diligently, and was remembered as quiet and likable by his classmates. Significantly, his social acumen was not as obvious. He did not participate in athletics during his first two years at West Texas, nor did he actively assume other leadership roles at that time. Limited by his status as one of the younger boys, it is possible that his new scholarly efforts also demanded much of his time. For the first time in his life, though perhaps still inspired by his older brother's example, he no longer felt the pressures of comparison which had earlier been intensified by Arthur's immediate presence. As the younger child, moved frequently from post to post, he had naturally relied to an exaggerated degree on his family for support, guidance, and established values. Slowly, now, he began to look outward and to seek peer confirmation for his own self-definition. To an unusual extent, however, his friends and new role models only reinforced the earlier guidelines set by his family. The military atmosphere of his school, the uniforms worn by his friends, and the social and religious values conveyed by the faculty of the church-supported institution did not confuse his earlier understanding of what was important and good.

As did many of the youths of his class and period, Douglas accepted, with little apparent conflict, the social values, the career choice, and, indeed, the world view which was presented to him. Once comfortable with this outlook, he went on in his last two years at West Texas to succeed socially and on the athletic field to a remarkable degree. In his final year, he directed the football team as quarterback, managed and played shortstop for the baseball team, served as first sergeant of his military company, and was chosen for membership in the elite Crack Squad, an exhibition group made up of only ten cadets. In addition, his academic achievement reached new highs. He was chosen valedictorian of his class and won medals in three special areas. In deportment, his final grade was 100 percent. Even for one so clearly talented and hard-working, the determination to succeed evidenced by this record was unusual.

The period of development through which Douglas was moving during the years in San Antonio required that he come to terms with himself in a number of ways.[44] He needed to find a place in his world into which he could fit his own predilections and natural abilities with reasonable ease. West Texas and Fort Sam Houston seemed to provide a context which particularly encouraged this achievement. Yet the effort needed for the feats of those years clearly surpassed that usually expended by most young men of his age, and suggested a source of energy derived from an unresolved conflict somewhere within the developmental process. A comment he made while describing the honors he garnered in these years is revealing in this regard. ". . . my marks went higher, and many of the school medals came my way. But I also learned how little such honors mean after one wins them."[45] Even at this young age, Douglas MacArthur was driven to a success which, once attained, felt empty. Clearly, the inner need, which inspired the young man to these excessive efforts, was not satisfied by the socially accepted rewards bestowed as their result. He may have needed something else, something which he could not recognize, and which the world could not allow.

If, as has previously been suggested, Douglas MacArthur failed in his earlier years to define clearly the extent to which he was a separate and independent being, the heightened tensions of this later stage of development may have dredged up the prior confusion. As a little boy facing the terror brought on by his brother's death, he had localized this unresolved conflict by carefully adhering to the warnings and admonitions of his parents. He felt free to exert his own efforts at independent action only in areas acceptable to them. Once again, when the pressures of adolescence required further definition of himself, he

Mary, "Pinkie," MacArthur, c. 1925
Brown Brothers

Louise Cromwell Brooks MacArthur,
c. 1925   *United Press International*

Jean Faircloth MacArthur, 1944
Brown Brothers

Isabel Rosario Cooper
Used with permission of the family

was at a loss. This may have been particularly evident in connection with his relationship to his mother, the strongly dominant woman who, as the first woman in his life, served for most of it as the model in his mind for all women.

Pinkie MacArthur became, if anything, even more strong-willed and overpowering as she grew older. With one son safely away at school and well on the road to success, she could now focus her considerable energies entirely on Douglas's life at school, his social activities, and his unparalleled efforts to achieve success. Major MacArthur, distanced by professional responsibilities, his own austerity, and often by temporary assignments away from home, provided scant buffer for her efforts. Indeed, there is every reason to believe that both of his parents were in essential agreement concerning Douglas's upbringing. Consequently, Douglas's need to assert himself, so natural to all young people at this age, was frustrated by his own inability to risk conflict in certain areas. Unlike his parents at the same age, he chose not to break away from the values and options they suggested, but to accept them fully. His larger culture, the immediate friends and mentors whom he found during this period, and his family all reinforced one of the possible directions he could choose. In many ways, this configuration of influences allowed for a comfortable and successful adjustment. At some inner level, however, the self-definition necessary at this point was not of his own making. He did not experiment with alternate possibilities, discarding them later if he chose. At an even deeper level of awareness, he may never have established clearly the lines of separation from his mother, the original source of his security.[46] It was during these years that he first demonstrated an interest in girls. It was also at this time that he established a long-held pattern of brief, simultaneous courtships with many young women, which precluded the necessity for real closeness. His later apparent inability to achieve intimacy with members of his own generation may have been the ultimate result of this conflict.

Whatever the psychic reality of these years, their importance cannot be discounted. Here the young MacArthur began his long ascent to success and power. Here he demonstrated for the first time the enormous energy that he could always muster under challenge. His inner needs and abilities joined successfully with the needs and values of his society to produce an individual who at this point exhibited great promise. He too understood the significance of this period. In a later discussion of the West Texas Military Academy, he stated with unusual simplicity, "this is where I started."[47]

After the successful conclusion of his years at West Texas Military Academy, Douglas and his family were once again on the move. In October 1897, the newly promoted Lieutenant Colonel MacArthur was transferred to the Department of the Dakotas in St. Paul, Minnesota. Pinkie and Douglas, intent on the next phase of their jointly held career plan, decided not to accompany him. Rather, they would settle into the Plankinton House, a fashionable hotel in Milwaukee, where they hoped to obtain for Douglas a congressional appointment to West Point through the auspices of Representative Theabold Otjen, an old friend of Douglas's recently deceased grandfather. The Colonel visited on weekends.

In the spring of 1896, while still in San Antonio, the MacArthurs had begun a concerted attack on their next objective. Bringing to bear all the influence they could garner, they sought to capture for Douglas a presidential appointment to West Point. Letters from many state and federal officials to President Grover Cleveland urged his acceptance, but to no avail. Undeterred by this disappointment, Pinkie and Douglas devised another plan. They continued, still unsuccessfully, their efforts to attain an appointment-at-large from the next President, William McKinley. In the meantime, they designed a strenuous program that they hoped would assure his success in the competitive examination for Congressman Otjen's 1899 appointments. Complicating their project was the fact that Douglas not only had to pass the academic examination successfully, but he also somehow had to correct a slight curvature of the spine, which had caused him to fail his first physical examination for the appointment. To pass the competitive examination, he studied under a tutor and attended refresher courses at a local high school. To correct the physical deficiency, he undertook a therapeutic program under the direction of a Milwaukee doctor familiar with such cases. Admitting later that "I never worked harder in my life,"[48] Douglas exercised and studied with an intensity which was now characteristic. It paid off, and in May 1898, just after the United States entered the Spanish-American War, the young man passed the congressional examination with high marks. He scored 93.3 percent, far surpassing his nearest competitor. His physical therapy was apparently just as successful, and his appointment, which would begin in June 1899, was now assured.

The twenty months that Douglas spent in Milwaukee at this time provided further opportunity for the young man to grow. He used this late adolescent period, between the ages of seventeen and nineteen, to complete the preparations which had started with the move to San Antonio. The successful work habits and clear direction he developed at West Texas were again in evidence. Although disappointed when his parents refused to let him give up his appointment to West Point in order to volunteer for service in Cuba, he, unlike his father almost forty years before, acquiesced with little conflict. On the surface, his adjustment to the expectations of his family and culture appeared complete.

In May 1898, Colonel MacArthur was appointed brigadier general of Volunteers and transferred to Camp Thomas at Chickamauga, Georgia, where the freshly mustered troops of the newly expanded United States Army were preparing for an invasion of Cuba. After this date, the senior MacArthur's visits to his wife and son in Milwaukee were even less frequent, and after his assignment to the Philippines in June of that year, they were totally separated for over three years. During this period, Douglas and his mother remained together, first in Milwaukee, and later at West Point where Pinkie settled into Craney's Hotel, just outside the academy grounds. The symbiosis that this arrangement suggested reflected still another aspect of Douglas's development.

During the sojourn in Milwaukee, Pinkie quite naturally provided Douglas with the encouragement he needed at that crucial time. She shored up his occasionally waning self-confidence, and when he suffered the first of many attacks of nausea produced by the anxiety of examination day, her words urged him on. " 'Doug,' she said, 'you'll win if you don't lose your nerve. You must believe in yourself, my son, or no one else will believe in you. Be self-confident, self-reliant, and even if you don't make it, you will know you have done your best. Now, go to it.' "[49] These words, while probably like those spoken universally by mothers in similar circumstances, contained a contradiction. The underlying message was clear. Douglas's self-reliance must not cancel his need for his mother. Alone with her now, her son could not complete the task young men face in adolescence. He could not, and did not, differentiate himself from her powerful personality. Apparently, he did not even try. The young ladies he met in Milwaukee were of little interest to him during this period. While he enjoyed their attention, he may have tried to escape its implications by playing the field.[50] On many levels, mother and son needed and wanted each other. While the relationship disturbed Douglas's later attempts at intimacy with women of his own age, it provided much of the impetus for his success in other fields. To outside observers, Douglas's devotion to Pinkie was noteworthy, and seemingly conflict-free. At other levels, it was perhaps ambiguous. Within these confines, his need to establish a sense of his own independent being may never have been fulfilled. His unrecognized, but nonetheless real, resentment at this injustice may explain one of the sources of his amazing energy.

In June 1899, Douglas, accompanied by his mother, set off for the adventure for which he had so long prepared. During the months in Milwaukee, they had kept track of General MacArthur's Philippine exploits.[51] His reputation was nationally known now, and this reality both eased and complicated Douglas's entry into life at the military academy. On the one hand, his father's position brought the young cadet to the attention of his superiors perhaps earlier than it would otherwise have occurred.

Conversely, General MacArthur's fame encouraged the upper-classmen to come down hard on the plebe in a period when hazing was still widely accepted. Both he and his classmate, Ulysses S. Grant III, were frequently singled out for this special attention. Douglas often had to recite his father's military record, only one of the milder forms of hazing to which he was subjected. Nonetheless, despite the pain and resentment this experience must have caused him, he survived this indoctrination and went on, as usual, to win the respect and friendship of most of his fellow cadets.

The next year, when a congressional investigation into hazing procedures required testimony from Cadet MacArthur, he was forced to chose between informing on his classmates and probable expulsion from the academy. Stricken again with the nausea which always signaled a state of intense anxiety for him, he entered the examining chamber in a quandary. Pinkie came to the rescue when she sent in a poem, which sixty years later MacArthur still claimed told him what to do. Whether or not this was actually the case, the poem is important if we are to understand more fully the relationship between the two:

> Do you know that your soul is of my soul such a part
> That you seem to be fiber and core of my heart?
> None other can pain me as you, son, can do;
> None other can please me or praise me as you.
> Remember the world will be quick with its blame
> If shadow or shame ever darken your name.
> Like mother, like son, is saying so true
> The world will judge largely of mother by you.
> Be this then your task, if task it shall be
> To force this proud world to do homage to me.
> Be sure it will say, when its verdict you've won
> She reaps as she sowed: "This man is her son!"[52]

Whether Pinkie authored, edited, or simply found this verse, its meaning exactly suited her immediate and extended purposes. Douglas survived the inquiry, although not, as he remembered, by refusing to reveal the names of his friends involved in the hazing. Indeed, he and several other classmates reluctantly revealed the names of the hazers, and then were allowed to return to the academy. Although he later conveniently forgot his testimony, it is much more significant that for sixty years he carried in his mind the admonition and responsibilities conveyed to him by this verse. Admittedly sentimental in the vein of much turn-of-the-century popular poetry, it was nevertheless meaningful to both the mother and son whose attitudes toward life were no less romantic. They both accepted the close relationship the poem portrayed, and the vision of honor and responsibility described in its middle lines. Most revealing of all, however, was their acceptance of its final idea. Underlying their joint and impressive effort of these years was, indeed, the intent "to force this proud world to do homage to me."[53] For the rest of his life, Douglas would attempt to assuage Pinkie's insatiable need for honor.

Buttressed by the daily walks with his mother during the half-hour free period allowed the cadets each evening, Douglas's determination to succeed soon became obvious to all who observed him. He spoke glowingly of his father and clearly patterned his efforts at the academy after this model. He got up before reveille to study, and was permitted an extra hour at the books in the evening due to his fortunate selection as roommate of an upperclassman. The hard work paid off, and he was number one in his class for three of his four years at West Point, maintaining an average higher, with one exception, than had any cadet in the one-hundred-year history of the academy.[54] The few demerits he earned were for trivial offenses, and only one other serious conflict with authority developed during the four years. In a dispute with his mathematics professor at the end of his second year, MacArthur was infuriated to learn that he would have to take the final examination in the course, although his average was the highest in the class. He threatened to resign. For twenty-four hours, a stalemate existed. Ten minutes before the final was to begin, MacArthur was excused. His honor appeased, the young cadet uneventfully continued the regime of hard work to which he was now accustomed. But he learned one important lesson from this episode. When pride and honor are at stake, confront the problem. In the usual course of events, a strong will carries the day. Perhaps it was an inaccurate assessment, but it remained foremost in his approach to life, and it certainly reflected his mother's beliefs.

In June 1903, Douglas MacArthur graduated from West Point before the proud gaze of both his parents. His father, now a Major General and returned from his Philippine assignment, commanded the Department of the Pacific, and was stationed in San Francisco. His son stood before him as first captain of the corps of cadets and first in his class in academic rank. Under his mother's guidance, he had achieved all that the General had hoped for during the years of his absence. Indeed, this absence may have encouraged Douglas's success. In any event, the elder MacArthurs, once again united, accepted their son's triumphs with pride, and readied themselves for his now seemingly assured future.

At twenty-three, the newly commissioned Second Lieutenant looked ready to assume the responsibilities for which he had so long and devotedly prepared. Tall, straight, and handsome, his dark brown eyes dominated a face which had taken on the fine aquiline features of his mother in her youth.[55] He wore his recently acquired uniform proudly, but always managed to inject some personal note to differentiate himself from all the others in khaki. The successes of the last decade had provided a veneer of assurance, which was only occasionally called into question. But beneath this almost overconfident appearance lurked an insecurity from which he never escaped. This reality was seldom recognized in the years to come; but one man, for a long time perhaps his closest friend, explained it convincingly.

In a conversation with Charles Burton Marshall just after World War II, Brigadier General Thomas J. Davis, MacArthur's longtime aide and friend from the twenties and thirties, suggested that "the MacArthur he knew, far from epitomizing certitude, was deeply unsure of himself. The goal instilled into him was to be Superman. He felt inadequate to the part but did not know how to get out of it. . . . MacArthur's tie to his mother was the key to Davis's interpretation . . . the relationship represented possessiveness and dominance, with the son never free of an imposed destiny or from fear of failing it."[56]

Although this understanding neglected to emphasize the importance of MacArthur's father in the shaping of his son, it contained much that is true. Even though the career he chose and the goals he set for himself were patterned after his father, his mother's forceful mediation, particularly during the General's absences, shaped the specific ways in which he would achieve those goals. Their relationship, molded during the tragic period after Malcolm's death and tempered by their closeness during the years in Milwaukee and West Point, helped to create a lifelong struggle within Douglas MacArthur. Unable to separate himself psychologically from his mother, a tension developed within him which forced him to strive again and again for greater success. Once achieved, it never satisfied him. Often actually present during his first fifty-five years, Pinkie was always there in the inner recesses of his mind. If he often asked, "Governor, how about it?" after each new venture, we can be sure that another question was asked as well. Was this success enough? Did the "proud world" now "do homage?" Sometimes, his efforts to please this loving but demanding taskmaster led to misjudgment and defeat.

(2)

The First MacArthur
in the Philippines

The Philippines charmed me.... and
fastened me with a grip that has never
relaxed.
Douglas MacArthur
Reminiscences, 36.

WHEN SECOND LIEUTENANT Douglas MacArthur left for his first
assignment to the Philippines, in October 1903, he was already
predisposed to fall subject to the charm of the archipelago so
distant and different from anything he had previously known. In
part, he was responding to his country's increased awareness of
the outer world, which resulted from the United States' entry
into the international scene during the Spanish-American War.
In addition, during his years at West Point the curriculum had
been expanded; it now sought to prepare the new officers for
service in the tropical jungles of the southwest Pacific. Finally,
his knowledge of the Philippines was informed by discussions
with his father regarding the senior MacArthur's longstanding
interest in Asia and his unique experience in the Islands between 1898 and 1901. Although conditions in the Philippines
changed between 1901, when Arthur MacArthur left Manila,
and 1903, when Douglas first saw the archipelago, the changes
were subtle and did little to alter the shared opinions the two
men held. All these sources, intensified by the anticipation and
fear brought on by this first assignment away from country,
home, and family, formed the basis for the younger MacArthur's
initial perception of the country, which would eventually play a
vital role in his future. From the outset, the Islands provided
a special attraction to which he always responded. After his
first year there, he welcomed each opportunity to return. To

understand this "grip that . . . never relaxed," it is necessary to examine in detail all the influences upon which it was based.

When Commodore George Dewey swiftly destroyed the Spanish fleet guarding Manila Bay on May 1, 1898, most Americans, including President William McKinley, were forced to check their atlases hastily before they could be sure exactly where or what "the Philippines" actually were. This cursory research led most to the conclusion that the archipelago, set in the western Pacific just southeast of Hong Kong and farther southwest of Japan, was peopled by exotic heathen, surrounded by tropical greenery much like that described by Robert Louis Stevenson in his then popular *In the South Seas.* Encouraged by the mistaken assumptions of American missionaries, most of those concerned concluded that, four centuries of Spanish-Catholic colonization notwithstanding, the Islanders eagerly awaited the arrival of the Christianizing and civilizing progressives from the United States. A more thorough investigation of the complex history of the Philippine Islands might have helped to avoid the painful bewilderment that most Americans felt when their attempts to shoulder "the white man's burden" were so abruptly rejected by General Emilio Aguinaldo, his 30,000-man army, and the many Filipinos by whom they were supported. Such an investigation would have revealed almost four hundred years of colonial domination and a recently developed, but strongly held, determination to submit to such domination no longer.

On March 17, 1521, when Ferdinand Magellan's Spanish expedition first sighted Samar, easternmost of the group of islands which would later be called the Philippines, he might well have heeded the advice given another European conquerer concerning the Ides of March.[1] In just a little over a month, on April 27, 1521, Magellan met his death in the form of a poisoned arrow shot by one of the followers of Lapulapu, chief of Mactan, and later considered the first hero of Philippine nationalism. Although Magellan's death demoralized his followers and led to their departure shortly after this engagement, he had succeeded in converting to Christianity nearly 800 members of a rival native group, and laid the foundations for Spain's subsequent claim to the Islands. The archipelago, originally peopled by Negritos, had witnessed successive immigrations of Indonesians and Malaysians as early as 3000 B. C., and the arrival of Chinese and Japanese traders sometime after A. D. 700, and of Moslem Arab missionaries in the fourteenth and fifteenth centuries. But it was this brief Iberian incursion that brought the Islands to the attention of Western geographers and colonialists.

For the next three and one-half centuries, Spanish colonialism in the Philippines developed slowly, following patterns similar to those in Latin America and the Caribbean. Sequestered by Spanish mercantile theory, Manila served as entrepôt on the Acapulco-China galleon trade route. During the nineteenth century, Filipino fortunes waxed and waned in direct relation to the occasional upsurges of liberalism in Spain, but for the most part, the indigenous inhabitants did not benefit from the Spanish-imposed system of encomiendas, caïques, and friar-controlled provincial governments. Although localized rebellions led by native chieftains and religious leaders occurred regularly, traditional ethnic animosities militated against any united actions. Only after Philippine ports were opened in 1834, expanding economic opportunities for both Spanish *peninsulares* and the growing class of Philippine-Chinese-Spanish mestizos, was it possible for the rising tide of social liberalism in Europe to affect the Philippines.

Many of these newly advancing mestizo families acquired wealth by accumulating land not controlled by the small Spanish ruling class. Since social acceptance was denied them by the *peninsulares* in Manila, they used this new wealth to send their sons abroad. There they found less prejudice and an intellectual stimulation, which encouraged their dreams of equality at home. This small group of *illustrados,* as they came to be known, provided the theoretical and propagandist framework for the growing reform movement in the Philippines. With brief exception, the Spanish colonial government, encouraged by the friar semi-theocracy, overreacted to this originally peaceful reform effort.

Creating martyrs in 1872 with the garroting of three native priests, the Spanish contribution to Philippine nationalist mythology culminated in 1896 with the public execution of José Rizal, the leading *illustrado* spokesman and a Philippine novelist of some repute. Although Rizal had not advocated violent revolution, his death served as the kindling point for a fiery union of the *illustrado* elite and the peasant masses. This union provided the basis for an on-again-off-again rebellion directed by Generals Emilio Aguinaldo and Antonio Luna, and advised by the *illustrado* thinker, Apolinario Mabini. It was this revolutionary movement which was both encouraged and confused by the sudden American naval interest in the southwest Pacific in early 1898.

In late 1897, Aguinaldo and several of the other revolutionary leaders agreed to what became known as the Truce of Biyak-na-bato. According to this agreement, the insurgent leaders would go into temporary exile in Hong Kong and direct their followers to give up their arms in return for ₱800,000 to be supplied in three payments by the Spanish government. The Spanish believed that the revolution was at an end, while Aguinaldo and his compatriots spent the time in Hong Kong arranging for additional arms paid for with the ₱400,000 first payment, which they deposited in Chinese banks. Although historians disagree about the details of the truce and its subsequent breakdown, it is clear that both sides felt that the other had broken its word and that Biyak-na-bato was merely a temporary lull in the overall Philippine fight for independence. In the meantime, Commodore Dewey and several minor U.S. State Department officials stationed in Hong Kong and Singapore saw in the presence of Aguinaldo and his companions an ideal opportunity for an alliance which might aid the still-undefined American venture into Pacific colonialism.[2] Consequently, in late April 1898, when Dewey received the go-ahead from Washington, a later denied but clearly negotiated agreement had been reached between the insurgents and the representatives of the United States government. Afterwards, Aguinaldo would claim that he had been encouraged to believe that the United States had no permanent interest in the Philippines. Pressure from Washington forced the emissaries in Hong Kong and Singapore to deny that they had negotiated along these lines. Whatever the case, it is certain that Dewey arranged for Aguinaldo's return to the Philippines on the revenue cutter *McCulloch* in mid-May. When he arrived in Cavite on May 19, he was welcomed by Dewey on the *Olympia* and immediately set about reorganizing his army to participate in the final dissolution of the Spanish reign in the Islands.

Meanwhile, half a world away in Washington, United States leaders grappled with the implications of their newly won role among the major actors on the world stage. President McKinley and his cabinet had reluctantly entered what became known as the Spanish-American War on the crest of a wave of popular jingoism encouraged by journalistic fantasies and a decade of domestic economic and social upheaval. While the Teller Amendment denied the nation's expansionists any long-lasting colonial influence in Cuba, it soon became clear that other benefits might accrue from what was most often described by its advocates as an altruistic attempt to aid our hemispheric brothers in their efforts to throw off the heavy yoke of Spanish rule. Although this argument was in conflict with a growing anti-imperialist movement and was weakened by the news of Dewey's victory in the far-off Pacific, it did not die but was simply enlarged to suggest that American efforts must expand to encompass additional responsibilities for those darker-skinned Filipinos so obviously in need of Anglo-Saxon inspiration and guidance. Urged on by Rudyard Kipling and William Randolph Hearst, most Americans believed that Dewey's exploits already had delivered the Philippines into their hands and that it was only their Christian duty to do their best by them. If, in the process, the United States stood to gain economically and strategically from the Islands' natural resources, cheap labor and well-placed ports, these gains were only the rightful due of a nation so beneficently inspired.

If Douglas MacArthur thought at all about the Philippines during this early period, it was almost certainly in these terms. Informed only by limited newspaper reports from the area, and busy preparing for West Point, his attention was more than likely focused on the Caribbean aspect of the war which received much more coverage in the early months. All this would change during the next year when his father was reassigned to the Philippines, and when the younger MacArthur's experience at West Point began to incorporate a Pacific perspective.

In addition to the personal reasons which inspired Cadet MacArthur's interest in the Philippines, the Spanish-American War and the subsequent acquisition of the Philippines provided the entire Regular Army with fuel to feed the long-banked fires of military ambition. Future historians would deride the "splendid little war" as either an aberration and a blot on the national tradition, or as the logical, if shameful, outgrowth of the theories of manifest destiny, the close of the continental frontier, and the need for new markets. Contemporary expansionists, however, both in and out of the military, viewed the U.S. entry into Cuba as an opportunity for the country to take its rightful place as a world leader and, at the same time, to rebuild a long-neglected defense system which was the necessary support upon which this newly acquired mantle of leadership might rest. Alfred Thayer Mahan and Theodore Roosevelt argued for an impressive Navy and coaling stations with which to supply it; Secretary of War Russell A. Alger, and his much more influential successor, Elihu Root, urged an expanded Regular Army and worked to establish the system which would support it. When the volunteers began to return at the end of their brief enlistment periods, and when, from the Philippines, General Ewell S. Otis and later General Arthur MacArthur continued to request additional troops to quell the surprisingly stubborn Filipino revolutionaries, the incentive was finally provided for a reluctant Congress to vote for the expansion of the army.[3] This series of events was not lost on those preparing for leadership in the new army, nor did their teachers ignore the problems posed by the attempts to fight a conventional war in an archipelago with few roads, minimal alternative transportation, an unsupportive native population, and enemies which included not only tropical disease but adversaries who refused to respond to conventional attacks in conventional ways.

In February 1901, Colonel Albert L. Mills, superintendent of the Military Academy, requested permission of the Adjutant General's office in Washington for Professor Gustav J. Fiebeger, head of the Department of Civil and Military Engineering, to visit "our possessions in the Pacific." Although the Professor was forced to travel at his own expense, he was to be allowed military transportation, and, Mills argued, the experience could not "but operate to enhance his usefulness as an Instructor at the Military Academy."[4] In his fourth year, when Douglas MacArthur achieved third place in this Civil and Military Engineering class,[5] many of Professor Fiebeger's experiences must have been included in the curriculum. Graduating at the top of his class, the young Second Lieutenant chose assignment with the Corps of Engineers, generally considered the branch where promotion was most likely, and volunteered for duty in the Philippines—the only opportunity for active duty, and a route which also would enhance the ambitious young soldier's chance for advancement.[6] By this time, the Philippine Islands had become a reality for him.

The third and most important influence on Douglas MacArthur's initial perspective of the Philippines developed out of his father's extended experiences there. Although shaped by his unique service as military commander in the Spanish-American War and the Philippine-American Revolution which followed, and by his tenure as military governor of the Philippines in the early years of the American colonial regime, the elder MacArthur's philosophy had developed much earlier. In the early 1880s, frustrated by his personal lack of advancement, he undertook a scholarly examination of the Asian question in some depth. By the time of his young son Malcolm's death in 1883, he had prepared a forty-four page report entitled "Chinese Memorandum and Notes" which he attached to his request to former President Grant for an assignment as military attaché to the U.S. legation in China.[7] The carefully prepared report reflected a familiarity with many of the contemporary economic discussions of the period. Although not entirely original in its conception, it represented sincere convictions, which MacArthur continued to hold over the next two decades. He did not specifically identify the Philippines as an important part of his expansionist outline in 1883, but by 1898, the General and many of his fellow expansionists were quick to see how Dewey's victory could help to realize the goals of the philosophy stated earlier.

Written in his traditional "ponderous" style,[8] much of this report illustrated his romantic perspective and the widely accepted beliefs espoused by the Social Darwinists. Referring to Asia as "now the true region of romance, where the heated imagination can indulge the boldest assumptions, since it is essentially an unknown country," MacArthur went on to predict the eventual clash of Russia and the West. Foreseeing "a struggle for . . . supremacy" between Russia and Great Britain, wherein Asia would become "the theatre of gigantic political, and perhaps warlike operations," the Captain argued that this "collision . . . would resound on the shores of the Pacific, and affect the commerce of the world." Obviously, it was not in the best interests of the United States to allow this struggle to impede the development of its own relationship with Asia. "It is now apparent to thinking men," he continued, "that we cannot attain our natural growth, or even continue to exist as a commanding and progressive nationality, unless we secure and maintain the soverignty [*sic*] of the Pacific."

Defining China as "the real stepping stone to supremacy throughout the commercial world," MacArthur went on to suggest that continued national development hinged upon the government's encouragement of this expansion, arguing that George Washington's advice concerning no international entanglements had been put forth "simply as an expedient of weakness." He continued, "The principle of non-intervention handed down by the Fathers, was hardly intended to abrogate or in any way diminish the right of national development, or of self defense. Hence, the principle cannot apply to the question under discussion; as to possess a state of neutrality in the east, where our material interests are paramount, would in effect be an abandonment of most precious rights."

MacArthur argued that U.S. involvement in Asia was inevitably based on what he saw as the Asian tendency toward inertia and the law of historical change. In addition, he believed that America's 1500-mile Pacific coast required a more extensive defense system. The most important reason for expansion, however, was that "the extension of our commerce is absolutely essential to the prosperity and happiness of our citizens." Establishing to his satisfaction the argument for Pacific expansion and the potential for Asian conflict thereby induced, the Captain concluded the report by pointing out the need for "competent Army officer[s]" to observe the military development of the Chinese.

In the first of the appended notes to the report, MacArthur illustrated his awareness of the need for colonial annexation by discussing the possible annexation of Korea by Russia. In the fourth and final note, the most revealing of his arguments, he predicted that "a condition of over-supply is established as a permanency, which in all probability will take place in many industries in the not distant future, the pressing necessity of the hour will be an extension of our markets. No matter how rich we may be in accumulated capital, restriction of production, by reason of restriction of markets, means stagnation of business, increasing pauperism, and social disturbances." Referring to the recent discontent in the anthracite coal region of Pennsylvania where he had served during the great railroad strikes of 1877,[9] MacArthur concluded ominously that without an increased international market, "the mass of unemployed will amount to a considerable fraction of the whole, large enough perhaps to cause universal uneasiness." The solution was obvious: "We will have to seek trade everywhere. We must have new and ever-expanding markets to meet our ever-increasing powers of production; and these seem to lie principally in the far East, and there, we naturally and inevitably must go." He believed, as did a growing number of American businessmen, policy makers, and theorists, that the tide of international development was moving west, and that if the United States did not want to be left in the backwater of the future, it must turn from its preoccupation with European concerns to a new awareness of the potential of Asia.[10]

Thus, in June 1898, when General MacArthur's orders were changed from his expected duty in Cuba to service in the Philippines, he was not adverse to nor totally unprepared for the new assignment.[11] His still-intense ambition was encouraged by the opportunities that he believed awaited him in the Philippines, and his earlier interest in Asia was reawakened. His father's change of station undoubtedly increased young Douglas's awareness of the occurrences in the Pacific as well, and there is every reason to believe that from this point on, both MacArthurs' general interest in the Orient became specifically attached to the Philippine archipelago.

By the time General MacArthur arrived in Manila on August 4, 1898, it had become abundantly clear to the commanders of the American, Spanish, and Filipino forces involved that the Spanish hold on Manila was extremely tenuous.[12] Consequently, during the first days after the full complement of American troops, approximately 11,000 officers and men, were finally encamped around the capital city, General Fermin Jaudenes, commanding the Spanish forces in Manila, regretfully agreed to participate in a "mock battle," which was to allow the Spaniards to surrender Manila with the honors of war. Aguinaldo, always hopeful that his cooperation would bring American support to his country's movement for independence, agreed to allow a portion of his forces to move aside so that the American troops under Brigadier General Francis V. Greene would have clear access to the Spanish. During the second week of August, after a polite exchange between Major General Wesley Merritt, in overall command of the American land forces in the Philippines, now Rear Admiral George Dewey, and Governor General Jaudenes, the ceremony was initiated. Four of Dewey's ships began to shell the Spanish defenses. On every front but one, the struggle proceeded as planned, with white flags unfurled and multiple Spanish surrenders in rapid succession. On the road to Singalon, south of the Walled City held by the Spanish, however, the brigade under newly promoted Major General MacArthur's command ran into heavy fire. The Spanish in that area were either uninformed of the previously arranged agreement or angered at the shelling that Aguinaldo had begun at daybreak. In any event, by early afternoon, Singalon was subdued, Intramuros had surrendered, and American troops were deployed in a way which effectively blocked insurgent access to Manila.

General MacArthur's first real engagement in thirty-four years, although accidentally bloody, had primarily been part of a ritualized exchange wherein one Western power gave up its control of a subject people to another Western power, while successfully denying those subject people any influence over the details of that exchange. The idealism of the young brevet Colonel of 1864, partially dissipated by ensuing years of thwarted ambition, was further diminished by these realities of colonial warfare. Arthur MacArthur continued to support his country's emerging international goals, but he, out of all the American military leaders close enough to the Philippines to understand what was really going on, refused to deny the true nature of the undertaking. He knew that his Philippine adversaries had both the reasons and the ability to make America's quest for President McKinley's "benevolent assimilation" a long and bloody struggle.

Word soon arrived in Manila of the August 12 cessation of hostilities in the Spanish-American War, rendering the August 13 Battle of Manila unofficial at best. Instructed to wait until the Treaty of Paris was negotiated, General Merritt and his successor as military governor, Major General Otis, settled their troops into an uneasy truce, hoping through a series of vague promises to keep Generals Luna and Aguinaldo under control. The Spanish troops, although theoretically prisoners of war, remained at liberty and largely assumed the position of disinterested observers, believing that the final treaty would send them home.

Appointed by General Merritt to serve as provost-marshal-general of Manila, General MacArthur was given the opportunity to observe, at first hand, the results of the prolonged siege of the city. The responsibilities of this position extended well beyond its traditional concern with the judiciary and included at least sixteen departments, forcing the General to oversee public instruction, prison reform, and many other details of municipal government.[13] As military Chief of Police, he was given three regiments of infantry and ordered to bring the chaotic situation under control. The municipal water supply, held by Aguinaldo's forces, had been cut off for two months. The food generally supplied from the provinces had been sharply curtailed, leading to a noticeable lessening of the numbers of ponies and pets usually seen in the narrow streets of the Walled City. The Spanish system of garbage disposal, which consisted of dragging the refuse to the edge of town and leaving it to rot, had completely broken down. In addition to the stench and discomfort, constant vigilance was required to forestall sudden bolo attacks from the many unfriendly citizens. Malaria, dengue fever, and dysentery were daily companions, and the specter of the dreaded cholera was never far away. There was little effective fire-fighting equipment, the city was overcrowded by Spanish refugees from the provinces, and to magnify the misery beyond belief, two hundred lepers, generously freed from the hospital by the Spanish, roamed the city for the next four months. Nevertheless, order was quickly restored, and Manila seemed to return to a nearly normal condition with native shops, banks, and customhouses open for business; public transportation moving once again; newspapers readily available; and direct communications with the United States restored.[14] In this period between battle assignments, the accomplishment of these tasks gave Arthur MacArthur and the men he commanded more than enough to keep them busy.

One of those men, young William Compton, described this interlude in detail in a letter to his fraternity brothers in St. Paul.[15] On patrol one day, fatigue the next, and off duty on the third, the volunteers were finding service in the tropics much more rigorous than they had expected. They spent their off duty hours in the Luneta, a park just south of Intramuros, watching "Spanish lovelies" and enjoying the sight of Filipinos riding a "regular steam American merry-go-round" as often as they could. Stationed in Tondo, one of the rougher districts in old Manila, Compton and his fellow infantrymen found themselves the frequent targets of roving bands of Macabebes[16] with "long, dangerous-looking knives [which they knew] how to use." Mentioning the concern over a recent outbreak of smallpox, Compton admitted that venereal disease was also a problem. On the whole, however, he found much improvement in conditions in Manila during the four months he had been stationed there. Better food, real cots to sleep on, cleaner streets, more equitable conditions in the Spanish prisons, and better communications were among the things he praised. In commending General MacArthur's "brave manner" during the Battle of Manila, the young foot soldier conveyed respect for his commander. He acknowledged the necessity of the work they were doing, but he longed to return to cool St. Paul, more than anything else.

Although this "police action" was undoubtedly one of the more unpleasant assignments during this period of waiting, it provided Arthur MacArthur an excellent opportunity to confront at first hand several of the problems which would be his twenty months later when he was appointed military governor of the entire archipelago. He kept his eyes open, saw more of the Filipinos than his superiors, Merritt or Otis, and recognized their obvious desire for independence. He did not support the Philippine goals, but he never underestimated them. He, unlike most of the Americans already present or on their way to Manila, accepted the fact that most Filipinos preferred to undertake the responsibilities of self-government rather than to follow the dictates of another white colonial master, no matter how benevolent. He believed that the process of changing their minds would be long and costly, politically as well as militarily. In these assessments, MacArthur proved more farsighted than most of the American policy makers involved.

On February 4, 1899, the tensions which had been developing between the Filipinos and the Americans exploded into actual combat, engaging MacArthur's command on the north side
of the Pasig River that evening, and the entire American force
in Manila early the next day. Ostensibly resulting from a misunderstood sentry signal, the eruption was not unexpected, and
marked the point at which the Spanish-American War really
ended in the Philippines (the U. S. Senate was, at that moment,
in the process of ratifying the Treaty of Paris) and the Philippine-American Revolution began. General MacArthur's active
participation in this three-year struggle, both as combat leader
and military governor, provided him with the basis for the final
conclusions concerning the Philippines he presented to the Senate in 1902,[17] and conveyed to Douglas after his return to the
states.

Prior to the February 4 engagement, General MacArthur
had been placed in command of the Second Division of the VIII
Army Corps.[18] For the remainder of the winter, his forces pursued Aguinaldo and his cabinet in an attempt to capture the
Filipino leader through conventional military maneuvers.[19] Despite a massive effort on the part of the American command,
Aguinaldo escaped the U.S. trap in late March, 1899, and retreated into the mountains to reconsider his strategy.

By November, however, it appeared that U. S. efforts were
finally meeting with some success. There were sporadic examples of guerrilla-like atrocities, but the diminishing conventional
response of Aguinaldo's army convinced MacArthur and his
fellow officers that the Philippine revolutionaries were indeed
persuaded that further resistance was futile. From that point on,
MacArthur believed and acted upon the belief that the active
phase of the insurrection was ended and that the remaining
problem was merely one of convincing the populace that the
Americans meant no harm. He had expected acquiescence once
the Philippine civilians became aware of the good intentions and
strength of the Americans, and apparently he was right. With
General Otis's concurrence, MacArthur spent December occu-
pying Zambales and Bataan provinces. The new year, the first of

the twentieth century, would prove this assessment wrong; Aquinaldo and his armies had not given up. Instead, at a meeting of the Philippine Council of War on November 12, the revolutionaries reassessed their strategy and decided that the only response still open to them was to revert to the guerrilla tactics which had proven so successful against the Spanish in 1896. They expected and quickly received loyal support for this decision from most Philippine civilians.

In the period between January and May, 1900, regular military resistance on the part of the Filipinos ended. By February 13, all of Luzon was ostensibly under American control, and by May 5, when Otis was relieved as military governor and replaced by Arthur MacArthur, commanders in the field reported that all the major islands were occupied and civilians were returning to their homes. This proved to be merely a lull before the storm, and the early months of MacArthur's tenure as military governor were marked by bloody guerrilla attacks leading to American casualty figures nearly double that of the previous year. The American military responded in kind: McKinley's policy of benevolent assimilation was replaced, at least temporarily, by heightened force, and accusations of war atrocities arose on both sides.[20] General MacArthur, who had sincerely believed in the earlier, more benign policy, was frustrated by the necessity for this reversal in strategy. His respect for his adversaries increased even as his patience diminished. But this was not to be the only source of frustration for the new Military Governor: On June 3, 1900, the second Philippine Commission, headed by former federal Judge William Howard Taft, arrived aboard the *Hancock,* and a situation which was to prove General MacArthur's bête noire was about to develop.[21]

The arrival of the six-member Philippine Commission aroused a variety of responses. To the Filipinos who observed them, they were indeed impressive. As one historian observed, "the aggregate weight of the five members of the commission and its secretary was 1,362 pounds, an average of 227 pounds each. The Filipinos, who are small people, regarded the commission as an imposing spectacle."[22] The American military government, on the other hand, was neither impressed nor pleased with its new advisers. Conflict had already arisen between General Otis and the first Philippine Commission (the Schurman Commission), when Otis questioned the status of the group and argued against its policy of negotiation and concessions to the Philippine revolutionaries.[23] To further complicate the issue, instructions to the second committee had been issued in Washington before the shift in the nature of the Philippine offensive had become clear. Consequently, when the commission arrived in June, they were faced with a new set of circumstances, and forced to work with a new military governor who did not underestimate the serious nature of the military situation as had his predecessor. Even if the two men directly involved had possessed complementary personalities, which they did not, conflict would almost assuredly have developed.

Focused around the central issue of authority and the question of when civilian rule should occur, the disagreements between MacArthur and Taft illustrated the widely varying backgrounds and expectations of the two major participants. Taft, politically knowledgeable and judicially experienced, preferred an informal system of communication in direct contrast to MacArthur's longstanding experience with strict military protocol. Although the two men had initially set out to cooperate, Taft was almost immediately put off by what he believed was the U. S. military's overreaction to the new guerrilla tactics. He had been led to believe by Otis's mild communiques and McKinley's politically inspired policy that the revolution was merely the response of a small faction of Filipinos. MacArthur's experience had convinced him that just the opposite was true. In the early months of his administration he was forced to use more stringent military tactics than ever before against the many Filipinos who acted in concert with their guerrilla leaders. Convinced that he understood the situation more completely than did the new commission, MacArthur had apparently chafed in the long months of subordination to Otis's ill-advised command, and looked forward to being able to initiate policies of his own. He saw the complex issue of civil-military authority as a direct personal humiliation and, additionally, was not convinced of the legality of the commission's increasing assumption of power. This underlying attitude displayed itself in disputes over questions of appointments, the formation of a native constabulary, and the treatment of suspected insurgents. Again and again, MacArthur characteristically tried to define formally the responsibilities of his office and those of the commission. Each time, the six members of the commission indicated that they preferred a more pragmatic, less systematic procedure. Even in the Taft descriptions of the conflict, however, it is clear that, just as often as MacArthur stiffly refused to cooperate, he made efforts to achieve harmony.

Although there is no doubt that tension existed in the thirteen months during which the two men shared authority, the picture of the stuffy, proper martinet harassing the big, bluff negotiator is overdrawn—the product of stereotypical assessments rather than a close examination of the facts of the case. Still, there can be little doubt that this tense, long-lasting dispute convinced MacArthur that frequently civil administrators did not understand the realities of military necessity. The conflict ended only when the General was reassigned to the United States in July 1901. Later, when Taft became Secretary of War, and did not select General MacArthur as chief of staff of the Army,[24] he undoubtedly based his decision at least partly on his personal experience with the General in 1900–1901. To the intensely ambitious MacArthur family, this provided one more example of misjudgment in Washington, a lesson not lost on the younger MacArthur as well.

By the time Arthur MacArthur was called to Washington in the spring of 1902 to testify before the Senate committee investigating affairs in the Philippines, he had taken the time to evaluate his experiences and to draw firm conclusions concerning the Islands, their people, and the value of the United States colonial experiment. Many of his opinions reflected little change from the attitudes he conveyed in the "Chinese Memorandum and Notes" of 1883. Now, however, the locale from which the

United States must launch its Pacific venture had become specific and was, obviously, the Philippines. In his attitude toward immediate independence, in which the Democratic minority on the committee was interested, MacArthur differed little from the position taken by Taft and other members of the McKinley-Roosevelt administrations: While the Filipinos should be given greater participation in the newly introduced democratic institutions of government, immediate independence would lead to "chaos."[25] The Filipinos, whom he saw as romantic and sincere, but naive, had, he believed, little experience in the pragmatic necessities of the politics of self-government. The General appreciated the Islanders' desire for democracy, their ability to work hard when adequately rewarded, and their ultimate potential as citizens and officials of an independent nation. In this opinion he differed once again from Taft, who had earlier testified before the committee, and was somewhat less impressed by Philippine abilities.[26]

MacArthur, considered by some of the members of the committee as the "fairest witness" they had heard, obviously possessed a sincere attachment to and respect for the Filipinos with whom he had been in contact.[27] Unlike his peers, he believed that the Filipinos were different from Americans due to their long experience under Spanish rule rather than from any racial inferiority.[28] His evaluation of the Filipinos' inept fighting skills was based on an understanding of their lack of adequate training rather than the commonly accepted view of racial cowardice.[29] On the paramount question concerning the strategic importance of the Philippine Islands to the United States, however, he expressed the majority opinion that, for its advancement as a world power, the United States must hold the Islands for the foreseeable future. Indeed, he argued

The archipelago['s] . . . strategical position is unexcelled by that of any other position on the globe . . . relatively better placed strategically than Japan . . . likewise, India. . . . The Philippines are the center of that position. It affords a means of protecting American interests which, with the very least output of physical power, has the effect of a commanding position in itself to retard hostile action. Our presence in the Philippines, possible without the employment of any physical effort at all, will always insure . . . all that we need, all that we can possibly require.[30]

This declaration was characteristically overstated. Nonetheless, it illustrated a point of view which, while widely held in the early years, became increasingly unpopular, even within military circles, as Japan developed into a competitive world power, as the importance of aviation increased in defense considerations, and as the United States became further entangled in the economics of colonialism. It was, however, one of the strongly held viewpoints that, along with his attachment to the romance of the Islands and islanders, Arthur MacArthur would impress on his son. Thirty-five years later, when that son was offered the opportunity to build an army for the newly formed Philippine Commonwealth, he would make the same argument: that the mere presence of an adequate defense force (supported by the United States) would forestall invasion by a hostile nation.[31]

In the period between General MacArthur's return from the Philippines in the summer of 1901 and Douglas's departure thereto in the fall of 1903, father and son frequently discussed the Islands. Although academy restrictions forbade Douglas leave to visit his father, there is reason to believe that the General visited West Point to reclaim his wife in the period between his arrival in the States and the assumption of his new command of the Department of Colorado.[32] During this visit, while his impressions were still fresh, he and Douglas no doubt began their discussion, and the opinions and expectations Douglas would take with him on his first trip to the Islands began to form. Visions of tropical beauty, so different from the gray skies and windy plain of the academy, must have been inviting, and descriptions of the fiery and romantic temperament of the Filipinos appealed to the young cadet's already well-developed propensities in that direction.[33] General MacArthur's recollections undoubtedly provided a valuable balance for the views which Douglas may have formed from often distorted press accounts of the revolutionary setting. Recounting his views of Aguinaldo and other Philippine leaders, the General would have persuaded Douglas that the Filipinos were both skilled militarily and loyal to a vision of their national destiny. By the time Second Lieutenant MacArthur sailed on the *Sherman* in October 1903, in contrast to many of those accompanying him, he expected a diverse society, a setting of incomparable beauty, and a citizenry still intent on self-government. In sum, the Philippines seemed likely to provide an appropriate setting for the adventure and advancement for which the young soldier longed so intensely.

In the more than two years between the MacArthur visits to the Islands, the Philippine situation changed. One historian has described this time as the beginning of a period of "suppressed nationalism,"[34] and, indeed, the Filipinos had switched their strategy. Because of necessity, the mood of the nation began to swing from active support of Aguinaldo's guerrilla tactics to limited participation in the political connections established by the new civil administration.

Accounts of life in the Philippines between 1901 and 1903 vary depending upon their source.[35] Clearly, vast shifts occurred during this period as military influence diminished and Taft's civil government attempted to develop in the Filipinos the American vision of progressive democracy. Although rebellion continued at least until 1907 in the more remote provinces, most of Luzon during this period was involved in another kind of upheaval: one of conflicting political goals, cultural misunderstandings, and economic struggles.

The Taft Commission, acting upon the McKinley-Root instructions, began immediately to incorporate sympathetic members of the Philippine elite into the government.[36] By appointing a Philippine minority to the commission, and allowing the formation of a political party composed mostly of Spanish mestizo members of the Philippine ruling class (the *Partido Federal*), they developed a body of ambitious Filipinos from which Taft could fill the reorganized courts and expanding civil service. By placing these Filipinos in public positions, the commission hoped to convince the general populace that cooperation with the Americans was acceptable and rewarding. Since this cooperation permitted a return to business as usual, at least in metropolitan areas, the tactic for the most part succeeded.

Pockets of resistance remained, however, particularly within the literate segment of society. Encouraged by a tradition established during the revolution against Spain, many playwrights and newspapermen fanned the revolutionary flame through symbolic dramas and editorials, despite a continuing policy of press censorship. In addition, attempts were made to establish other political parties, which would draw popular support by advocating immediate independence. After a sedition act was passed in November 1901, efforts of this sort were punished by fines and imprisonment. Outright military rebellion and guerrilla strategy no longer existed in the more populated areas. Governor Taft attempted racial and cultural compromise, and was supported by that segment of the Philippine society which had the most to lose through further violence. Nonetheless, Philippine nationalism was still a factor with which to reckon during this period. Passage of the Brigandage Act in November 1902 and the Reconcentration Act in June 1903 provided the civil authorities with the legal bases necessary to suppress undesirable political activity wherever it occurred.

Within this framework of political conflict and compromise, the Manila-American community of which Douglas MacArthur would become an active member in 1904 began to take form. As the volunteer units of the U.S. Army were returned to the states in 1899, 1900, and 1901, some of those to be mustered out chose to receive their discharges in the Islands and remain there to make their fortunes. According to the statistics compiled in one analysis,[37] the majority of these men were originally from the southern and western United States but in most other ways represented a wide spectrum of American society at the turn of the century. Their racial and ethnic origins were diverse; most had some education and a religious affiliation; few were married; and their mechanical and professional skills added much to the modernizing process just beginning in the Philippines. Perhaps five to six percent of the discharged volunteers chose to remain

in the Islands. While a few would move out into the less populated areas, most of those who stayed began almost immediately
to put down roots in Manila where opportunities for advancement were greatest. Although it may be argued that these men
were probably the most adventurous of their lot, their quick
efforts to organize the institutions of American culture in this
new setting suggested that the main reason for their decision
was not additional adventure but a simple recognition that the
Islands provided a wider opportunity to succeed according to
American standards. As might be expected of young bachelors
of recent military experience, their conservative influence was
manifest in their investments and the small businesses that they
established, and was not of a social nature. The stringent social
codes which developed in the Manila-American community during this period were encouraged by other newly arriving
groups.[38]

Although the members of the Philippine Commission, their
staffs, and families exerted some social influence during these
early years, the nature and scope of their social responsibilities
allowed them little experience in common with the other members of the American community. Taft, from personal preference and his understanding of his office, chose to mingle
democratically with members of the Philippine elite in a manner
which was altogether foreign to the majority of the new immi-
grants. Instead, the former volunteers, increased in numbers by
the influx of nearly 1000 government-sponsored American
teachers, additional civil servants, missionaries, and more businessmen, and their families, chose to develop an enclave which
would provide a haven for American values. As might be expected, these values and the institutions they spawned discouraged the frivolity which had been present in the saloons of the
Escolta during the active phase of the Revolution. In addition,
the American schools, churches, and social organizations were
closed to Filipinos, a predictable decision, but one frowned
upon by the civil government and resented by the surrounding
Philippine society. These attitudes tended to place the majority
of the Manila-Americans at odds with the policies of the civil

government, and when the Taft administration tried to control the more visible examples of American economic exploitation, the up-and-coming American boosters resisted emphatically in their newspapers and public meeting places.

Of course, most of the day-to-day immigrant experience was focused upon more mundane concerns. In these early years, a newly arrived family was faced with immediate problems which seldom left time for political awareness. Although Manila hotels and restaurants provided comfortable quarters and adequate fare for the incoming settler, the prices charged usually precluded an extended stay. Since housing adequate by American standards was scarce, makeshift apartments appeared over local stores, in the homes of the tiny Philippine middle class, within the few existing schools and churches, and, indeed, wherever a room or two became available. The American community began to expand out of the Walled City into the adjoining district of Ermita.

The need for safe water and familiar recipe ingredients was a difficult problem in the early period, and would quickly provide an area of opportunity for the burgeoning class of American entrepreneurs. In the meantime, the newly arrived housewife generally settled for canned goods, including dairy products, which she could buy in the exchanges of the still extensive military establishment. If tempted by the succulent foreign fruits and delicacies, she risked bouts of severe dysentery for the entire family. When a frightening cholera epidemic developed in Manila in early 1902, many of the Manila-Americans must have had at least momentary regrets about their new adventure.

Although many of the more superficial traditions of the Manila business community seemed to adapt easily to the habits and rulings of the new colonial government, longer working hours and shortened siestas were not entirely effective in turning the local shopping districts into copies of Main Street. Native vendors from the provinces began to bring their produce into the city as soon as conditions allowed. The crowded native markets in Quiapo and along the Escolta thronged with Philippine peasants much different from the more sophisticated Manila urbanites. With the conflicting dialects, crowded and disordered stalls, and the vendors' obvious enjoyment of the haggling process, the consequent melee caused many young wives from small towns in America to retreat in confusion. Although unfortunate, their resulting determination to establish recognizable American supports for their new existence is perhaps more understandable in the light of the tremendous cultural chasm they were required daily to bridge.

While the domesticated segment of the American community struggled with these concerns, the large bachelor population accepted cultural differences with much more ease. The young men seldom resisted the enchantments provided by the local saloonkeepers who had had much experience in fulfilling the similar needs of the Spanish occupiers, and until Governor Taft ruled that the taverns on the Escolta must be removed to a less obvious location, the pesos spent there were welcome additions to the process of postwar economic rehabilitation. Generally boarding in local Philippine homes, many of the newly discharged soldiers were also not as impressed by racial differences so obvious to the more conservative members of the American community, and throughout the war and the occupation, marriages and common-law liasons were not uncommon. In an attempt to provide what was considered a more salutary environment for these presumably misguided young men, one of the earliest objectives of the missionaries who descended on Manila was the establishment of clubs which would provide more appropriate refreshment and social activity. In addition, the commissioned ranks of the still large military establishment were provided with a new Army-Navy Club where they could gather in grand isolation to refurbish the tenets of their faith and shore up the occasionally besieged walls of imperial superiority.[39]

Because the needs and goals of these various groups were so diverse, the potential for ideological conflict existed within the three major segments of society. The experiences of the enlisted men often led them to conclusions sharply in contrast to those of their commissioned officers. The Manila-American business community was frequently at odds with the civil government, which it felt should protect American commerce more completely. Finally, the Philippine elite, newly participating in the offices of colonial control, could seldom identify with the longing for immediate independence which characterized the older Philippine revolutionaries and their followers. But conflicts between these groups developed slowly, and in 1902 and 1903, appearances in Manila seemed to reflect cooperation. Nowhere would the mingling of these newly created interest groups be more symbolically represented than in the early evening social hour on the centuries-old Luneta, facing Manila Bay.

This popular gathering place, bordering Intramuros, welcomed much of the Manila population at the end of the working day. Here civil servants, merchants, local housewives, and peddlers gathered to watch the magnificent sunsets over Manila Bay, listen to the pleasant melodies produced by a local band in the nearby bandstand, and relax over casual conversation and tiny ice cream cones. After the arrival of the Americans, the scene contained fewer Spanish soldiers admiring the local beauties, but other men in uniforms joined the throng, and by the time the Tafts arrived in Manila, the Philippine Constabulary Band, under the direction of Major Walter Loving, provided music almost every evening. Much to the delight of one chronicler,[40] Governor Taft refused the coach-and-four, which was a prerogative of his office, and chose to drive a regular carriage and pair to the left, with the crowd, rather than to the right, as had the former Spanish governors. The symbolic nature of this choice was not lost on his newly acquired subjects. As he, Mrs. Taft, and the young Taft children arrived on the Luneta for the late afternoon drive and concert, the young Tafts were often allowed to play with their classmates from the nearby American School. At these times, the Philippine crowds were more likely to cheer than were the Americans.[41]

By 1903, these symbolic gestures and the other efforts of Governor Taft and the members of his civilian colonial government were at least partially accepted by the urban Philippine society. The conflicts which faced General MacArthur during his tenure in Manila two years earlier had become more subtle. In the outlying islands, however, guerrilla activity continued. The problems that the military leader had foreseen in 1901 remained subjects for serious consideration. In the months between Douglas's graduation from West Point and his departure for the Philippines, the General undoubtedly conveyed this perspective to his son. Although altered somewhat by his own experiences during the next year, his father's point of view, buttressed by Douglas's experience at West Point and his understanding of the goals and values of his society, provided the basis upon which the young soldier would build his own understanding of the archipelago. In combination with his personal needs, his expectations of the Islands defined what he found there. For Douglas MacArthur, the Philippines came to represent a romantic setting within which he might achieve the deeds of valor which were so important to his self-image. There a different and valiant people, weakened by colonial exploitation, would pose small threat to a young man destined in his own mind and the mind of his family to fulfill the MacArthur heritage—yet still unsure of his personal right or ability to do so.

(3)

First Assignments

We sat in the charmed circles of the
chancellories of the strong and the weak.
Douglas MacArthur
Reminiscences, 39.

BETWEEN THE Spanish-American War and World War I, the Philippine Islands provided the American military establishment with its primary training ground. There, during the first decade of the twentieth century, almost all of the officers who would later shape the modern army first faced problems of command, terrain, and logistics in an alien country. For many of these young men, Manila was their first foreign post, the "insurrectos," their first enemy. While very different from the situation they would later confront in Europe, their Philippine experience nonetheless provided an additional bond which helped to cement the collective world view of the American military establishment.[1]

Douglas MacArthur, a major influence on the development of the U.S. Army in the twentieth century, was also shaped by this shared background. During his year in the Islands, from October 1903 to October 1904, he had his first real taste of the workings of the establishment to which he would devote his life, and the first practical opportunity to assess his father's view of the importance of Asia to the United States. In combination with his superior talents and capacity for hard work, this experience allowed him to draw conclusions upon which he would base future political, military, and diplomatic successes. In addition, the Islands were particularly important to Second Lieutenant MacArthur because for him they fulfilled a personal need.

Until his departure for the Philippines at the age of twenty-three, Douglas MacArthur had led a remarkably protected life. All his extensive travel and education had occurred in the company of one or both of his parents. During this year, he would be given his first opportunity to test, and either confirm or deny, the views and values they had imparted to him. The Philippine Islands provided the young man with an environment which, in its complexity, was particularly suited to the ambiguities of his own inner needs. On the one hand, the archipelago was far away and very different from anything he had previously experienced. It thereby provided him with an opportunity to test his budding abilities free, for the first time, from close parental supervision. On the other hand, because of his father's unique experience there, Douglas could not escape either the shadow of the MacArthur name, nor the influence of the elder MacArthur's firmly held opinions. Once again, the conflict between his need to become himself and the fear of going beyond the security of parental direction was reaffirmed. Because the Islands were changing during this period, the young Second Lieutenant might have redefined his views and responses to the situation there had he stayed longer or been allowed to remain away from his parents after his return to the States. But he returned home quickly and this assignment was almost immediately followed by an extended family tour through the Orient. Thus, the first chance for self-definition was cut short.

In another way, too, this first experience in the Philippines highlighted the dual nature of Douglas's inner needs. Almost half of his time there was spent in the still partially subdued provinces. The dangers he saw and experienced there encouraged his perception of the Islands as a place suitable for the heroic deeds which would support his view of himself as a brave warrior. In many ways, the jungles of Panay and Samar provided him with his own personal western frontier, complete with still uncontrolled natives and unruly outlaws. Born too late to fulfill the fantasies of his early childhood in the American Southwest, he had been given a second chance.

The second half of his assignment in the Islands brought the young man into contact with colonial government officials and military commanders in Manila. In these "charmed circles," he performed administrative duties successfully, was promoted for the first time, and met men who would later be helpful in the advancement of his career. The city reflected a unique combination of ageless oriental mystery and twentieth-century American progress. As such, it was ideally suited to serve as context for the dual tasks dictated by Douglas's childhood and previous developmental experiences. On one level, the conflict inherent in his inner assignment precluded its successful resolution, and demanded its repetition throughout his life. He could not entirely define himself and still always submit to the dictates of his parents. Nonetheless, the Philippines, as the scene of the first of many such efforts, took on a special significance for the young soldier. For the rest of his life, and on many levels of his consciousness, he perceived the Islands as the most appropriate stage upon which to act out both his personal and public dramas. There he could participate in adventures which would reinforce his shaky self-esteem in an arena made safe by his father's still-remembered presence, and the warm support of many Filipinos. Just a little more than a year later, the young man would glimpse even more impressive "circles" of power. The impressions he gathered during his year in the Philippine Islands and the seven-month Asian tour which followed were vital to his still forming world view. It is for all these reasons that a detailed examination of this period is necessary.

Boarding the U.S. Army transport *Sherman* on October 1, 1903, MacArthur spent approximately four weeks at sea, glimpsing, for the first time, the island of Guam where the ship stopped to refuel. Accounts from the period emphasize the camaraderie which developed during these long journeys, enhanced by the similarities of background, training, and values of the voyagers. In close quarters—each small cabin contained four bunks—the days were long, and increasingly hot. While Douglas was excited about the adventures and opportunities that he expected in the Philippines, and was made more comfortable by the companionship of many of his classmates from West Point,[2] his anticipation was clouded by the reality of his first separation from his family. The length of his stay had not yet been determined, and while this foreign service was necessary for the young officer's advancement, the distance and dangers made so real by General MacArthur's discussions of his experiences there heightened any misapprehensions that his son secretly harbored. For the first time, the young officer was faced with the conflict inherent in the life he, and his family, had chosen—the success they all so ardently desired for him could only be acquired far from the secure maternal haven which provided some of the impetus for its achievement.

The days on ship passed quickly, lightened by card games, group singing, and the antics of still unseasoned young soldiers. Some of the more experienced officers worried over reports from Samar and Mindanao describing the bloody efforts of still active revolutionaries. Talk of increasing conflict between Russia and Japan was fanned by colorful press accounts in old newspapers picked up in Guam, and many of the young officers on board hoped for a closer view of the now certain war. These heady concerns served to heighten the sense of adventures to come for these recent graduates on their way to Manila.

On October 28, the *Sherman* entered the mouth of Manila Bay, and within a few hours the increased traffic occasioned by the many small sailboats, inter-island steamers, and native bancas foretold the first view of the capital city of the Philippines.[3] Since the docks were not large enough to accommodate a ship the size of the *Sherman,* it anchored at some distance from shore. Immediately it was surrounded by the native cascos, anxious to unload the passengers and their baggage and convey them to the Custom House, farther up the Pasig River. Once this was accomplished, the young officers set off to report for duty. Although originally assigned to Luneta Barracks in Manila,[4] Douglas MacArthur's orders were changed two days prior to his arrival, and when he reached Manila he found that he would have to leave almost immediately to reach Iloilo, on the island of Panay. There he was to join Company "I," Third Engineer Battalion, and to assume "duties in connection with the completion of wharf retaining wall, and earthen fill at Camp Jossman Landing.''[5] Manila, to young MacArthur's brief glimpse, was undoubtedly a swirl of narrow, crowded streets, old Spanish buildings topped with red Chinese tiles, and bustling calesia drawn by diminutive ponies carrying other new arrivals on sight-seeing jaunts. His own rushed efforts to retrieve his luggage and see it securely placed on the inter-island steamer he would take to Panay precluded further investigation. It would be another four months before he would be given opportunity to acquaint himself with the city which would later play such an important part in his life.

The period between November 1, 1903, and March 12, 1904, was filled with high adventure for MacArthur. Assigned to the Department of the Visayas, he saw duty on Panay, Samar, Cebu, and Leyte, the four major Visayan islands just south of Luzon. His first post, Camp Jossman, on Guimaras Island five miles off Panay, was a reservation of about 3400 acres housing a headquarters, band, and ten companies of infantry nestled in the hills of the small, green island. Several of these companies were frequently sent to Leyte or Samar, where the attacks of the *ladrónes* (outlaws) were more intense.[6] Situated in one of the healthier climates, Camp Jossman provided nipa quarters and barracks, which were gradually being replaced by buildings of American lumber. There was a good macadam road from the dock at Buena Vista to the post, and the water supply was adequate. Most of those who visited during this period agreed that the camp, and the nearby city of Iloilo, were among the more attractive spots in the Islands.

The harbor at Buena Vista was not sufficient for future military plans, however, and Lieutenant MacArthur was to oversee its improvement. In connection with this assignment, he was required to find timber for pilings, and took a small company of men into the woods for that purpose. While they worked, he carelessly wandered some distance away and found himself suddenly face to face with two *ladrónes*. Before the young officer could draw his pistol, one of the outlaws fired his old rifle and succeeded in knocking off the top of MacArthur's campaign hat. According to Douglas's account, written some years later, "like all frontiersmen, I was expert with a pistol," and he responded by killing both his attackers instantly. Although this account of the incident did not reveal MacArthur's emotions at the time, it is probably reasonable to assume that even though his first assailants were easily vanquished, he was shaken by the event, and very grateful that, as his father had often pointed out, the Filipinos were sorely lacking in "firepower" training.[7] In addition, Douglas's success in felling the two men added one more bit of evidence to support his growing assumption that his identification with the western heroes of his youth was accurate, and that he was indeed meant to survive in order that he might achieve that for which he was preparing.

The remaining days of 1903, while not as exciting as the Guimaras incident, were filled with a constant awareness of potential danger. In mid-November, he spent two weeks surveying the military reservation at Tacloban on the island of Leyte where Pulajane activity was at its height. Nearly 3500 *soldados,* or native bolomen, led by local "popes" and strengthened by *antinganting* (talismans guaranteeing indestructibility to the wearer), frequently attacked coastal Filipinos and Americans alike from their strongholds in the island's interior. Although this activity was inspired by class and religious concerns rather than any particularly political perspective, the Constabulary forces were hard put to control the violence and needed frequent support from other military contingents in the area.[8] There is no indication that MacArthur was actively involved in this conflict, but certainly his assignment at Tacloban gave him ample opportunity to savor the ever-present threats nearby.

On January 26, 1904, his twenty-fourth birthday, MacArthur was on the island of Samar, making a survey of the military reservation at Calbayon. Although his status as engineer seems to have prevented active participation in the American struggle against the religious rebels in the area, combat was intensifying all around him. In fact, MacArthur's year in the Philippines coincided almost exactly with a major policy change in this part of the Visayas. The area had been racked by violence almost continually since 1901. As in Panay, the official end of the insurrection in that year had brought no peace to Samar. By late 1902, the coastal areas had begun a painful effort at "Filipiniza-tion" when martial law was ended and American military forces were replaced by Constabulary from surrounding areas. This cosmetic effort did little for the reality of "bloody Samar," as it was known in the Manila newspapers, and after an unsuccessful two-year attempt by the Constabulary to control the ferocious attacks of armed bands of Pulajanes, remnants of guerrilla forces from the revolution, and starving peasants, the Filipiniza-tion process was put aside temporarily, and American combat troops reentered the scene.[9] By the time this final decision was reached, Lieutenant MacArthur was back in Manila, nearly ready to return to the United States. There can be little doubt, how-ever, that his opportunity to observe this situation in Leyte and Samar, at the very height of this conflict, convinced him that his father's predictions that military control would be necessary for years to come, had been borne out by time. Since Washington still supported the opposing point of view, as did the Manila press, young MacArthur's growing suspicions of the judgment of the civil arm of the government were again confirmed. This view gave added support to his self-confidence, which needed much selective reinforcement.

After the Calbayon experience, MacArthur was once again temporarily assigned to more civilized surroundings. After mak-ing boundary surveys at Camp Connell and Bumpers, he was ordered to the city of Cebu. Cebu, early center of the Spanish colonization effort and one of the oldest cities in the Philippines, had undergone little violent upheaval during the war and subse-quent revolution.[10] A thriving economy, based largely on the increased demand for hemp during these years, aided the devel-opment of a merchant class. In addition, the large and long-standing religious community was undergoing transformation as the Vatican, at the urging of the United States government, assigned increasing numbers of American clergy to the area. Both of these groups, in combination with the U.S. Army officer corps stationed there, provided a cosmopolitan milieu and am-ple social stimulation in contrast to the garrison life of MacArthur's recent experience. Although his visit was brief, the opportunities to view the fine old Spanish churches and local shops and to enjoy the amenities of the officer's club in the evening served as pleasant contrasts to his more daring adventures. More importantly, experiences of this kind provided the young officer with the opportunity to keep his social skills honed for the next phase of his personal Philippine campaign.

On March 12, 1904, the young soldier was relieved from duty in the Department of the Visayas and ordered to Manila "to report to Division Engineer as Disbursing Officer and Assistant."[11] Although his duties as disbursing officer would be interspersed by frequent brief assignments into the undeveloped areas surrounding the capital city, MacArthur was finally to have the opportunity to explore Manila, establishing a familiarity which, coupled with his exceptional memory for detail, was to stand him in good stead on each subsequent visit. Manila, a city of complex tradition, centered both by history and by geographical location as a cultural nexus between East and West, offered an unparalleled variety of experience. In the next seven months, the young man who was as yet relatively untouched by urban sophistication had occasion for enormous social growth.

The long, quickly paced walks to which he was already addicted often led him from the crowded Luneta along Malecon Drive (later Dewey, then Roxas Boulevard), which bordered the bay and provided a spectacular view of the sunset over Mt. Mariveles to the west. As he entered the Walled City, the streets narrowed, forcing close contact with the cigar-smoking shoppers in jusi or piña shirts and blouses. Tall, bearded *frailes* (friars) in brown or white cossacks mingled with the soldiers, schoolchildren, and shopkeepers in twilight negotiations. The old Delmonico Hotel provided a way station and meeting place for officers and their families on the way to other posts in the islands, and the Spanish governmental offices, often built atop the great wall, were now peopled by Philippine and American civil servants just leaving for home at the end of the long business day.[12] Twenty years later, as Commander of the Military District of Manila, MacArthur would live and work in these same

buildings. Unaware of this possibility in 1904, the young ex-
plorer wandered on, undoubtedly sometimes repelled by the
general disregard for order, but for the most part intrigued by
the mystery and romance engendered by the fascinating contrasts around him.

For the present, however, new family concerns were developing. In mid-December, 1903, while Douglas was still in the
provinces, a front-page article in the *Manila-American* announced that "[General] MacArthur stirred up all the animals;
his Honolulu talk became a topic for discussion in Washington."
The incident referred to in this and another article a week later
followed the pattern of conflict between the General and the
War Department which had its roots in his time as military
governor of the Philippines.[13] By the time Douglas reached
Manila in March, the matter was almost settled, but undoubtedly
it provided a subject for much conjecture in the military circles
that he frequented.

The core of the issue centered around an Associated Press
dispatch which stated that General MacArthur, at the time attending a military conference in Hawaii, predicted that "the
Pan-Germanic doctrine which is being spread throughout [the]
world. . . . presage[s] another testing and straining of the
Monroe Doctrine and in all probability [a] contest of arms between that Power and [the] United States in the near future in
which event no one can now forecast [the] attitude [of] England
and other European powers."[14] A detailed investigation inspired by Secretary Root in the War Department (and instigated
by the German-American Central Bund in Minnesota) revealed
that this prescient statement (which the General never officially
confirmed) had been made in a private conversation, which was
later transcribed and accidentally made available to a local reporter. After much debate and attempted clarification, General
MacArthur received a presidential protest.[15]

His superiors in Washington had one more reason to distrust this outspoken and high-ranking member of their military
establishment. This incident, coupled with the glorified accounts of Governor Taft's departure from Manila to become the

Secretary of War, and the news, shortly thereafter, of the appointment of Major General Adna R. Chaffee as chief of staff of the Army,[16] may have caused some discomfort for the young Lieutenant so ambitious for himself and his family. The new Secretary of War was clearly perceived as an antagonist, and Chaffee, his father's immediate successor in the office of military governor of the Philippines, was outranked by the senior MacArthur. Chaffee's appointment as chief of staff in 1904 and the subsequent and continued passing over of the General for this office during the remainder of his military career were bitter pills for all the MacArthurs to swallow.

Another major topic of discussion in military circles during this period was the possibility that Major General Leonard Wood, who was serving as the first civil governor of Moro Province, would succeed Governor General Luke E. Wright as chief administrative officer of the Philippines. Wood was popular in the Islands, but he had made enemies in the military establishment because of his close alliance with Theodore Roosevelt. He was generally judged an able candidate for the position, but since the appointment would require an Act of Congress or his retirement from active duty, most believed that he was more likely to succeed General Wade as division commander. Those who made this argument were proved correct when it was announced in February 1904 that Cameron Forbes would be the new governor general.[17] Although only peripherally engaged in this controversy in 1904, Douglas MacArthur apparently took note of the debate, and incorporated it into his campaign for the high office in 1929 and again in 1935.

Although many of the young Lieutenant's observations during this year would influence his future career in the Philippines, his day-to-day experiences were those of a typical junior officer. Off-duty hours were filled with frequent visits to the theatres in Manila. The well-known Zorrilla, the Orpheum, and later, the Paz, which opened in June 1904, offered a wide vaudevillian fare. Valmore, the "celebrated English ventriloquist," vied with Miss Gertie Maisie, "berlo-comic," and Conto, the "marvelous juggler," for popular approval on the Paz's first bill.[18] Dances, drives, and opera performances also provided entertainment, and one of MacArthur's friends still recalled, after more than half a century, "the little Tamanti, as gorgeous in person as in voice," who performed at the opera house that he and MacArthur frequented.[19]

Much of the social life for the military in this period centered around the activities of the Army-Navy Club, one of the first American social clubs in Manila.[20] Douglas MacArthur joined the club in 1904 and lived there when in Manila during that year.[21] Although bedroom space was limited and the plumbing somewhat inadequate, the club was relatively inexpensive and the food was superior. Another young officer who lived there at the same time as MacArthur recalled that his expenses ran between $4.50 and $5.00 per day, "counting room meals—and carriage hire."[22] In an economy upset by postwar inflation, thrift was an important consideration to young officers on limited incomes. MacArthur and his friends saved money by sharing the purchase price of a "victoria calesa" [sic] and three ponies, and by organizing a poker room in one of their bedrooms "so that military officers coming in from the islands or ships would have a decent place to play and not go to gambling joints."[23]

Although MacArthur welcomed these shared pleasures as a respite from the long hours spent in his new duties as disbursing officer, he would find that this close camaraderie accentuated the alienation which was so often a problem for the military community. Throughout the first decade of American rule, the efforts that Governor Taft had inspired toward social integration seldom succeeded. One historian has referred to the "white colony [as an] incestuous island of superiority."[24] In this period, although military leaders, high civil government officials, and some of the Filipino elite made gestures toward social intercourse, differences of custom, combined with all too recent memories of the Philippine attempt at independence, inhibited such impulses.

There were occasional exceptions, however, and when Lieutenant MacArthur prepared "brief notes on field reconnoissance [sic] and sketching," as an addendum to a newly issued Constabulary map of the Philippines, he was asked by Captain

James G. Harbord, then serving as Colonel in the Constabulary, to dinner at the Army-Navy Club as a reward. When he arrived, he found two young Filipinos with Harbord. The two young men, already friends of the Captain, were both in their early twenties and were laying the groundwork for careers which would lead to future acclaim. Although one was already involved in the defense of a well-known nationalist playwright and the other was the founder of *El Nuevo Dia,* one of the earliest nationalistic papers, both understood the realities of the American occupation and did not hesitate to form friendships which would aid their rise to national prominence. Throughout the dinner, which MacArthur later described as "gay," Harbord, Manuel Quezon, and Sergio Osmeña shared experiences, political insights, and gossip. None of this was lost on the young Lieutenant busy preparing for the future. The friendships thus begun with two future presidents of the Philippine Commonwealth proved to be long and very rewarding.[25]

This period was propitious for MacArthur in other ways as well. In late May he had been ordered to appear before a board of officers to be examined for promotion. Characteristically, he scored well on the examination, and in early September he was notified of his advancement to first lieutenant, effective April 23, 1904. According to one story, he had been wearing the first lieutenant bar since May.[26] Initially under the command of Major Curtis Townsend, chief engineering officer of the Division, and then later under Captain Harry Taylor, MacArthur served throughout this period with Company "M," 3rd Battalion, Corps of Engineers. The company was stationed in Manila proper, and MacArthur's office was in the Santa Lucia Building, on Malecon Drive, conveniently located near his room in the Army-Navy Club. His duties in addition to disbursement included keeping engineering records for the Division, and supervising occasional surveys in the surrounding areas. In April 1904, he surveyed the military reservation at Caloocan, scene of one of his father's early victories, and in June he was sent to survey the reservation at Mariveles, the small harbor town on the tip of Bataan just across Manila Bay. Here he began to familiarize himself with the terrain which would be the context of so much of his tragic defense of the Islands nearly forty years later.[27]

MacArthur's expanded duties did not apparently infringe on his extra-curricular activities. Long hours were spent exchanging stories with friends visiting Manila from outposts in the provinces. At other times, the young men explored the city with an eye toward adventure. Once MacArthur rode to Pasig with his friend, Perry Boyer, a young medical officer stationed in Manila, to attend the hanging of "insurrecto" Faustino Guillermo. Several thousand people observed the event, watching Guillermo die bravely, and Boyer recorded in his diary that it "from [a] spectacular standpoint was a disappointment."[28] Whether this implied that he had witnessed several of these affairs and had a basis for comparison, or whether he and his companion had simply expected more fanfare, neither he nor MacArthur ever explained. The incident does, however, reflect the aura of violence which surrounded life in the Philippines in those early years.

Although much that augured well for MacArthur's future had occurred since his arrival in Manila, the remaining months of his assignment were occasionally unpleasant. The rainy season in the Islands that year was the worst on record and during a typhoon in June, the area near Malecon, where he was stationed, suffered severe damage. Eleven people died, and one account reports that MacArthur was in the area at the time.[29] Shortly after this month-long torrent, the Manila-Americans joined together for a celebration of "Occupation Day." The festivities, commemorating the sixth aniversary of the Battle of Manila, included the usual patriotic speeches by government officials, parades, and galas in the evening. Although the inclement weather of the season may have been one factor in the disappointing turnout recorded, one also suspects that this event was not one in which the Filipinos could honestly participate with much enthusiasm. Manila in 1904 was still very much a colonial outpost.[30]

In addition to his encounter with the typhoon that summer, MacArthur was stricken with the bane of tropical service, his usually robust health deteriorated, and he had to spend several days hospitalized for malaria.[31] Although he would occasionally have recurring attacks of the fever, the illness was not serious, and did not interfere substantially with his other professional and social activities.

As his final days in the Philippines approached, MacArthur was faced with the pain of separation from one very pleasant person in his social circle. There is no indication that MacArthur, who had enjoyed a wide variety of feminine companionship since his days at West Texas,[32] had yet developed any serious romantic involvements. During his last months in the Philippines, however, he was seen increasingly in the company of Florence Adams, the sister-in-law of the Auditor of the Philippine government. For the first time, MacArthur did not play the field but concentrated on one woman. She appears to have been the only one he escorted to dances and was his frequent companion on drives in the calesia he shared with Lieutenant Bell. In addition, she was described as "an entertaining talker and an excellent chess player." Whatever her attraction, it is perhaps significant that it was during this first separation from his mother that MacArthur attempted a more intimate relationship with a woman his own age. Whether he genuinely wanted to continue it, or felt relieved at having to leave, cannot be known. In either case, he wanted to make his final leave-taking memorable. Consequently, he asked Bell to arrange for a special boat to take Miss Adams and himself to the transport which was to carry him back to the United States. Although the farewell could have taken place on the regular quartermaster boat used by everyone else, as Bell said, "he liked to do everything in a grand-stylish way." It was the beginning of a pattern of poignant farewell scenes he would continue for the next thirty years, and apparently it was very effective. Years later, in correspondence with Bell, Florence Adams, still single, recalled those last days in Manila with particular fondness.[33]

On September 24, 1904, MacArthur was transferred out of the Philippine Division, and after conveying the records for which he was accountable to his replacement, Lieutenant John

H. Poole, he prepared to return to San Francisco. The first available transport appears to have been the *Thomas,* and on October 10, 1904, accompanied by some of the young engineers who had been with him in the Islands, he set off for the States.[34] Amidst the final round of farewells and duties which filled his last fortnight in Manila, MacArthur probably had little time to read the local newspapers carefully. If he had, however, he could not have missed the October 5, 1904, *Manila-American* front-page story: "No more presents to officers will be tolerated by War Dept. The presentation or acceptance of any gifts will expose an officer of the Army to a court martial." The article charged that Section 1784 of the Revised Statutes was being "violated in spirit and letter," by an increasing number of Army officers.[35] This problem of gifts, with roots extending far back in the American military tradition, would plague the Philippine command during these years. Although there is no indication that the matter was one of immediate concern to Lieutenant MacArthur, the investigation, the source of this story, continued over the next few years and eventually touched his father. In 1907, in response to a War Department inquiry concerning certain wooden articles he had brought out of the Philippines in 1901, the General was required to pay for the services of the quartermaster department and for the material involved. Along with his check, the elder MacArthur included an indignant response.[36] While there is no indication that the younger MacArthur ever discussed this issue with his father, in this area, as in so many others, his own life experience repeated and surpassed that of the older man.

When Lieutenant MacArthur arrived in San Francisco in mid-November, 1904, he found his welcoming celebrations complicated by his parents' still uncertain plans concerning the General's next assignment. Dissatisfied with the inactivity entailed by his responsibilities as commanding officer of the Division of the Pacific, General MacArthur had requested assignment as military observer of the Japanese forces almost immediately after the outbreak of the Russo-Japanese War in

February 1904. Although the United States government had already sent eight other officers as observers, the Japanese seemed reluctant to allow these men adequate opportunity for frontline observation. Consequently, in December 1904, Secretary of War Taft agreed to MacArthur's request, arguing "that the high rank of General MacArthur would secure him opportunity for observation which the Japanese military authorities might deny to an officer of less rank." On January 21, 1905, Military Secretary Fred C. Ainsworth notified General MacArthur of his new orders.[37] The General, Mrs. MacArthur, and the General's aide-de-camp, Captain Paul W. West, began immediate preparations for the departure, which was scheduled for mid-February.

During this period of uncertainty, Lieutenant MacArthur began a new assignment with the Corps of Engineers in San Francisco. Serving under Colonel Thomas H. Handbury, his first stateside professional experience was a positive one, and Colonel Handbury reported that "he was bright and intelligent, regular in his habits, not disposed to idleness but studious." The Colonel continued his description by stating that the young officer spent "his time while under my observation in the office, in reading engineering literature and studying office methods and records, and generally improving himself in that line."[38] When Handbury left the district office of engineers in San Francisco, he was replaced by Colonel William H. Heuer, who also seemed pleased with MacArthur's behavior.

After a quiet winter spent in preparation for more active duty, however, Douglas was once again stricken by malaria, and hospitalized for ten days. This illness, coupled with subsequent "trouble with his eyes" led to his request in June 1905 to be transferred to "outside work." Complying with the request, the Department assigned him to duty with the California Debris Commission under the direct command of Major William H. Harts. Instructed to regulate gold mining operations in the Sacramento and San Joaquin valleys, the commission was established as a federal agency, utilizing the Army Engineering Corps to devise methods by which the debris from the hydraulic mining could be cleared from the local rivers. The work promised to be interesting and offered the young officer an opportunity to supervise excavation at Dagueree Point, site of the largest work under Harts' direction. Harts "believed that the best instruction in engineer work is by having responsible charge of some work where there will be opportunity for original observation, and Lieutenant MacArthur seemed to be pleased with this opportunity."

Before long, however, the young engineer requested a new assignment since "his departure for so long a time from San Francisco would be impossible owing to his father's absence and the necessity he was under of attending to some of his father's affairs."[39] With remarkable cooperation, the Department once again complied and reassigned MacArthur as an inspector of hydraulic mines, a position which would involve only occasional trips out of the city. Through the rest of his stay in San Francisco, MacArthur seems to have fulfilled his duties satisfactorily and even served briefly as acting chief engineer of the Division of the Pacific, a position of responsibility that one biographer has suggested was "rarely, if ever, given to a lieutenant."[40] It is significant, however, that MacArthur, in memoirs written sixty years later, chose to remember only "the stagecoach trips through Strawberry Valley that recalled my early days in the West."[41]

Following family tradition, MacArthur had obtained special privilege. Although this pattern was certainly not exclusively MacArthur's in the American military establishment of this period, his successes in these attempts reinforced for him the idea that even an institution as all powerful as the Army might bend to his will. Not only was he able to achieve his immediate desires by this method, but, indeed, he was given no reason to believe that this pattern would ever work to his disadvantage—for only a few months after these rearrangements went into effect, MacArthur received orders to report to his father in Tokyo for service as aide-de-camp.[42] Once again, family influence had achieved a desired goal. This experience, strengthened, as we have seen, by similar occurrences in his youth, and further reinforced in later years, encouraged a philosophy that MacArthur was never able to put aside.

During the ten months that the younger MacArthur spent in San Francisco, the rest of his family was undergoing an enjoyable, if somewhat strenuous, period of adjustment in the Orient. While Mrs. MacArthur and several other military wives set up temporary quarters in Tokyo, the military attachés began the often difficult task of negotiating with the cordial but secretive Japanese so that they might actually fulfill their role as military observers of the Russo-Japanese conflict.

When Japanese torpedo boats attacked the Russian fleet at Port Arthur on February 8, 1904, the resulting war came as a surprise to no one. The Japanese had long been angered at Russian refusal to leave Manchuria, which they considered theirs as a result of their participation in the Boxer Rebellion. The Japanese forces were not discouraged by either England or the United States in this action, which was, as Theodore Roosevelt would later come to see, a relatively painless way to achieve a balance of power in that area.

Many American imperialists saw the venture as a necessary deterrent to the growing Russian threat in Asia, assuming that, unlike Russia, Japan's entry into imperial competition could be controlled whenever necessary. One of these theorists was General Arthur MacArthur, who would now have an opportunity to observe at first hand the conditions he had studied so thoroughly since the early 1880s. Indeed, this was the argument he had put forth in his request for the assignment when, in December 1904, he sent Chief of Staff Chaffee a brief report entitled "Memorandum in Respect of the Organization of a Field Army." In this essay he discussed the effect of army organization on tactical operations, and suggested that "the Japanese at critical moments have been incapable of the celerity of movement essential to the full achievement of decisive results." Comparing the present conflict to the American Civil War, MacArthur believed that Marshal Iwao Oyama was mistaken when, after the battle of Liao Yang, he did not move a column "as General

Grant moved Sheridan" in the Appomattox campaign. Moving on to another historical parallel, the General argued that the advantages of flexibility far outweighed "minute instruction of officers and men," and supported his statement by alluding to the victory of the French militia against the Prussian Army in the Napoleonic Wars. The "apparent failure of the Japanese" proved his point and had serious implications for "the question of the most effective organization for our volunteers in future wars." Suggesting that his views had been "confirmed and strengthened by the progress of the war in Manchuria," he went on to request the opportunity "to continue further investigations on the spot."[43] Shortly after this request was received and approved in Washington, the tides of war changed and the Japanese began to prove that they, too, understood the advantages of flexibility in the field.

Instructed to investigate and study "the organization of the Japanese and Russian armies, with a view to a detailed and complete report thereon, together with such deductions and recommendations with respect to our own Army as, in your judgment, conditions warrant," General MacArthur arrived in Tokyo on March 5, just as General Oyama wrapped up his victory over the Russians at Mukden. MacArthur reported to Ambassador Lloyd C. Griscom at the United States Legation in Tokyo, and four days later, after a banquet in his honor given by the Japanese Minister of War, the General was allowed to go to the front, accompanied by Captain West and a Japanese lieutenant, also serving as aide.[44] Embarking from Shimonoseki, in southwestern Japan, on the eleventh, he was unable to reach Mukden until the twentieth, eleven days after the major battle of the war was concluded. Reporting that "the military environment is very inspiring and affords a fine scope for professional study and military reflection which I am enjoying to the full limit,"[45] MacArthur remained in Manchuria and Mongolia for the next six months, and was once again far away when the Japanese in the naval battle of Tsushima Straits finally annihilated the Russian fleet and forced the Tsar to the bargaining table. As the Treaty of Portsmouth was signed, on September

5, General MacArthur was en route back to Tokyo. He arrived there on the tenth.

Although invigorating and enjoyable, MacArthur's travels thus far had not "confirmed and strengthened" the views he had put forth prior to his assignment, and his observations provided little information to which the War Department was not already privy. Shortly after his return to Tokyo he forwarded a summary of a lecture upon the Battle of Nan-shan Hill to the G-2 Section of the General Staff. He argued that this narrative "should be accepted wherever it differs from any heretofore published."[46] Disregarded in Washington because "both combatants were too prone to cover up discreditable incidents and to work in self advertisements,"[47] this summary and an October 3 report on the use of machine guns in the Japanese Army seem to be the only reports that the General sent.

Nevertheless, General MacArthur's tour of observation in the East had just begun. Prior to his departure from San Francisco in February 1904, he had made one more request of Secretary of War Taft: "If I emerge from Manchuria alive, and in good health, it might be agreeable to authorize me to make a general confidential reconnaissance of the entire theater of interest, by visiting such parts of China as are accessible, and possibly continuing observations into India."[48]

Taft, who was faced with the difficult problem of what to do with this senior officer of the Army, whom he believed, from personal experience, not suited temperamentally to serve in the high administrative post in Washington for which his rank made him eligible, was perhaps relieved to make the assignment. In any event, Taft conferred with President Roosevelt, noting on February 17 that "the President thinks it wise to grant the request." On February 24, the Military Secretary's Office issued the order, and MacArthur was told that after "relief from duty as military attache, you will proceed to Peking, China, and to such places in Indo-China and India [on a] confidential tour directed by the President."[49] By September 10, then, MacArthur had fulfilled the first part of his assignment, and he and Mrs. MacArthur began preparations for the tour.

While the General visited Manchuria and Mongolia during the first six months of his assignment, his wife remained in Tokyo, exploring the Japanese capital on what was her first trip abroad. She had been the object of Japanese hospitality, and particularly enjoyed renewing a friendship with railroad magnate Edward H. Harriman, whom she was seated beside at a luncheon given by Ambassador Griscom.[50] Only one cloud threatened the horizon—the continued separation from her youngest son. Indeed, based on her previous behavior, it is likely that she had only agreed to accompany the General to Japan because she believed that it would provide an opportunity to be with Douglas again.

Although it was not uncommon for wives of officers to accompany their husbands on these assignments, it was an unusual decision for Mrs. MacArthur, who had earlier chosen to remain with Douglas at West Point rather than serve as official hostess for her husband during his tenure as Military Governor of the Philippines. Since the General's efforts to achieve assignment to Tokyo began well before Douglas was ordered back to California, and since at least one biographer reported that the younger MacArthur "tried without success to wangle his way to the fighting along the Yalu River," which occurred in May 1904,[51] while he was still in the Philippines, it is possible that Mrs. MacArthur's original plan to accompany her husband to Japan was contingent upon an opportunity to have Douglas nearby. The delay in Washington concerning General MacArthur's assignment and Douglas's somewhat unexpected orders to return to the States may have upset her hopes, but Mary MacArthur was not one to give up easily. It is very likely, therefore, that the six months she spent in Tokyo while her husband fulfilled his official duties allowed her further time in which to develop plans for an officially sanctioned and long-term family reunion. Word from California of Douglas's illness and the subsequent professional disruption it caused could only have encouraged these efforts.

Consequently, when Secretary Taft visited Yokohama on September 17, 1905, General MacArthur met with him to make one more request. On that same day, the General wrote to the Military Secretary in Washington, referring to "a conversation with the Sec. of War," and requesting that he be given "authority by cable to order Captain P. W. West, ADC to return to the U.S. and that another officer be ordered to report to me at Tokio, to accompany me on the journey [through China and India]."⁵² Although this cable did not refer to the other officer by name, the arrangements for Douglas to replace West were clearly understood. In fact, in a letter written two days later to Major William D. Beach in the War Department, West stated that "I am to return home and Douglas MacArthur to accompany the General on the China-India trip." Explaining the arrangements with Taft, West went on to assure Beach that "the General's relations and mine are of the best but for reasons which I will explain when I see you it is absolutely necessary that Douglas take my place and I want to do all I can to arrange it so."⁵³ We can be reasonably sure that motherly concern and pressure were part of what made the exchange "absolutely necessary." On October 3, the War Department issued the order which completed the arrangements.⁵⁴

Young MacArthur left San Francisco almost immediately after receiving this order and arrived in Yokohama on October 31, 1905. After resting at the Oriental Palace Hotel briefly, the reunited MacArthur family left in early November on the *Korea,* bound for Hong Kong. Captain West returned to Washington via Europe, carrying with him "maps and [a] list of killed and wounded of 2nd Army at Mukden and . . . notes on the battle made up from a lecture given after we left the front."⁵⁵ While awaiting Douglas's arrival, the General caught up on his paperwork, bought (and presumably read) several books on the areas he would soon visit, and made a series of official calls in Tokyo. The MacArthurs attended official receptions given by Marshal Aritomo Yamagata and the Minister of War and, on October 19, made a formal call on the Emperor. In addition, the General continued to increase his knowledge about the Japanese military establishment through inspections of hospitals, troop barracks, and the Cadet School in Tokyo.

En route to Hong Kong, the MacArthurs stopped at Kobe, spent a day going cross-country from Kobe to Kyoto and back, visited Nagasaki and Shanghai briefly, and arrived in the British colony on November 11 for a week's stay. This jewel-like island, set into a landlocked bay and capped by the exquisite city of Victoria, captivated the visitors immediately. Nothing in Manila or Tokyo had prepared them for the dizzying heights from which they could view the crowded markets of the city, the South China Sea, or the hilly outlines of southern China. Precariously perched in sedan chairs, the family made its official calls on the American Consul General, the British Governor General and, finally, the Commanding General of the British garrison. On the eighteenth, they reluctantly left Hong Kong, and journeyed across the South China Sea to Singapore.

Here, the General and his aide spent eight days visiting the British fortifications, making official calls, and acquainting themselves with the 220-square-mile island at the tip of the Malayan peninsula. They spent the day of November 26 visiting Johore, just across the causeway in Malay, and then returned to Singapore to prepare for the forthcoming excursion to Java. On November 30, the MacArthurs began the two-day trip, during which they were increasingly uncomfortable due to the intense tropical heat. From Batavia (now Jakarta), the General reported that the heat and "irregular connections" had slowed his progress, but that he was "covering the ground thoroughly with some professional benefit and considerable general interest and instruction."[56] Although nearly a month behind schedule by this time, the family visited most of the major cities in Java and garrisons in Batavia, Buitenzorg, and Tjimahi where they were appropriately received by the Dutch colonial officials. After almost three weeks in Java, they returned to Singapore on December 23.

The first family Christmas in many years was cut short by the necessity of leaving Singapore on Christmas Day to begin the next leg of their journey, which would carry them north through Malaya, the Siamese peninsula, and into Burma. With brief stops in Kuala Lumpur and Penang, they arrived in Rangoon on New

Year's Day, 1906. The next ten days were spent more or less independently traveling through Burma, visiting British posts in the interior, and making a pleasant riverboat trip to Mandalay and Bhamo, near the northern border, accompanied only by an interpreter. On January 11, they left Rangoon, moving west to India, and arrived in Calcutta on the fourteenth.

During the seven and a half weeks the MacArthurs spent in India, they were cordially welcomed by the British civil and military authorities, and provided with ample opportunity to enjoy the comforts which had accrued to station in this colony in which the British had most securely defined the benefits of imperialism. Although Douglas would at one point recall that the major impression he received was of the impoverished masses, his recollections at the end of his life remember with pleasure the royal welcome given the family.[57] In Calcutta, they were warmly received by Lord Kitchener, in the midst of his term as commander-in-chief of the British forces in India, and embroiled in a well-publicized feud with Lord Curzon, who, as a result, had just resigned as Viceroy of India. Although Douglas later claimed to have "listened to both sides of the famous Curzon-Kitchener feud—that age-old struggle between the civil and the military to fix the exact line of demarcation between executive control and the professional duty of the soldier," he must have heard the civil perspective indirectly, since there is no evidence of a meeting with Curzon, already back in England.[58] It is much more likely that the MacArthurs listened with sympathy to Lord Kitchener's viewpoint, since the General's Philippine experience as military governor had left him predisposed in that direction. Certainly, Douglas's observance of the abortive "Filipinization" process in the Islands two years before, coupled with a profound respect for his father's outlook, must have confirmed this view in his mind as well.

Both the General and his aide were delighted to have the opportunity to retrace the great colonial expeditions which had secured India for the British. On their first excursion, by riverboat up the Ganges to Darjeeling in the north, they listened to stories of Sir [*sic*] Francis Younghusband's quest of the

"Grand Llama" two years earlier. Returning to Calcutta in order to pick up what MacArthur would later describe as "the Grand Trunk Road of Kipling's *Kim*,"[59] they traveled by rail westward through the great Indian alluvial plain, stopping frequently to inspect British military posts, where they were cordially received. On February 11, they arrived in Peshawar and spent two days with Sir Bindon Blood, "King of the Khyber," visiting the famed pass into Afghanistan. Retracing their steps to Lahore, they changed trains, boarding the branch line which traversed the Thar Desert and arrived in the port city of Karachi on February 20. From there they sailed to Bombay and boarded the train which would carry them on the last leg of their Indian adventure southeast through Secunderabad, Bangalore, and Madras. Moving south to Tuticorin, they embarked on a brief side trip to Colombo, Ceylon. Three days later, on the eleventh of March, they began their return trip to Singapore, and arrived there on the sixteenth.

By this time the MacArthur family had traveled nearly 20,000 miles by rail, riverboat and ocean liner, made countless official calls, studied guidebooks and maps assiduously, and, if their expense memorandum was accurate, been forced to rely on local medical facilities frequently in order to maintain their arduous itinerary. Still they were behind schedule. In Secunderabad and Bangalore, the commanding officers had "practically put their commanders under emergency orders," General MacArthur reported, "and thus enabled me to accomplish in a few hours what otherwise would have taken days." Nevertheless, he found it useless to try "to hurry the East," and therefore was resigned to arriving back in Singapore two weeks later than he had planned.[60]

Father and son had clearly enjoyed their reception. The romantic predisposition so strong in both of them had been encouraged by "the lands so rich in color, so fabled in legend," and their enormous need for deference and regard had certainly been fed by the formal protocol of the British colonial system. Nevertheless, and perhaps emphasized by hindsight, the young Lieutenant, as an old man, pointed out that "the colonial system . . . brought law and order, but failed to develop the masses along the essential lines of education and political economy."[61] Part of this insight undoubtedly derived from the long years of experience and study between the time of the trip and the writing of the memoirs. But another influence must be admitted. His father, both privately to his son and publicly in his testimony before the 1902 Senate Committee, had delineated this exact problem in the Philippines and urged its solution through further involvement of the Filipinos in the workings of government.[62] The plight of the masses in India must have underlined this inequity and been the subject of many MacArthur conversations as they journeyed from one colonial outpost to another.

The dual and contradictory nature of these observations may have gone unnoticed by the father and son, but it certainly created an ambivalence for both of them which would influence and complicate their future judgments as military officers in a democracy. On the one hand, they clearly came to believe in the importance of long-term Western control of certain Asian countries, and to respect, and indeed enjoy, the firmness, ritual, and order of the British approach to this necessity. On the other hand, the philosophy of democratic opportunity was also a factor in the background, experience, and education of both men. They had been influenced enough by the progressive milieu then current in the United States and by their Philippine experiences to believe that something must be done to alleviate the impoverished condition of the Asian poor. Even though they enjoyed the luxuries and tribute offered them by the British class system superimposed on the rigid castes of India, at the same time they deplored the economic base which made this system possible. It was a quandary which would provide Arthur MacArthur a subject for the philosophical and theoretical examinations of which he was so fond. For his son, these parallel, equally attractive and yet opposing, concerns would be cause for a much more serious and concrete response in later life.

After a brief respite in Singapore, the MacArthurs left the island and arrived in Bangkok, Siam, on March 27. Here they would have an opportunity to observe a noncolonial Asian empire as the guests of King Chulalongkorn, son of the famed King Mongkut, the subject of Margaret Landon's *Anna and the King of Siam*. Chulalongkorn (also known as Rama V) ascended the throne of Siam in 1868, and during the years which followed, he had successfully warded off the imperial interests of both France, to the east, and Great Britain, on the west, through careful negotiations and the institution of liberal reform. Skill-fully taking advantage of the competition between the European powers, he lost territory occasionally, but managed, throughout his forty-two-year reign, to maintain control of central Siam. At the time of the MacArthur visit, he was enjoying a period of consolidation, and looked forward to showing his Western visitors his country's recently built railway network, its new telegraph and telephone systems, as well as the small, but well-disciplined, Siamese army.[63]

The twelve days spent in and around Bangkok provided the MacArthurs, and particularly Mrs. MacArthur, with a marvelous contrast to the long series of British and Dutch garrisons they had visited during the past four months. In a letter to Elihu Root, then Secretary of State, Ambassador Hamilton King reported that

> the Siamese Government showed him [General MacArthur] great respect and rendered him every assistance in their power. He was given Audience by His Majesty the day following his arrival and dined at the Royal Palace a week later. His reception by the Crown Prince was most cordial and the courtesies shown him by the Princes at the head of the several Departments were marked. Indeed outside the reception given His Royal Highness Prince Heinrich of Prussia and Prince Waldemar of Denmark on their visit to Siam some years ago, no man has been accorded such a Royal and generous welcome as was the General since I have been in this country.[64]

The diary of Mrs. Cora Lee King, the Ambassador's wife, confirms this assessment in great detail.[65]

Mrs. King, as the official American hostess in Bangkok, spent many hours each day in the company of the MacArthurs during their visit, and to her fell the responsibility of entertaining Mrs. MacArthur while the General and his aide accompanied Ambassador King and the Siamese officials on various state duties. These duties included formal calls on the heads of the Siamese governmental departments, the commanders of the army and navy, and inspections of military barracks, schools, and prisons in the surrounding countryside. The MacArthurs stayed in a comfortable guest house in the U.S. legation compound. After spending their first two days in Bangkok, where they visited the new wat recently built in Dusit Park, the General, accompanied by Douglas and a Siamese aide-de-camp, was taken by private railcar to Rat Buri. Along the way, they visited prisons and barracks and also had time for a brief call on several Protestant missionaries serving in the area. After a quiet weekend, the Kings and the MacArthurs embarked on a two-day trip to Ayutthaya. There they were royally entertained by the Siamese High Commissioner. The men inspected the Gendarmerie, and watched the regular drill. Then the entire party boarded a "picnic boat" for a visit to the old wat to see the largest sitting Buddha in the world. Although the temperature reached 102 degrees during the afternoon, a breeze could be felt, and the "Royal bungalows where they were quartered for the night were surprisingly comfortable."

The following day provided the highlight of the trip for Mrs. MacArthur. After returning by launch to Bangkok, the party rested during the afternoon and prepared for the state dinner to be hosted that evening by King Chulalongkorn. Escorted by the Kings and other embassy officials, the MacArthurs were entranced by the Siamese Princes who greeted them at the Palace, and delighted by what Mrs. King described as "a most delicious dinner with all the 'delicacies of the season' most beautifully served on a table decorated with the King's wonderful red gold vases and urns full of tropical fruits and flowers." After this exquisite display, the group was escorted by the King on a tour of the Palace. In such a setting, the aging southern belle from Norfolk, Virginia, directed all her substantial charms toward the usually dignified and highly respected King of Siam.

Mrs. King, appalled at the effrontery of the General's wife, described the scene which followed:

> Passing through the throne room Mrs. MacArthur . . . said to him
> [the King], "Oh! I should like to see you on your throne!" He,
> entering into the joke of the thing, seated himself on the Royal
> throne! & when we entered the room there He was, smiling at Mrs.
> MacA. who in turn was making long bows to him! . . . Mrs. MacA.
> seemed utterly unconscious of having done anything out of the
> ordinary and [later] took the King's arm as though it were the only
> thing to do, where no one ever does it!

Later, when the King requested the visitors to write their
names and birth dates in his autograph book, once again Mrs.
MacArthur responded informally. "Mrs. MacA. beseeched him
to exempt her from this, which he graciously did. She grasped
his hand and said, 'Oh! Your Majesty, you're a darling!' at which
he laughed heartily but it nearly took our breaths away." Following this episode, the gentlemen retired to the smoking room and
the ladies were entertained by visits from "a number of little
Princes." It was perhaps at this time that another incident,
recalled with pleasure by Douglas MacArthur much later,
occurred. Apparently the lights suddenly went out, and the
alert young Lieutenant, having earlier noted a nearby fuse box,
remedied the situation with alacrity. The King, as Douglas
recalled, was delighted and offered to decorate the General's
aide on the spot. Uncharacteristically, Douglas MacArthur declined.[66]

The rest of the visit seemed not to have contained any other
untoward incidents, in Mrs. King's eyes, and included other
formal dinners given by various Siamese and U.S. officials, as
well as an invitation to be the guests of the Crown Prince at a
kite-flying contest. Two days before their departure, the MacArthurs received the news that the General had been promoted to
lieutenant general, increasing his pay, as Mrs. King noted, from
$7,500 to $11,000 per annum. Although Mrs. King reported
that "they were all very happy," the General's future responsibilities had still not been defined, and his news undoubtedly

provided the family with another reason to get on with their trip so that they might return home on schedule.

During the seventeen months that the General spent in Asia, the office of chief of staff became vacant twice, and correspondence from that period indicates that General MacArthur, and his supporters in Washington, still harbored some hope that he would receive the assignment. The status of his position as commander of the Pacific Division was uncertain, and in January 1906, just prior to the temporary appointment of Major General John C. Bates as chief of staff, Colonel Beach wrote the General that "personally we have all hoped that you would succeed General Bates but we are very dubious as to the result. . . . The outlook at this time seems to be that General Crozier will be Chief of Staff and that you will command a division as Lieutenant General. This, however, may all be upset and, for many reasons, I hope it will be."[67] Instead, Major General J. Franklin Bell replaced Bates. As in the case of Chaffee, Bell had served under MacArthur's command in the Philippines. General MacArthur, sixty-one at the time, could only hope that Bell's tenure would be brief. It soon became clear that this would not be the case.

In early 1907, War Department reorganization did away with the division as an administrative unit, and the General, once again in command of the Pacific Division, was offered the newly created Department of the East. He refused, and in March, took the bull by the horns and wrote to Secretary of War Taft.

"I have," he began, "been painfully conscious for some time that my present assignment is not compatible with the traditions of the Lieutenant Generalcy. The further purpose to abolish divisions, and thereby reduce me to Command of a Department emphasizes the incongruity." As solutions to the problem, MacArthur offered two alternatives. He could either retire early, or be given special duty, "with station outside of Washington, and not at the headquarters of a geographical command." Dismissing the first option as one which would result in "unenviable notoriety," he offered, subject to Taft's approval, "to submit

a project, calculated to serve as a basis for primary discussion,"
in connection with the special assignment. He concluded his
request with a statement which clearly indicated his understanding of the situation:

> I doubt Mr. Secretary if you fully realize the professional aspect
> of the dilemma which now confronts me. The office of Lieutenant
> General which I now hold, was originally intended to subserve
> only the highest purposes of military expedience. In consideration
> of past achievements, and of the possibilities of usefulness in
> future emergencies, the place has, perhaps, at times, been unduly
> magnified; but on the other hand it is now so much depressed, that
> in effect it has become merely a title. By process of current events
> it has been mediatized, and divested of prestige, dignity and influ-
> ence.
>
> I am reasonably concerned in respect of the partial restora-
> tion of the first two of the foregoing attributes; and as such a result
> can be accomplished without interfering in any way with the policy
> of the Department to have the army represented at Washington
> by a junior officer, I am decidedly of the opinion that such a
> readjustment of the professional status of the Lieutenant General
> would be of material advantage to the service.

Secretary of War Taft accepted the General's argument without
comment, and invited him to submit "a statement on the
project."[68]

Two weeks later, MacArthur sent Taft a definition of his
proposed special assignment:

> I propose that I be detached from command and assigned to a
> station in some central part of the country, with a view to employ-
> ment from time to time on such special work as the Department
> may deem expedient; . . . possibly representing the army on such
> occasions as the presence of the Senior officer thereof would, in
> the opinion of the War Department, be appropriate and desirable.

In addition, the General argued that this arrangement
would allow him to complete the report on his trip through the
Orient. The request was granted, and shortly afterward he
moved to Milwaukee and established a small office there. From

this time on, he participated very minimally in War Department affairs. In 1909, just after William Howard Taft became President, the General retired from the Army, having served the last two years of his tenure as lieutenant general with no substantial responsibilities.[69]

At his retirement, the rank of lieutenant general was abolished and not restored until World War I.[70] When he died three years later, in September 1912, the measure of his bitterness about the situation could be gauged by the fact that he left instructions forbidding a military funeral or burial in the National Cemetery at Arlington, Virginia.[71]

But all this was in the future, and when, on April 7, 1906, the MacArthurs once again began their trek eastward, they were encouraged by the latest promotion. They stopped briefly in Saigon and arrived in southern China in midmonth. In Canton the General visited a military academy and garrison and found the latter to contain "about 2000 fairly good looking modern-type soldiers, quartered in really good, clean, sanitary barracks."[72] Moving slowly up the coast of China, they passed the rest of April and all of May in visits to the various foreign garrisons in China, including Tsingtao, the German post on the Shantung peninsula, and Tientsin, which was jointly occupied by the Western powers during the recent Boxer Rebellion, and later would be the home of the U.S. 15th Infantry. Stopping briefly in Peking, the MacArthurs completed their tour of China by rail, visiting the various Chinese posts between Peking and Shanghai, from which city they embarked for Japan in late June. On July 17, 1906, they boarded the *Manchuria* at Yokohama, en route to San Francisco.[73]

What conclusions had the MacArthurs drawn from their long journey? Both father and son have left clear statements of their response. Arthur MacArthur, his career almost at an end, never wrote the final report he had promised the War Department. Nevertheless, after his return to Milwaukee, he was given an opportunity to voice those views. By the time he addressed the 1907 Annual Convention of the Wisconsin Bankers Association, the philosophy he had begun to develop a quarter of a

century earlier was firmly fixed in his mind. He chose as his
subject, "The United States in the Philippines," and, as usual,
approached the topic from two perspectives, "one . . . more or
less academical, the other intensely practical." In line with the
"academical" aspects of the question, he devoted approximately
two thirds of his time to an argument which pointed out the
semantic difficulties inherent in the recently assumed United
States responsibilities to the Philippines. After eliminating as
dangerous and misleading the two currently popular names for
the Islands, "territory," and "colony," the General suggested a
word which he had invented himself. The word, "tuitionate,"
would neither lead the Islanders to hope for statehood, as did
"territory," nor connote the evils usually linked with the term
"colony." Rather, it would describe "a territory the inhabitants
of which are being tutored in the art of self-government," and
would encourage loyal cooperation on the part of the Filipinos
whenever the defensive needs of the United States demanded it.
His suggestion was not taken seriously at the time, and is relevant primarily because it provided him the opportunity to define
the situation in the Islands as he saw it and to formulate future
Philippine policy in the rest of his discussion. It is interesting to
note in passing, however, the similarity between MacArthur's
plan for "tuitionates" in 1907 and Woodrow Wilson's proposed
mandate program more than a decade later.[74]

In the remainder of his address, the experiences derived
from his recent Asian tour were apparent, and, for the first time,
provided a frame of reference and comparison for his Philippine
views. He admitted "the general good administration apparent
in certain colonial territories," but emphasized that "self-supporting, germinal ideas, have not been introduced into any
sphere of influence in the East, excepting in the Philippines."
This situation, he continued, would weaken the position of
"these ostentatious colonial governments . . . in the final struggle with the Orient," leaving the United States as the only Western power of significance in the area—a significance achieved
because it had planted "imperishable ideas upon which free
institutions are based." Consequently, necessities of defense,

which might occur later, would be aided by "the loyalty and valor of the Filipino people themselves." Arguing against exploitation and in favor of free trade with the Islands, the General seemed to foresee with amazing clarity the situation with which the nation, and his son, would be faced thirty years later—a need to defend America's interests in the Pacific in a world of weakening European colonialism and increasing Asian demands for autonomy. He concluded, as he had in his other two public statements on the problem, that "the American occupation of the Philippine Islands may possibly transcend in importance any event recorded in the annals of mankind since the discovery of this continent." Although a typically MacArthurian overstatement, this conclusion reflected the intensity with which the General held his views.

Douglas, stationed in Milwaukee in 1907, may very well have heard the General's speech, but even if he did not, there is every reason to believe that he agreed with his father on the subject of America's interest in the Pacific. The younger MacArthur always described the Asian trip as very significant to him, and believed that "the experience was without doubt the most important factor of preparation in my entire life." Although his journey through the European colonies had demonstrated to him both the efficiencies and inadequacies of European imperialism, there can be little doubt that he enjoyed the amenities to which he became accustomed then, and which he would enjoy in much greater measure in the Philippines later. On the other hand, the visit to Siam certainly convinced him that a well-governed nation, no matter how small and inconveniently located, could survive through careful planning and diplomacy. His belief that the Pacific frontier was vital to American interests was firm:

The true historic significance and the sense of destiny that these lands of the western Pacific and Indian Ocean now assumed became part of me. They were to color and influence all the days of my life. Here lived almost half the population of the world, and probably more than half of the raw products to sustain future generations. Here was western civilization's last earth frontier. It was crystal clear to me that the future and, indeed, the very existence of America, were irrevocably entwined with Asia and its island outposts. It was to be sixteen years before I returned to the Far East, but always was its mystic hold upon me.[75]

Finally, and perhaps most importantly, he was impressed by the "boldness and courage" of the Japanese soldiers and realized that as a result of their recent victories over the Chinese and Russians in Asia, this island nation would never again be satisfied with a secondary position in world affairs.[76] This awareness, coupled with the firm conviction that America's needs were also paramount in this arena, provided the impetus for his lifelong fight to influence the American military establishment's policy toward the East. When frustrated in this direction, Douglas MacArthur, characteristically, would take the responsibility into his own hands, and despite inadequate strategic capabilities, attempt to hold America's Asian outpost against the Japanese through the strength of his own personal will. But this situation would not present itself until thirty years later. In the interim, the young Lieutenant would fight a war, become a general in his own right, and command the Department of the Philippines. Along the way, his emerging attitudes and responses, apparent only in dim outline during this first Asian period, would clarify and determine the direction of his future.

(4)

The Middle Years

... The laughter of children at play on
the green,—
Insist on a picture so cheerful, so fair,
Who ever would dream that a grief could
be there?

Douglas MacArthur
c. 1908[1]

THE YEARS WHICH separated Douglas MacArthur's first Asian
adventure and his second assignment to the Philippines provided much of the material for the MacArthur myth. Duty with
Teddy Roosevelt in the White House, heroic action at Veracruz
in 1914, outstanding bravery during the Great War, and a coura-
geous, though ill-fated, attempt to revamp his beloved West
Point, all established the young officer as one of the most promising in the twentieth-century American military establishment.
These were the episodes which future biographers would stress,
the experiences to which the mature MacArthur would attribute
his success. His outstanding efforts, talents, and ability to insure
the furtherance of his career, combined with the singular opportunities he was given by the events of the era, all contributed
to the accomplishments of these years. And yet, when all
this is understood, other problems arise. For the man who
achieved prominence and maturity between 1906 and 1930 was
still faced with the insecurities of his childhood. Within the
success story can be found a continuing thread of ambivalence
and confusion which threatened both his personal and professional advance. The tension engendered by these conflicts
produced much of the energy reflected in his achievements.
To clarify and explain this contradictory force is this chapter's
task.

Following his arrival in San Francisco with his family in August 1906, Lieutenant MacArthur was assigned to the 2nd Engineer Battalion in Washington Barracks, D.C.[2] Chosen as one of the eleven officers to attend the Engineer School of Application at the post, the young officer began his studies with his usual enthusiasm. After the first month, however, his interest waned, and the commandant of the school, Major E. E. Winslow, later reported that "his work was far inferior to that which his West Point record shows him to be capable of."[3] This uncharacteristic lack of effort foreshadowed the onset of a difficult five-year period for Douglas, and represented, in its entirety, one of the most significant phases of his internal development. Once again he would wrestle with his own need for independence. When the struggle was over, he had again acquiesced to the will of his strongest adversary. Consequently, the battle was not decisive.

Other factors naturally played a part in the unsuccessful tenure at Washington Barracks. Having just returned from exciting and highly flattering experiences in Asia, the young officer found it difficult to settle down to the routine demanded by his rank. In addition, the expectations that he and his family still held concerning his father's future may have led him to believe that this duty would be brief. Finally, his concurrent assignment as one of the junior military aides at the White House, requested directly by President Roosevelt, certainly provided a welcome diversion from the grind at school. Many of his evenings were spent attending social engagements at the presidential mansion, and these long hours certainly did not increase his efficiency the next day. The attention he received from his father's old friends in this capacity was comforting, and years later he would still remember that the President "was greatly interested in my views on the Far East and talked with me long and often."[4] This heady wine only encouraged MacArthur's taste for such special attention—a taste already nurtured by his recent Asian tour. Although he finally graduated from the school in February 1908, after assignment away from Washington, the experience was not to his liking and may have contributed to his decision later to leave the Engineers and join the Infantry at the beginning of World War I.

Midway through the younger MacArthur's year at the Engineer School, his father's future career was finally decided by assignment to "special duty" in Milwaukee. Consequently, when Douglas also was assigned to Wisconsin in August 1907, he was able once again to join his family in the comfortable three-story house they had taken on Marshall Street. On duty in the office of engineers, he reported to Major William V. Judson, commander of the district. Soon he was involved in plans for refurbishing several harbors on Lake Michigan. Again, his interest lagged. Shortly he was immersed in a conflict with Judson which would have a serious effect on his career. Undoubtedly sharing his family's dissatisfaction with the recent turn of events, Douglas may have felt that his new assignment paralleled his father's exile. Also, the attention he received in Milwaukee as son of a famous veteran annoyed Judson. Although MacArthur never explained or even mentioned this unsatisfactory tour publicly, his commanding officer made sure that his young subordinate's attitude became part of his record. He reported that MacArthur "exhibited less interest in and put in less time upon the drafting room, the plans and specifications for work and the works themselves than seemed consistent with my instructions. . . . he was absent from the office during office hours more than I thought proper." When Judson attempted to counter this disinterest with an assignment which would give the young officer valuable experience, "he remonstrated and argued verbally and at length against assignment to this duty, which would take him away from Milwaukee for a considerable portion of the time." Judson concluded that "Lieutenant MacArthur, while on duty under my immediate orders, did not conduct himself in a way to meet commendation, and that his duties were not performed in a satisfactory manner."[5]

The two men seemed unable to compromise their differences, and the affair ended only when Douglas was relieved from his duty in Milwaukee and transferred to the 3rd Engineer Battalion at Fort Leavenworth. This order was signed directly by

General J. Franklin Bell, chief of staff in Washington, an old friend and former subordinate of Arthur MacArthur. Whether or not his family had once more interceded in Douglas's behalf is not known, but the shift clearly worked to the younger MacArthur's professional advantage.

There is some reason to believe, however, that removal from Milwaukee interrupted an important development in the young man's personal life. For during the year in Milwaukee, Douglas, then twenty-eight, became romantically involved with a local young lady, Fanniebelle Stuart. The relationship, reflected in several poems the young officer wrote to Miss Stuart in 1908, was apparently more serious than any Douglas had previously known.[6] For the first time, marriage seemed to be a consideration. While no record remains of Miss Stuart's response, the various addresses to which the poems were sent suggest that either she, or her family, wanted to escape MacArthur's passionate attention. Early poems were sent to her Milwaukee address, later ones to New York City, and the final ones forwarded to Paris. The poems themselves revealed the intensity of Douglas's attachment, and indicated that during this year when his work continued to deteriorate, he was seriously examining the direction his life should take.

Written in the sentimental tone of the period, the verses traced the complicated inner processes through which Douglas was able to deal with his continuing ambivalent response to intimacy. Attracted by the possibility of marriage and family, he nonetheless harbored serious questions about giving up his independence to any woman. His mother's opinion, although unrecorded, may have added to his confusion. Consequently, if the poetry is an accurate reflection of the development of the relationship, he managed to both encourage and insure Fan's denial of his suit, assume the role of rejected lover, garb himself in a belated fin-de-siècle cynicism, and then, at least in his imagination, retreat into the romantic danger and security of the masculine, military world.

The earliest poem, a gargantuan twenty-six page epic, offered Fan a detailed picture of what she might expect as an

Army wife. In the note which Douglas attached, he explained that "it is only after much hesitation that I have forced myself to do this, for I feel that it probably takes away even my fighting chance." In fact, the bloody portrait which followed almost insured that possibility, and is important not only for what it revealed about Douglas's attitudes toward marriage and the military, but for its insights into his views on war and race as well.

Opening with a scene of idyllic devotion, complete with "songs of the birds and the hum of the bees," the poem quickly established its tragic undertone. The young warrior husband was about to leave for battle, and Fan, his steadfast wife, was tortured by the possibility that he would not survive. Although the battlefield was never clearly defined, it soon became evident that the war was being fought nearby, that Douglas, as had been his father, was a member of Wisconsin's "bravest and best," and that he was fighting

> For home, and for children, for freedom, for bread
> For the house of our God,—for the graves of our dead,—
> For leave to exist on the soil of our birth,—
> For everything manhood holds dearest on earth.

With those values at stake, Fan could only respond:

> I grudge you not, Douglas—die rather than yield,
> And, like the old heroes, come home on your shield.

The soldier departed, but soon he returned, seriously wounded. The period required for his recovery allowed the poet to portray more visions of domestic serenity, broken only by the feverish cries of the delirious soldier, still, in his fantasy, directing the efforts of his "brave Yankee laddies" who were attempting to "drive those brown beggars clean into hell!" Clearly, the poet was drawing from imaginative pools fed by his father's Civil War and Philippine experiences.

After descriptions of a long and rapturous convalescence, in which MacArthur seemed almost to suggest that the threat of his alter-ego's death made the recovery period most precious of all, he once again returned his poetic counterpart to the front. After an icy winter lull, the war resumed. Soon the engagement shifted to the area bordering the cottage of Fan and Douglas, and Fan and young Arthur (their son) were called to nurse the wounded. Finding "Colonel MacArthur's" orderly, they were told that

> The Colonel passed
> untouched through the battle, unhurt to the last.

Although her home and valley had been destroyed, Fan, who had finally come to realize the great losses she must face as the wife of a soldier, felt encouraged. Days passed before the final agony was revealed. At last a letter arrived which described the conclusion for which the reader has long been prepared:

> Our cavalry bore themselves splendidly—far
> In front of his line galloped Colonel MacAr;
> Erect in his stirrups,—his sword flashing high,
> And the look of a patriot kindling his eye,
> His hoarse voice rang aloft through the roar
> Of the musketry poured from the opposite shore;
> —"Remember Wisconsin!—remember your wives!
> And on to your duty, boys!—on—with your lives!"
> He turned, and he paused, as he uttered the call
> Then reeled in his seat, and fell—pierced by a ball.
> . . . .
> And here, as I write, on his face I can see
> An expression whose radiance is startling to me.
> His faith is sublime: he relinquishes life,
> And craves but one blessing—to look on his wife.

Fan, ever dauntless, arrived at the camp hospital in time to witness her brave husband's death, and the poem ended. Whatever the real Fan's involvement in the relationship, this bathetic vision could not have been encouraging, and apparently, shortly after receiving it, she fulfilled the poet's expectations and left for New York.

In late January Douglas tried again. Forwarding a brief reminder concerning his "House of Dreams," he revealed the ultimate outcome of his earlier vision:

> Why should I tell of my house of dreams?
> You have been with me there
> You know its walls of joy and pain
> And you did not find them fair.

Two days later, a brief quintain suggested that he was beginning to shift the responsibility for the situation to Fan's shoulders:

> Fair Gotham girl
> With life a whirl of dance and fancy free,
> 'Tis thee I love
> All things above
> Why cans't thou not love me?

His role in life was serious, and she had chosen another, more carefree way.

At the end of February, the young poet was beginning to accept what he apparently could not and probably did not really want to change:

> There is a fixed and moveless nature,
> 'Gainst which the tide of passion and desire
> Breaks useless as the water o'er the rock;
> And the warm glow of feeling burns alone
> On the soul's surface, leaving all beneath it
> Unmoved and cold as subterranean springs;
> Love hath no power o'er spirits such as thine.

By mid-April, 1908, Fan was enjoying Paris, and Douglas had become a cynic:

> Love is at best a tragic joke—
> Begun in flames it ends in smoke.
> But he who shuns its thrills and frets

And when in doubt takes cigarettes
Has fewer joys—but no regrets.

In a note enclosed with this poem, the first evidence of
MacArthur's need to reshape reality in order to make it coincide
with the necessities of his contradictory desires for the future
and his damaged pride came to light. Still hoping to appeal to
Fan's sympathy, he wished her "good luck and good bye," and
then went on to explain that

> the authorities could not agree with me on Panama; I could not
> agree with them on West Point; but we both agreed on my going
> back to the Old Battalion at Fort Leavenworth for a twelve month
> [*sic*] and then off again for the Islands. This means for me the
> whirling swing of the old life unless some day out there in the
> jungle a Moro bolo or a snubnosed forty-five changes it all—into
> still waters and silence.

Since he was not being considered for assignments to either
Panama or the Philippines at this time, Douglas was undoubtedly attempting to establish once and for all, in Fan's mind and
his own, that his choice was both brave and honorable.[7] He
could not admit to himself nor to her that his manipulations to
escape marriage were the result of his fear of intimacy. Certainly, at one level, his efforts may have been an attempt to
reconcile himself to what was very likely to be rejection on Fan's
part. Still, the ultimate result of the poetic adventure was to
reconfirm his earlier predilection toward the isolated, military
life—a choice that his parents, the dominant members of his
world, firmly approved. For now, only one woman would continue to have real influence over Douglas's life.

The end of the romance and Lieutenant MacArthur's new
assignment to Fort Leavenworth represented an opportunity to
reestablish the promise of his earlier career. While he spent the
early months in Kansas trying to counter Major Judson's unfavorable evaluation, he also attacked his new duties with the old
vigor. Although unable to convince the Chief of Engineers to

remove the Major's judgment from his record, the new surroundings, and the opportunity to command troops for the first time provided MacArthur with a chance to recoup his losses. His efforts, temporarily unalloyed by inner turmoil, soon met with success. Company "K," undisciplined and in disarray, offered a challenge that he eagerly met. As he later explained it, "by praising them when they were good and shaming them when they were bad, by raising their pride and developing their sense of self-respect, I soon began to convince them they were the best of the lot."[8] Soon they ranked first at general inspection.

The young leader found much greater satisfaction with men than with engineering plans, and the years at Leavenworth and farther west at Fort Riley were therefore a time of renewed achievement. He taught a course in pioneering and explosives at the Mounted Service School at Fort Riley, and then became instructor in demolitions at the Leavenworth schools. His commanding officers were well satisfied. By late 1909, he was serving as adjutant of the 3rd Battalion of Engineers, and in February 1911, he was promoted to captain. Shortly thereafter, he was assigned to head the department of military engineering of the Field Engineer School. Clearly, his outstanding abilities and renewed attention to his career were paying off. He enjoyed the easy camaraderie of the officers' quarters, and managed the post's baseball team. Only one cloud darkened the horizon. For just as Douglas seemed to be readjusting to his role as soldier, Pinkie began to rethink her former attitudes toward the military.

In the years between General Arthur MacArthur's return from the Orient and his retirement in June 1909, it became increasingly clear to his wife that her dreams of ultimate success for him in the Army were not to be fulfilled. Washington's final lack of recognition of the General's efforts and talents was bitter medicine for Pinkie, and when Douglas, too, seemed to be a target for this unfair treatment, she characteristically decided to do something about it. Although Douglas seemed happy and more successful at Leavenworth, his achievements there were a far cry from the expectations she held for him. Her husband was no longer in a position to correct this injustice. Consequently,

Mary MacArthur looked around her to find a new way to help her boy achieve the goals she had in mind. If the Army could not appreciate his talents, she would find someone who could.

With this in mind, she began another letter-writing campaign. Three months before her husband's final retirement she settled on a target and wrote to Edward H. Harriman, head of the Union Pacific Railroad. She had met Harriman in Tokyo three years earlier, and even earlier he had seen Douglas in his father's office in San Francisco, just after the younger MacArthur graduated from West Point. After reminding the railroad magnate of their previous meeting, Mrs. MacArthur reviewed Douglas's career of the past four years, and, admitting that she had not consulted her son concerning this request, asked Harriman to consider Douglas for a position within his enterprises. Conceding that Douglas could not be "regarded as an expert in any particular subject," she argued that "his splendid mathamatical [sic] and technical training, together with exceptional stability of habits and flexibility of mind, fit him for any work, especially of an administrative character."[9] Her dissatisfaction with the military was reflected when she stated, "Frankly, I would like to see my son filling a place promising more of a future than the Army does." On April 28, Harriman's secretary responded, promising that Mr. Harriman was "making an inquiry through our Western officers to see if there is any position which could be offered him." He suggested, however, that "unless a man of his years has had some preliminary training in railroad work, it would be very difficult for him to make a connection which would be at all satisfactory in view of his previous training and station in life."[10]

In the next two months, Harriman's lieutenants quietly investigated Douglas's background, turned up the record of his mediocre performance in Milwaukee, but concluded that this incident had "not impaired his standing whatever with the War Department."[11] Toward the end of July, they were ready to make an offer and visited Lieutenant MacArthur at his post. Much to their surprise, they found Douglas unwilling to consider ending his military career. "It is evidently a case where the mother wants to get her son out of the army, and not where the son is figuring on getting out himself."[12] With that, the Union Pacific concluded its efforts in Mrs. MacArthur's behalf. No record remains of her reaction.

For the first time, Douglas had chosen to reject his mother's advice. At twenty-nine, after several years of uneven progress in the Army, the young officer had found an assignment which provided full scope for his considerable talents. He, and his superiors, were happy with his work at Leavenworth. His recent close brush with matrimony had perhaps reinforced his desire to escape the control of not only that woman, but of all women, as personified in the formidable figure of his mother. Considerably removed from her day-to-day observation, he could control his own life more completely. By renewing his allegiance to a military career, however, he could maintain this sense of independence within a framework which had earlier been approved by both of his parents. In this way, the guilts aroused by this conflict with Pinkie could be controlled. If the uneasy inner balance between his need to exert his own manhood and his equally strong need to secure the approval of his mother was shaken by this disagreement, he was, at least, succeeding within the major realm of his experience: the military. While his father's opinion of this choice went unrecorded, it is possible that Douglas believed that his decision reaffirmed the value of the elder man's life. Certainly, if the action stirred up tensions harking back to his earlier, childhood uncertainties, it allowed him to resolve those tensions by concentrating on the arena which had earlier been defined as a safe testing field. The uneasy balance held fast.

The remaining three years in Kansas were interrupted by maneuvers on the Texas border in the first half of 1911, and then a brief hitch as instructor at a National Guard Camp in Michigan. At the beginning of 1912 he finally was sent to the Panama Canal Zone to observe and advise on the construction of fortification for the canal. The trip was brief, and by spring, 1912, he was back at Leavenworth, once again on the faculty of the Field Engineer School. Now a Captain, and head of his department, his decision of mid-1909 seemed a wise one.

On September 5, 1912, while addressing the remnants of his old regiment, the 24th Wisconsin, General Arthur MacArthur was striken by apoplexy and died almost immediately. His two sons returned to Milwaukee for the simple, civilian funeral the General had requested. They remained as long as they could, but were soon called back to duty at their respective posts. Almost immediately after her husband's death, Mrs. MacArthur's health began to deteriorate, and it fell to Douglas to arrange for some kind of care for her. His brother Arthur was serving aboard ship at the time, and although his wife and young family could perhaps have taken Pinkie in, she chose, predictably, to rely on Douglas. Although the nature of her illness remained undefined, its seriousness was obvious at the time of the General's death, and on September 10, Douglas, "with great reluctance," wrote to the Chief of Engineers, requesting "assignment in charge of the Milwaukee District," a position vacant at the time.[13] The appointment, which would have represented a substantial promotion for the Captain, was apparently considered unjustified, for he heard nothing concerning the request. Consequently, on October 19, he wrote once again, this time to his commanding officer at Leavenworth. Reiterating the seriousness of his mother's condition, he informed the Major that he had been forced to bring his mother to Leavenworth, but had immediately realized "how impossible it will be to properly care for her here." Once again he requested a change of station to a "city of such size as would furnish the needed requisites," adding that "Washington, on account of its proximity to Johns Hopkins Hospital, would offer more of advantage for Mrs. MacArthur than any other possible station." He did not add that his own fortunes might also be served to advantage by such a move.

Once again, friends in high places aided the MacArthurs. Sometime in late October or November, his case caught the attention of Chief of Staff Leonard Wood, a longtime acquaintance of Arthur MacArthur. On Wood's advice, and "in view of the distinguished service of General Arthur MacArthur," Secretary of War Henry L. Stimson recommended that a favorable response be made to the Captain's request. In December, Douglas was ordered to Washington to serve in the office of General Wood. Both he and his mother were delighted at this turn of events which eased the long trauma caused by his father's death.

For Douglas, the move to Washington represented a significant turning point in his career. It ended, at least for the next decade, the uncertainty which had surrounded his life since his return from the Orient in 1906. He had reexamined his goals, and found them satisfactory. He had risked failure, and successfully corrected his mistakes. He had considered marriage and once again managed to escape. He had even confronted his mother's will with a modicum of success. But in this part of his life, the domestic drama begun thirty-two years earlier continued unabated. Fifty years later he still could say of his father's death: "My whole world changed that night. Never have I been able to heal the wound in my heart."[14] And indeed, there is no reason to doubt his judgment. The loss of his father, complicated by his mother's ill health, almost immediately resulted in an unprecedented attack of insomnia serious enough to require medical attention.[15] Undoubtedly, this physical symptom reflected the much deeper effort at adjustment which generally follows the loss of a loved one.[16] Douglas, whose response to previous stress had involved extensive efforts to pattern himself after his father in order to please both his father and his mother, now redoubled his attempts to succeed in his chosen field. In this way, he could incorporate into his personality the characteristics most obvious in his dead father, thereby relieving his immediate sense of loss. By increasing his devotion to his mother, and moving back into the realm of her control both physically and mentally, he not only fulfilled his father's expectations for him, but was able to justify what must have seemed, at some level, a surrender to maternal dominance. For the next ten years, his only attempts at independence were within the safe arena of the battlefield. Because twentieth-century history provided vast opportunity for these acceptable attempts, his inner need for self-assertion in other areas diminished. It is to combinations of historical reality and personal necessity like this that the public success of leaders like MacArthur may often be attributed.

Douglas MacArthur's return to Washington in late 1912 marked the beginning of a period in which he would succeed in establishing himself as one of the "bright young men" of the newly professionalized Army.[17] Joining the staff of General Leonard Wood shortly after that officer had finally succeeded in modernizing the last remnants of the Army bureaucracy, Douglas quickly renewed the ties of family friendship which had developed earlier when Wood had served with his father at Fort Wingate. The dynamic and egocentric Chief of Staff appointed the Captain a member of his personal staff and undoubtedly reinforced many of the younger officer's views concerning the successful use of power. Intent upon insuring preparedness and restrained by a reluctant Congress, Wood fought long and hard for summer training camps, a larger Army, and a generally more efficient force with which to meet the international threats which were developing rapidly. Douglas admired Wood's confidence and would often refer to the lessons he learned from him in the years to come.

The young officer's personal life was also satisfactory. He lived with his mother in northwest Washington, and frequently used the family car and driver for excursions with a variety of young ladies.[18] Once again, however, he found safety in numbers and remained seriously involved only with Pinkie.

In the spring of 1913, MacArthur was appointed superintendent of the State, War, and Navy Building, a position which he fulfilled effectively, but which must have seemed unsatisfying, since his brother, on the General Board of the Navy, was assigned to one of the offices for which Douglas was responsible. With considerable relief, he left this post in September 1913 to become a member of the General Staff. With this official recognition, Douglas's future seemed promising. Only a war would have insured faster promotion.

Seven months later, in April 1914, even that possibility became a near reality. The Huerta regime in Mexico, already at cross purposes with President Woodrow Wilson in Washington, arrested several U.S. sailors, and refused to honor the Navy's request for a salute in apology. Neither side would back down, and soon Wilson had obtained congressional authorization to send American troops to the scene. On April 30, General Frederick Funston led one brigade of the 2nd Infantry Division into Veracruz. War seemed a distinct possibility. Secretary of War Lindley M. Garrison ordered General Wood to prepare to lead an expeditionary force, and with this in mind, Wood ordered MacArthur to Veracruz on a reconnaissance mission.

Captain MacArthur arrived in Veracruz early in May and immediately began to gather information. He soon discovered that the American force was very likely to be stranded upon arrival in the port city due to a lack of animal transportation. The railroad seemed to offer one solution, but no locomotives were to be found. Hearing of some engines hidden between Veracruz and Alvarado, he decided to see for himself. If discovered, however, his mission would have increased the risk of war and was therefore considered unwise by Funston's command. Deciding that his private instructions from Wood covered the mission, MacArthur hired three Mexicans and set out by handcar to locate the engines.

The trip was hazardous. Not only did MacArthur have to avoid the many Mexican troops in the vicinity, but he risked attack by the rebel bands as well. In addition, his three companions were none too reliable, and although he attempted to insure their support by proving to them that he had no money on him and that they would be paid only if they returned safely to Veracruz, he was forced to maintain a constant alert. Reaching Alvarado after midnight, they found three locomotives perfect for their purposes, and headed back. The rest of the trip was filled with adventure.

Attacked first by five armed men, MacArthur fired and two "went down." This was only a preview of what was to come; in the little town of Piedra, a much larger band approached. This time, as the Captain later described it, "I was knocked down by the rush of horsemen and had three bullet holes through my clothes, but escaped unscathed. My man was shot in the shoulder, but not seriously injured. At least four of the enemy were brought down and the rest fled. After bandaging up my wounded man we proceeded north with all speed possible." Finally, near Laguna, they were once again fired upon by yet another small group. Again shots were exchanged and another rebel fell.[19]

Since the locomotives were never needed, MacArthur never directly reported his findings to General Funston, who was known to have disapproved of the venture. Two other officers of the command, impressed by MacArthur's obvious bravery, did report the mission to General Wood and recommended that the Captain be awarded the Congressional Medal of Honor. Wood concurred, and after receiving a full report from MacArthur when he returned to Washington in August, made the recommendation. Funston, when questioned by the War Department Board appointed to examine the case, did not judge MacArthur's bravery, but indirectly suggested that the young officer's decision might have been an "error of judgment." The Board apparently agreed, because on February 9, 1915, they concluded that "to bestow the award recommended might encourage any other staff officer, under similar conditions, to ignore the local commander, possibly interfering with the latter's plan with reference to the enemy."[20]

A minority report filed at the same time also opposed the award, questioning whether or not the action was "extraordinary" and denying that there was "incontestable proof" of the incident. MacArthur's response to this action was immediate and indignant, reminiscent of his earlier rash response concerning the mathematics examination at West Point. In a detailed four-page argument, Captain MacArthur recounted his action, and then carefully listed precedents which seemed to clarify and justify his position.

It is with the greatest reluctance that I submit this memorandum, and only an impelling sense of injustice would make me do so. Such a complete reversal of precedent, such a disregard of judicial interpretation, such a sudden change of announced policy as would be involved in the adoption of the Committee's views, could not fail to leave such a sense of rankling injustice as would serve to embitter always the professional career of its victim. My military self respect forces me, against my desire, to speak in an effort to avoid such a state of affairs.

His argument fell on deaf ears and the honor was denied. Repeating the story in detail at the end of his life, MacArthur could only bring himself to admit "I may have been right or I may have been wrong,"[21] but the affair still rankled. He had tested his courage on the only battlefield available, and his bravery had gone unrecognized. Unlike his father, he would not receive the Congressional Medal of Honor in his first war. The intensity of his response reflected the depth of his need to measure himself against that model—to bolster the self-image of which he was never completely sure.

MacArthur's return to Washington in August 1914 coincided almost exactly with the outbreak of war in Europe. He became immediately involved in drawing up contingency plans in the War Department. Although President Wilson, who was determined to maintain a neutral stance, originally ordered the department to work quietly on these plans, by early 1916, the Army, under the leadership of Newton D. Baker, began to develop broad national defense legislation, which the President signed into law in June of that year. The National Defense Act of 1916 allowed an increase in the size of the Regular Army, a larger and more closely controlled National Guard, and permission to plan for the necessary economic mobilization in the event of war. MacArthur, now a major, helped to draft the act and was soon assigned to study the question of effective utilization of motor transportation. By early 1917, Major MacArthur was meeting regularly with his counterparts in the Navy on these questions, and it was at this time that he first met Franklin D. Roosevelt, then assistant secretary of the Navy.

MacArthur also received a new appointment from Secretary Baker. Assigned to serve as military assistant in the recently established Bureau of Information, he became, in his own words, "press censor . . . the liaison link with the newspaper men who covered the War Department."[22] A major part of his duties in this capacity consisted of convincing the newsmen, and through them the American public, of the necessity of the Selective Service Act of 1917. As might have been expected, this assignment in public relations suited MacArthur well, and provided experience and contacts he would use for the rest of his life.

On April 6, 1917, the United States entered the Great War. Douglas MacArthur, like many of his contemporaries, sought action in this war, for he understood, as Regular Army officers have always understood, that only in war are reputations established and careers secured. As a member of the General Staff, there was a real chance that he might be retained in Washington in a planning capacity. He escaped this possibility in his usual dramatic manner. When conflict developed within the War Department concerning the use of National Guard troops in the war effort, MacArthur found himself in disagreement with most of his superiors. Assuming the traditional Regulars' stance, they argued for an expanded federal contingent; MacArthur, on the other hand, believed that sufficient numbers could not be raised in this way and argued for the use of the National Guard. Conveniently, Secretary of War Baker agreed. Taking the Major with him, Baker brought the problem to President Wilson. Together he and MacArthur convinced the chief executive. They were then faced with the politically delicate problem of deciding which divisions should be used and in what order. At this moment, MacArthur's quick mind and talent for the well-chosen word became obvious. "I suggested that we take units from the different states so that a division would stretch over the whole country like a rainbow;—from that time on it was known as the Rainbow Division."[23]

In early August the 42nd "Rainbow" Division formed and shortly thereafter Major MacArthur was promoted to full colonel in the National Army and named chief of staff of the Division, under Brigadier General William A. Mann. Strangely, Baker gave the new Colonel the opportunity to remain in the Engineer

Corps or to transfer to the Infantry. MacArthur chose the Infantry, remembering later that he "could think only of the old 24th Wisconsin Infantry."[24] Certainly his father's influence was always important to MacArthur, but the fact that advancement in wartime generally was most rapid in the line did not diminish its attraction.[25]

The years of the Great War had a profound impact on American society, and most certainly on the American military establishment. While the war ended before American participation could achieve its ultimate potential, the mobilization effort established precedents that the federal government would use for a variety of purposes in the twenties, during the New Deal, and in preparation for World War II. For the individuals involved in this planning, this vital experience would serve as a paradigm after which they would pattern many of their professional and personal tasks of the future. For Douglas MacArthur this was particularly true. From the time he left Hoboken on October 19, 1917, until he sailed home from Brest on April 18, 1919, he seemed intent upon using this war, perhaps the only one he would ever have, to his best advantage. If he had long been seeking a testing ground, no better one could have been found. This need to test, coupled with a belief in the war and his capacity to help win it, shaped the pattern of his participation.[26]

In outline, MacArthur, who achieved rank as brigadier general in June 1918,[27] saw action in eight major engagements, was frequently commended for his personal bravery, and was awarded seven Silver Stars, two Distinguished Service Crosses, two Purple Hearts, one Distinguished Service Medal, and several French honors. As chief of staff of the 42nd Division, he clearly established an administrative reputation. When allowed to command a brigade, the 84th, he soon became respected as a combat leader by his peers, and popular with the men he led. Since he was one of the few regular officers allowed to keep his wartime rank after he returned to the States, and since both the press and Secretary of War Baker often referred to him as "the greatest fighting front-line general" in the A.E.F.,[28] the war years served MacArthur well. The fame and fortune he had so long sought were now, apparently, his.

Several of the incidents which helped to establish MacArthur's reputation, however, need close examination. For it is by tracing the patterns of adaptation he developed under the pressures of warfare that the links to his past and future behavior become most obvious.[29] All these patterns reflected in one way or another the lingering influence of Arthur MacArthur upon his son. In addition, they illustrated the intensity with which Douglas wished to achieve the fame which was so important to his mother. Finally, his behavior foreshadowed the belief in himself which later led to the tragedy of Corregidor and to the glory of Inchon. Three patterns emerged in his career at this time: (1) excessive—and premeditated—bravery, (2) spontaneous conflict with authority, and (3) exaggerated quest for attention. Obviously, many of the examples which illustrate these tendencies apply to more than one category. All these patterns were motivated by both realized needs in the present and unrecognized tensions from the past.

Throughout the war, the most notable MacArthur attribute was his determination to accompany his front line into the foray. Again and again, in the offensives at Baccarat, Champagne-Marne, Aisne-Marne, St. Mihiel, and, of course, Meuse-Argonne, he plotted his tactics in advance, leaving careful plans with his subordinates so that when the battle began he could be beside the troops, unencumbered by last-minute decisions of command. In each of these adventures, he refused to carry arms or wear appropriate protective garments. His soldiers and the correspondents who reported the war applauded his action, and certainly it was heroic. It may have been unique. Although remarkable acts of bravery were not unusual in this war, they almost always occurred in the pitch of battle when the rational veneer wore thin. Not so for MacArthur. He planned his bravery, and there is reason to believe that much of his courage derived from the fantasies of this premeditation. Certainly, his promise to General Charles Summerall that "if this Brigade does not capture Châtillon you can publish a casualty list of the entire Brigade with the Brigade Commander's name at the top,"[30] suggested a rather extreme vision of what was to come. Châtillon, which the 84th took after three days of intensive effort and severe losses, remained one of MacArthur's most significant memories, and his description of the final victory suggested that this experience paralleled for him his father's glory more than half a century before: "Officers fell and sergeants leaped to the command. Companies dwindled to platoons and corporals took over. . . . That is the way the Côte-de-Châtillon fell, and that is the way those gallant citizen-soldiers, so far from home, won the approach to final victory."[31]

If this premeditated bravery worked to the General's advantage, another of his developing traits certainly did not. From the outset of his experience in France, MacArthur continued his earlier habit of spontaneous conflict with authority. Now he did not hesitate to use his recently learned media skills to buttress his attack. When the 42nd arrived in France in November 1917, it became immediately apparent that headquarters at Chaumont intended to break up the division, requisitioning both officers and equipment for divisions scheduled for earlier combat. Units of the Rainbow Division would be used as replacements where most needed. MacArthur was enraged. As a consequence, he told the story to American reporters, journeyed to Chaumont in protest, and most effectively loosed a barrage of cables to Washington. Public reaction in the United States was immediate and soon the War Department bowed to the pressure. Pershing was instructed to keep the 42nd together, and this incident may have been the root of the various conflicts which later developed between these dashing and determined leaders. Certainly, MacArthur always believed that this was true.

Other incidents of a similar nature characterized MacArthur's service in France. Frequently, he took unnecessary risks against the stated or implied advice of his superiors. Sometimes he chose to accompany French units on reconnaissance. Almost always he refused to wear the gas mask and helmet that he insisted his men have always with them—and he continued not to wear them even when headquarters at Chaumont questioned him about it. His devotion to his men also led him into conflict with authority when he issued passes to Paris after Aisne-Marne. The passes were cancelled by higher command. Although he achieved favor with the Brigade, Chaumont saw the incident as one more example of MacArthur's disrespect. Finally, although certainly not alone in this instance, his was one of the loudest voices to question the Allied decision to halt before Metz after the success of St. Mihiel. It seemed almost as if some inner need propelled MacArthur into these conflicts. He fulfilled the larger goals of the Army brilliantly, but he could accept its dominance only if he could interpose occasional outbreaks of independence. Sometimes, these encounters were serious; often they were only eccentric.

The third pattern most obvious during this period, an exaggerated quest for attention, both led to and grew out of MacArthur's personal eccentricity. This quest showed itself most clearly in his unorthodox attire, but also vented itself in impromptu speeches and interviews he frequently gave. Taken together, these actions represented a serious effort on MacArthur's part to call public attention to himself.

Prior to the war, Douglas had often been commended on the neatness of his appearance. In fact, throughout his life, and even in the heat of battle, his freshly laundered appearance was subject to much comment. During the period in France, however, he gradually altered his standard uniform until it became distinctively his own. First, he discarded the metal support inside his cap. Now his headgear assumed a rakish tilt, easily adjustable to suit his mood. In addition to the unusual hat, MacArthur was seldom seen without his riding crop. For an officer who had never seen service in the Cavalry and who was participating in the war without horses, this prop caused some stir. Explaining it years later, the General attributed the usage to "long habit on the plains."[32] Since he refused to be encumbered by gas masks, helmets, or weapons at the front, the need for the riding crop was even more in question. Completing his unorthodox gear, Douglas usually wore highly polished puttees, a brightly colored turtleneck sweater, and a long wool muffler draped around his neck. Although the cold French winter provided some reason for these items, they nonetheless were unusual and revealed more about MacArthur's obsession for attention than any desire for additional warmth. And he defended his behavior vehemently. When Chaumont appeared to be questioning his habits, he grew increasingly defensive, and finally threatened to shoot one of the Inspector General's emissaries if he appeared again.[33]

Coupled with his outlandish garb, MacArthur's dramatic rhetoric also brought him special attention. Both in the line of duty and in afterhours interviews, he managed to answer simple questions with unparalleled flare. His response to Summerall at Châtillon was only one example of this tendency. After that mid-October battle, the Division was scheduled to move forward again in early November. Division Commander Charles Menoher worried that the recent losses would render the force less than effective. Calling his brigade commanders together, he questioned them on this possibility. MacArthur responded brilliantly and at length, finishing with the assurance that his Brigade was "fully capable of playing its part in such an advance."[34]

When the fighting ended in mid-November, the 42nd was transferred to the newly created Third Army, the American occupation force. Although this would mean a longer stay in Europe, MacArthur was undoubtedly consoled by the fact that he could keep his wartime rank a little longer. He put the time to good use, and once again emphasized his own best qualities at every opportunity. Finally settled in a grand chateau in Sinzig in the Ahrweiler district, the General and his Brigade enjoyed what he later described as "a beautiful spot filled with the lore and romance of centuries."[35] Soon he became a favorite focus for American journalists who now were given much freer range for their inquiries. Although twice stricken with throat infections for which Pinkie's muffler had proven no defense, MacArthur quickly recovered in time to greet the many visitors to Sinzig. Foremost of these was William Allen White. Ever perceptive, White later described MacArthur as "a bachelor, with the grace and charm of a stage hero. . . . all that Barrymore and John Drew hoped to be."[36] Interviews like this one both underlined and helped to fulfill MacArthur's intense need for attention.

   In April 1919, the Rainbow finally started for home. For a brief moment, it looked as if MacArthur would not accompany them, but remain in France on special detail. Once again, Pinkie's health took a turn for the worse, and her son wired Washington.[37] He sailed from Brest on April 18 on the *Leviathan,* and arrived in New York a week later. Pictures of the Brigadier General en route show him in a full-length raccoon coat, his mother's muffler tied rakishly around his neck.[38] Chief of Staff Peyton March, an old friend of Arthur MacArthur, almost immediately assigned the returning hero to a new post which would allow him yet another opportunity for conflict and fame. Beginning in June 1919, he was to become superintendent of West Point. In January 1920, this position justified his permanent promotion to brigadier general.

   The Academy on the Hudson was one of the casualties of the Great War. The school's four-year curriculum had been reduced to one year in order to meet the war's demand for officers. In addition, the courses taught by its superannuated faculty had undergone little revision since shortly after the Civil War. Faced with a conflict between morale and tradition, the new Superintendent was expected to upgrade the institution and establish a new, three-year program. But he had little actual power over the securely tenured faculty, many of whom had been his instructors almost twenty years before. The ensuing battle, which lasted for the next three years, ended in a standoff. Although able to accomplish certain changes in cadet life, MacArthur never imposed a modernized curriculum. In 1921, when General Pershing replaced March as Chief of Staff, support from Washington diminished. These problems, coupled with a now frequently noted loneliness and newly serious demeanor, may have made MacArthur particularly vulnerable to an attack from an entirely new quarter.

   MacArthur, like many other veterans, returned from the war sobered by what he had seen. Describing this feeling years later, he admitted "perhaps I was just getting old; somehow, I had forgotten how to play."[39] Whatever the cause, the effect was widely noted. His aide at West Point, Captain Louis E. Hibbs, described MacArthur during this period as "one of the loneliest men I have ever known."[40] Others found him "a changed individual," and attributed this change to the fact that "he had come face to face with the awfulness of war."[41] Undoubtedly, this had an effect, but the difficult position in which he found himself during the years at West Point was also a contributing factor. Accompanied only by his mother, now sixty-seven, his isolation in the superintendent's house was emphasized by the contrast of this period with the memories of his earlier years at the Point. Despite his continued effort, he could not succeed on this front as fully as he had hoped. Faced with this reality after 1921, he sought solace elsewhere.

Louise Cromwell Brooks was a product of the best social background that money could buy. Stepdaughter of Edward T. Stotesbury, and, for a time, Doris Duke's sister-in-law, Louise, after a spectacular entry into Washington society, married Walter Brooks, a wealthy contractor from Baltimore, in 1908. The marriage ended officially in 1919. Louise, even richer now, and the mother of two children, spent the war years in Paris. There she hobnobbed in Parisian society, established her credentials as an early flapper, and met General John J. Pershing. A friendship developed, and when Pershing returned to Washington after the war, Louise came too. Sometimes she served as his official hostess, and soon there were reports in the press that they would marry.[42]

In January 1922, just as MacArthur was beginning to realize that his assignment at West Point was less than a success, he met Louise Brooks at a holiday party nearby. She often stated later that if he had not proposed almost immediately, she would have asked him to marry her. Taken with his prestige and good looks, Louise announced the engagement on January 15. Two weeks later, Pershing announced MacArthur's transfer to the Philippines. Immediately rumors sprang up to the effect that Pershing's reaction was that of a jilted suitor. In a statement to the press, the Chief of Staff rejected this idea, and pointed out that General MacArthur was due for overseas duty. Although both MacArthur and Pershing continued to deny that the forthcoming wedding had anything to do with the new assignment, nearly everyone else questioned this explanation, since traditionally the post of superintendent was held for four years.[43]

On February 14, 1922, Douglas MacArthur married Louise Cromwell Brooks at her mother's fashionable home, El Mirasol, in Palm Beach. Of the two hundred guests who attended, only one, the West Point chaplain who performed the ceremony, was linked closely to the groom's old life. His mother, who had rejected the wedding plans from the outset, refused to attend, and spent the honeymoon period packing and moving out of the superintendent's house at West Point.

For the second time in his life, Douglas MacArthur, now forty-two, had rejected his mother's advice. This decision, which he would later regret, suggested that once again Douglas was uncertain about his future. As in the 1909 debate concerning his continuation in the military, his career as Superintendent at West Point had been less than spectacular. General Pershing, whom he already considered an adversary, had recently been appointed chief of staff, and his old friend, Newton Baker, was no longer Secretary of War. Undoubtedly at some level, these changes reminded MacArthur that the establishment in Washington was really never to be trusted. Once again, as in the 1880s and in the period just prior to his father's retirement, important people in high places had not recognized the MacArthurs' achievements. In mid-life, with almost all of his energy invested in his career, this realization must have been disconcerting to the General.

On a more personal level, his mother, the strong woman on whom he always relied, seemed to be weakening. At sixty-seven, she was obviously no longer the robust and vivacious companion with whom he had toured the Orient. She could not live forever, and for her son, who had returned from the war with a more highly developed sense of mortality, this was a terrifying prospect. If she died, he would not only lose the mainstay of both his conscious and unconscious strength, but he would be forced to face the ultimate reality of his own death. There was no one else from whom to draw comfort. Into this potential vacuum, Louise Brooks entered with all the force of a tropical typhoon.

She was not young. In fact, despite statements in the press to the contrary, she was only six or seven years MacArthur's junior. Although fashionably dressed in the boyish, youthful styles of the twenties, her solid, even heavy frame offered an obvious contrast to MacArthur's tall slimness. She was a mother, and if the accounts of MacArthur's devotion to young Walter and Louise during the marriage are to be believed, this too was a point of attraction. Most of all, she was cheerful, fun-loving, and determined—all the characteristics which MacArthur associated with his mother in earlier years. She flirted, but so had Mary MacArthur in Siam in 1906. She demanded and cajoled, but so too had his mother. Indeed, in many ways, there was a great similarity between Louise and Pinkie. For just this reason, and because they were both determined to have Douglas, their courses were bound to conflict. For the same reason, Douglas found himself unable to resist the initial onslaught of Louise's attentions.

After the honeymoon, the MacArthurs returned to West Point to finish out Douglas's term. In June they left the Hudson, and after several weeks on leave, embarked from San Francisco for Manila. When they arrived in Manila in October 1922, MacArthur welcomed the opportunity to revisit familiar places and renew old friendships which had lapsed in the eighteen years since his last tour in the Islands. Here he expected warm recognition based not only on his own now established reputation, but on the still strong memories of his father's years there. He looked forward to renewing his earlier relationship with Leonard Wood, now Governor General of the Philippines, and with General George Read, an old friend from the Leavenworth days who now commanded the Philippine Department.[44] Louise's first impressions went unrecorded, but based on later ac-

counts of her accomplishments while in Manila, there is reason
to believe that she faced this new challenge with her usual verve.
As one of the perquisites of Douglas's new office as commander
of the Military District of Manila, they were to reside at 1 Calle
Victoria, known locally as "Casa on the Wall." Originally a
Spanish cavalry barracks and prison, the dwelling, high atop the
Intramuros wall on a "ravelin opposite the San Pedro bastion,"
had been turned over to the Philippine Constabulary at the time
of the American occupation. In 1920, it was transferred to the
Philippine Department and was thereafter used as a residence
and military headquarters for the District of Manila.

Louise redecorated the Spanish adobe quarters with Chinese rugs and heavy carved furniture, all highlighted by the
unusual circular doorway which looked out over the street.[45]
When this was done, she found another focus for her restless
energy in a small nipa bungalow on the beach at Pasay that she
rented from a local resident. Only a few miles from their official
home, the two-room cottage was used on the weekends for the
frequent entertainment which Louise enjoyed. Since she had
managed to have the woven interior walls painted black and
hung with large silver ornaments, the house provoked some
comment from the neighbors.[46]

Finding that her new husband's work habits permitted little
time for shared social activity, she pursued several interests in
which he seldom participated. Concerned over the treatment of
orphans fathered by American soldiers, she helped organize and
maintain an orphanage in their behalf. She also sympathized
with the plight of the often mistreated ponies whose job it was
to pull the local calesas. Soon she had herself sworn in as a
policewoman so that she could officially arrest the drivers guilty
of this mistreatment.[47] Not all of her adventures were benevolent, however, and occasionally she found herself in conflict with
local Filipinos. Such was the case when she attempted to organize a dancing class for her daughter and several friends and to
hold the class in the Constabulary Band Barracks at Fort McKinley. An anonymous patriot complained to Manuel Quezon of
this misuse of Philippine property: "Are we afraid of Gen. McAr-

thur [*sic*] and let his daughter dance on expenses of Juan de la Cruz?"[48]

If some Filipinos criticized Louise's flamboyant taste or questioned her use of government property, others found her delightful. This was particularly true of Manuel Quezon, who, as President of the Senate during this MacArthur stay in the Islands, was the most powerful of the Philippine leaders. Touched by her kindness at the time of his daughter's death, a friendship developed which was strengthened by his appreciation of her determination and devil-may-care attitude—approaches to life which, in many ways, they shared. The MacArthurs and the Quezons saw each other frequently, and when Quezon was in Washington during the summer of 1924, he spent two days with Louise's parents. Even after the MacArthurs returned to the States in 1925, and Louise and Douglas were living separately, Quezon kept in touch with each of them.[49]

Although there were profound differences in the personalities of Douglas and Louise from the start, the major trouble spot in their marriage centered around Douglas's mother. Even from halfway around the world, her presence was felt. Douglas's concern over her health did not lessen in Manila, and in February 1923, when the MacArthurs were called home to her bedside, tensions heightened. This time, as usual, Pinkie recovered, but her obvious influence over her son did not enhance Louise's sense of security in the marriage. She had succeeded in temporarily winning the devoted son away from the maternal hearth, but it was becoming increasingly clear that her victory was hollow.

Despite the interruptions caused by Louise's high jinks and his mother's declining health, Douglas MacArthur managed to devote much of his time during this three-year period in the Islands to his work. He found an ally and ready confidant in Governor General Leonard Wood, the old family friend with whom he had become intimate during his experience in the War Department in 1912. MacArthur had maintained the relationship throughout the war years, and was particularly delighted when Wood wrote from the Philippines early in 1922, requesting a photograph of General Arthur MacArthur to hang in his official residence, Malacanang Palace.[50] The younger MacArthur had every reason to expect support from this quarter, and in this he was not disappointed.

Wood, after an unsuccessful attempt to gain the Republican nomination for president in 1920, had reluctantly accepted President Warren G. Harding's request to examine conditions in the Philippines as part of what became known as the Wood-Forbes Mission. Detailed to evaluate the eight-year Wilsonian attempt to encourage early independence, the mission found the Democratic program responsible for severe Philippine economic and political dislocation. Aided by the 1915 Jones Law, Wilson's appointee, Governor General Francis B. Harrison, further Filipinized the colonial government. He allowed the Philippine legislature more autonomy, broadened Philippine participation in the cabinet and civil service, and, as a consequence, strengthened the position of the two major Philippine political leaders, Manuel Quezon and Sergio Osmeña. Confusing Spanish and American traditions, the newly empowered Philippine leaders soon became embroiled in situations of questionable constitutionality. The government became involved in private business matters, and soon the Philippine National Bank was near bankruptcy. The Harding administration, following longstanding Republican policy toward the Islands, accepted the Wood-Forbes recommendation to slow the movement toward independence. In order to insure this program, Harding prevailed upon Wood to assume the office of governor general. After a period of hesitation because he was required to retire from the Army, Wood accepted.[51]

Assuming office in 1921, Wood faced a difficult situation. Although personally popular in the Islands because of his earlier experiences there, he represented an unpopular administration. In addition, the Harrison years had encouraged Philippine hopes and demands for independence. Both Wood's official assignment and his personal beliefs precluded a continuation of this more lenient policy and he soon found himself in the midst of a crisis of rising expectations. Working from a narrower interpretation of the Jones Law than had his predecessor, the Governor General consistently attempted to regain the power that Harrison had allowed to fall into Philippine hands. To further complicate the picture, Quezon and Osmeña, fearing a loss of their own personal power, decided to use the conflict as an issue behind which they hoped to unite the various Philippine legislative factions. By late 1922, when Douglas MacArthur arrived in Manila, Wood's less than tactful performance of his duties had created a political crisis of vast proportions. In July 1923, the breakdown of communications between the Filipinos and the American colonial government was symbolized by the dramatic resignation of the Philippine members of the cabinet. Infuriated, Wood accepted the resignations and ran the government on his own. In the process, he managed to reestablish the solvency of the Philippine National Bank, reconfirm the economy, and revive faltering governmental services.

Within this complicated situation, Douglas MacArthur walked a tight rope. Intent upon retaining his developing friendship with the Philippine leaders, and particularly Quezon, he found himself the target of "resentment and even antagonism" on the part of some Americans.[52] Nonetheless, he was able to retain Wood's support. Apparently, he achieved this balance by avoiding political issues and adhering strictly to his military responsibilities. Only once, in July 1924, did the two areas of concern overlap in a significant way.

Assigned originally to the newly established Military District of Manila, Douglas found upon his arrival in the Islands that he was to command only a battalion of troops. Incensed, he confided his dissatisfaction to Governor General Wood.[53] By June 1923, shortly after he and Louise returned from their trip to his mother's bedside in Washington, this situation was remedied and he was given command of the 23rd Brigade of the Philippine Division. The Division, established early in 1922, was "the main mobile tactical unit of the Philippine Department."[54] MacArthur's Brigade, consisting of two Philippine Scout Regiments, the 45th and 57th Infantry Regiments, was stationed at

Fort McKinley, the American post south of Manila. His duties were varied and included veterinary responsibilities, the organization of an R.O.T.C. unit at the University of the Philippines, a survey of Bataan, and occasional aid to the Philippine Constabulary in its efforts to control local disorder. In September 1923, MacArthur's troops aided the Department's efforts to send supplies to the Tokyo-Yokohama area, which had been stricken by a serious earthquake.[55]

Along with other members of the military establishment there, he struggled against reductions in the strength of the Philippine garrison brought about, in part, by the Five-Power Naval Treaty, which was signed in Washington in November 1921. As was often the case, the War Department disagreed with the Department of State. At the urging of Governor General Wood, military planners in Washington soon began to revamp War Plan Orange, the War Department plan for action in the event of a war with Japan. The plan, which had existed in various forms since 1904, was considered particularly inadequate in the face of the recent diplomatic developments.[56] Backed by Chief of Staff Pershing, the planners argued that since the treaty forbade the development of any other bases in the Pacific, those already established in the Philippines must be maintained at top strength. In addition, although the planners recognized the difficulty of defending the Philippines in the face of a Japanese attack, they maintained that loss of the Islands would "seriously affect American prestige and make offensive operations in the western Pacific extremely difficult."[57] Consequently, an outline was developed within War Plan Orange which called for the defense of Manila Bay by the Philippine garrison for six months until naval reinforcements could be rushed to the Islands from the United States. As history proved, the plan was inadequate because it did not consider the idea of a Japanese invasion at any other point in the Islands which might, in the face of the diminished Fil-American numbers, allow the Japanese to approach the bay area from another direction, nor did it consider the possibility that the U.S. naval reinforcements might be unable to come to the rescue. Even in 1923, although they did not foresee all these circumstances, Douglas MacArthur and many of his peers in Manila disapproved of the strategy.[58]

Throughout the rest of 1923, MacArthur pursued these additional responsibilities with his characteristic vigor. His relationship with Wood and, paradoxically, with Quezon remained on a solid footing. In December, when he received word of his brother Arthur's sudden death from appendicitis, both of these friends offered support, and Wood was particularly sympathetic. MacArthur, strengthened in this loss by his mother's unexpected composure, replied to Wood's letter of condolence by commenting that Arthur's death made "the world begin to seem a very lonesome place."[59] Now, more than ever, he alone faced the task for which his parents had prepared their sons; to him alone fell the burden of insuring that the MacArthur name would find its place in history. At this moment, Douglas undoubtedly felt a renewed need for maternal support.

MacArthur recovered slowly from the shock of his brother's death, but by early spring of 1924, he had reestablished a daily routine. He worked hard at his new post at Fort McKinley, but as had always been true for the American military in the Islands, there was plenty of time left over for relaxation. Much of the summer was spent in Baguio, the cool city which had become the semiofficial summer capital, and when in Manila, most officers enjoyed golf, swimming, and polo. MacArthur, who always loved athletics, joined in these pursuits, and, in addition, delighted in organizing athletic competitions for his troops.[60] On the surface, the early part of 1924 seemed relatively calm despite the continued political conflict. As a consequence, both General MacArthur and Governor General Wood felt free to enjoy the July 4 parade that year. As the units of R.O.T.C. and Filipino veterans passed before the reviewing stand the two men shared, Wood believed that the turnout "indicated a fine spirit on their part."[61] MacArthur, who organized and commanded the parade, saw no reason to disagree. Three days later, both men were disabused of these assumptions, and Douglas MacArthur was suddenly confronted with a situation which promised to complicate his previously successful efforts to remain apolitical.

The year-long conflict between Wood and the Philippine leaders, and the extensive press coverage which accompanied it, encouraged other groups in the Islands to seek more equitable status.[62] One of these groups was the Philippine Scouts, which made up the regiments of MacArthur's Brigade.[63] These crack native troops, enlisted shortly after the beginning of the American regime, had long been dissatisfied with their situation. Although they were considered vital to Philippine defense, they had traditionally received less than half the pay, not to speak of the professional recognition, given American regulars. Encouraged by rumors that they would soon be paid in dollars rather than pesos, which would double their salaries, the Scouts began organizing a group of the enlisted men into a quasi-union known as The Scouts Enlisted Men's Organization that they hoped would better their condition. Forbidden to meet publicly, the union leaders continued their organization in secret. When discovered, early in July, several were arrested. As a consequence, on the morning of July 7, 1924, nearly 400 members of the 57th Infantry Regiment staged a sit-down strike to protest these arrests. The next day, over 200 members of the 12th Medical Regiment (PS) joined the movement. In all, 602 men mutinied, but almost 400 returned to duty after the serious nature of their action was explained to them. More than 200 others continued their rebellion. As a consequence, these mutineers were brought before a general court-martial board and charged with violating the 66th Article of War. All were dishonorably discharged and sentenced to five years of hard labor. A separate court-martial of the mutiny leaders led to fifteen more convictions of dishonorable discharge and from five to twenty years of hard labor. The "mutiny," which was almost entirely nonviolent, ended two days after it began, and by late August, the court-martial, headed by Douglas MacArthur, was concluded. Shortly thereafter, the General was given full command of the Philippine Division.[64]

Although the American press paid very little attention to the affair, the popular, political, and military response in the Islands was overwhelming. The majority of the Scouts had not participated in the mutiny, but the numbers involved still worried the

American military establishment. Massive investigations followed, triggered in part by the Philippine Department's desire to forestall further dissatisfaction and in part by the fear of American residents that this passive mutiny would lead to a violent anticolonial rebellion. Since Plan Brown, the War Department Color Plan "for the reinforcement of the Philippine garrison to suppress seditious movements or a general insurrection requiring the use of military forces in excess of the regular garrison," relied to a great extent on the continuing loyalty of the Scouts, it was reevaluated. As a result, General Read, commanding the Philippine Department, "called for increasing the American component for the Philippine garrison to a reinforced brigade, peace strength." After an exhaustive study of comparable outbreaks elsewhere, the War Department suggested that pay increases be implemented, that officers trained in the language and cultural values of the Filipinos be assigned to the Scout troops, and that channels of communication between the Scouts and their American commanders be reinforced. Given the economic retrenchment in the War Department during this period, and the longstanding prejudice on the part of many American military officials in the Islands, few of these suggestions were ever implemented. As a result, service with the Scouts, long considered prestigious and honorable to many Filipinos, became less inviting. From that time on, recruitment efforts were necessary in order to maintain sufficient enlistments.[65] The Scout dissatisfaction remained as a low-keyed but still obvious influence well into the Commonwealth period.

On the political level, the mutiny added one more cause for conflict between the American and Philippine governmental factions. Governor General Wood believed that "the foundations for the mutiny were laid largely by the disloyal speeches by Roxas, Quezon, Osmeña, and others, advocating non-cooperation, reducing the authority of the Governor General to that of a mere figurehead, and impugning the good faith of our country, and has the effect of aligning Filipinos against the government and against Americans, through creating the opinion that Filipinos are being oppressed, unfairly treated, et cetera."[66]

While Quezon and his compatriots publicly supported the goals of the strike, they realized that too much emphasis on the mutiny would damage their quest in the long run. When the investigations began to suggest a connection between the Scout union and the Legionarios del Trabajo, "a radical labor society of which Mr. Queson [sic] . . . was Honorary Grand Master,"[67] the Senate President became genuinely concerned. The Legionarios were formed in June 1923 to provide Filipinos a less expensive counterpart to the Masonic Order and had been encouraged in the venture by Quezon, then Grand Master of the Philippine Masons. Soon, however, Americans began to suspect that one of the goals of the society was labor agitation.[68] Quezon, fearful that this belief would have serious ramifications for his larger goal of Philippine self-determination within the protection of American might, immediately sought to break the connection. Consequently, he ordered that ". . . legionario leaders should be advised to keep their hands off the scouts and constabulary. All should bear in mind that no excuse must be given for reports that there is insurrection or disloyalty in the Philippine Islands. This would prove fatal to our cause."[69]

This loss of Philippine political support, coupled with the serious military consequences of their act, further weakened the already waning Scout determination to continue the disobedience. The Philippine Scout mutiny ended with the imprisonment of most of the participants. Although several of the officers participating in the subsequent investigations recognized the essential justice of the Scout demands, few of their goals were ever achieved.

Douglas MacArthur never officially expressed his views concerning the mutiny and did not even mention the affair in the memoirs he wrote at the end of his life. Less than a year after the revolt, he returned to the United States. Nonetheless, his longstanding respect for the Philippine soldiers—a respect he and his father shared—and his continued friendly relationship with the Philippine leaders concerned with the incident suggested that he was sympathetic with the Scout demands. As the officer in charge of the court-martial proceedings, he was faced with the delicate problem of punishing the military infractions without further inciting the political situation. That he was able to achieve this end is a reflection of his skillful diplomacy. The reward for this effort included his assignment as commanding officer of the Philippine Division, and, more significantly, his subsequent promotion to major general in January 1925.

Continually concerned with the direction of his future career, General MacArthur had arrived in the Philippines convinced that the War Department and particularly Chief of Staff Pershing were conspiring against him. In a conversation with Governor General Wood in the summer of 1923, he confided that "the little clique which has gotten control of the General Staff [was] doing more to destroy Army morale and efficiency than any force or combination of forces for years." Regarding his own career, MacArthur had been informed indirectly that Secretary of War John Weeks had decided that his appointment as Brigadier General would be his last promotion for at least the next five years. For this he blamed Pershing and believed that the Chief of Staff, whom he described as "bitterly hostile," was responsible for his shortened tenure at West Point.[70]

Once again believing that advancement was being denied him by the establishment in Washington, MacArthur's original assignment in Manila was also a source of discouragement. Somewhat mollified by his transfer to brigade command, he still felt uncertain about what would happen next.[71] Driven by his desire to achieve further honor, two directions seemed open to him. On the one hand, he continued to cement the relationship with Governor General Wood, hoping that this influential mentor could influence the War Department on his behalf. On the other hand, if the Army continued to frustrate his career, he might perhaps establish another arena of achievement in the Philippines. Thus he made every effort to solidify his friendship with the Philippine leaders whose support would be necessary for appointment to colonial office in the Islands. With these two options in mind, he spent this three-year period in Manila carefully nurturing the individuals on both sides of the political conflict. Even his participation in the mutiny court-martial did not apparently weaken his position with either Quezon or Wood. Shortly after that incident, however, it became clear that this time, the Wood connection would be the most rewarding.

On May 9, 1924, Governor General Wood, with MacArthur's knowledge, made his first attempt to change the attitude of the War Department concerning a promotion. Writing to Secretary of War Weeks, he pointed out the General's "many excellent qualities and his qualifications for promotion." He recounted MacArthur's past career, including his successes in Mexico and France, and concluded with an evaluation which must have pleased Douglas: "He has great energy, courage and initiative and has those qualities which render him an excellent leader of men. He has rendered excellent service during his tour of duty here and has done his best to cooperate in every way with the Civil Government. He is a clean, straight-forward type of officer. I commend him to your favorable consideration when an opportunity for promotion occurs."[72]

Weeks responded that he "had to face the situation of a very young Brigadier outranking a large number of excellent brigadiers, who are almost old enough to be his father. In justice to those men," the Secretary explained, "it seemed to me they should be given the right of way before they went on the retired list." Nonetheless, the Secretary seemed to be weakening when he concluded that "his turn will come in the early future."[73] In the next three months, during which the General dealt effectively with the difficult Scout problem, the War Department reconsidered its position regarding MacArthur's possible advancement. When, in September, another attack came from a different quarter, its defenses seemed to break down completely. In the face of maternal devotion, even the strongest men sometimes bend.

Realizing that her last ally in the War Department would soon retire, Mary MacArthur, still in Washington and apparently once again in good health, determined to intercede for Douglas once more before Pershing left the office of chief of staff. After an unsuccessful personal meeting, she wrote still another of her very effective letters. Referring to their earlier "heart-to-heart chat" which had left her "particularly unhappy," she resorted to flattery:

> It is just because I know you to be such a noble, broadminded and just man and friend that I am presuming on long and loyal friendship for you—to open my heart in this appeal for my Boy—and ask if you can't find it convenient to give him his promotion during your regime as Chief of Staff? . . .
>
> Your own life is so full to overflowing with joys and happiness —and deserving success—that it may be hard for you to understand the heartaches and bitter disappointments in the lives of others. Won't you be real good and sweet—The "Dear Old Jack" of long ago—and give me some assurance that you will give my Boy his well earned promotion before you leave the Army? . . . God bless you—and crown your valuable life—by taking you to the White House.[74]

Ten days after Pershing retired, Douglas MacArthur was elevated to the rank of major general. As D. Clayton James has suggested, the relationship between the letter and the promotion was unclear. Nevertheless, Mrs. MacArthur could not help but believe that her well-timed requests generally met with success.[75] The new Major General, still in Manila and probably unaware of his mother's part in the episode, was undoubtedly also reassured in his belief that well-placed friends like Leonard Wood were an important asset. Newspaper accounts of the promotion announced that as the youngest major general in the Army, MacArthur could look forward to eventual assignment as chief of staff.[76] This was a consideration never far from MacArthur's mind in the next five years.

Shortly after MacArthur's promotion became effective, he was returned to the States. With Louise and the two children, he left Manila in the early spring. At the beginning of May, they were in Atlanta, where MacArthur was to command the IV Corps Area. Throughout the spring and summer, he fulfilled his new duties with the usual aplomb, and by fall was once again transferred. This time, as commander of the III Corps Area, around Baltimore and Washington, he would be near the centers of power. The MacArthurs moved into Louise's estate, Rainbow Hill, near Baltimore, not too far from the War Department and, more significantly, from the Washington home that Douglas's mother shared with her widowed daughter-in-law.

During the three-year period of MacArthur's command of the III Corps Area, one of his major professional concerns was a sustained battle against the pacifism now rampant in the United States. His frequent public warnings of the dangers of this stance earned him the respect of the War Department and wider recognition from the public. Along with this preoccupation and the regular duties of corps command, two special assignments required his attention. As he later recalled, one of these was "most disagreeable, one most pleasant."[77]

In October 1925, MacArthur was assigned to serve as one of the thirteen judges in the court-martial of Brigadier General William Mitchell, accused of eight charges of violating the Articles of War. Mitchell, an acquaintance of MacArthur's since their Milwaukee days, had come out of World War I convinced that all future military efforts would be dependent upon air power. While many foreign powers shared this belief, few military leaders in the United States agreed with him. Throughout the early twenties, Mitchell took his warning to the public. He criticized his superiors as negligent of the nation's defense, and as his advice went unheeded, he became more and more vocal in his attack. Finally, after a particularly strident statement to the press in September 1925, Mitchell was relieved from duty and summoned to Washington to stand trial.

The trial, which stretched out far beyond all expectations, received much public attention. Ostensibly an effort to decide if Mitchell was guilty of "conduct prejudicial to good order and military discipline," or "conduct of a nature to bring discredit upon the military service,"[78] the affair quickly turned into a judgment of his attitudes concerning air power. In this dispute, his antagonists included some of the most powerful members of the Army. This reality, emphasized by the widespread publicity surrounding the case, placed MacArthur, the youngest member of the court, in a personal quandary. If he supported his old friend's right to speak his mind, he risked angering many of the men who controlled his future. Moreover, his own attitudes concerning the effectiveness of air power were more or less in agreement with his superiors. Consequently, he remained discreetly silent. In later years, he would suggest that he had been one of the minority who voted against Mitchell's conviction.[79] There is little evidence to support this contention, but his success in extricating himself from a potentially difficult situation once again reflected his now highly developed skills at diplomacy and self-preservation. He had yet to reach the pinnacle from which his boundless ego needs could fully manifest themselves. In the meantime, he was very careful.

The "most pleasant" assignment given to MacArthur while he served in Baltimore grew out of his election as president of the American Olympic Committee in September 1927. His well-known interest and encouragement of athletics, coupled with support from his superiors in the War Department, led to assignment on detached duty to accompany the U.S. team to Amsterdam, where the 1928 games were to be held. As always, he was determined that his forces would be victorious, and after riding them "hard all along the line,"[80] he was successful, and so were they. While in Holland he dined with Queen Wilhelmina, and he returned to widespread praise in the press. It was a high point in what had otherwise been a dismal period in his life.

With the exception of the controversial Mitchell trial, the shadow over MacArthur during this time was personal. His marriage to Louise was breaking up, and although he continued to occupy the mansion at Rainbow Hill until his departure for Amsterdam, Louise had moved to New York City during the summer of 1927. From the outset, the relationship had faced difficulties involving contradictory social attitudes, Douglas's career responsibilities, and, of course, the influence of Mary MacArthur. The three years in Manila, while alleviating the latter pressure, had witnessed a widening gap between the husband and wife. In fact, shortly after their return to the States, Louise indicated in her letter of condolence to Pershing at the death of his former aide, Colonel John G. Quekemeyer, that she was having second thoughts about her marriage.[81] Louise, forceful and gregarious, resented her husband's devotion to his military career. She found it difficult to understand his loyalty to the Army at a time when civilian opportunities seemed so much more inviting. In this regard, she and her wealthy stepfather, Edward T. Stotesbury, attempted to convince MacArthur to investigate the possibility of joining the firm of J. P. Morgan & Company.[82] They met with no success. For Louise, this was particularly frustrating, since the General insisted that they live largely on his salary as major general.[83] The distance between the two widened once they returned to the Washington area and were in close contact with the elder Mrs. MacArthur. In later years, Louise would attribute the failure of the marriage to "an interfering mother-in-law."[84] There is reason to believe, however, that there was yet another source of tension between them, which manifested itself early and also may have been directly linked to Douglas's relationship with his mother.

At the time of the marriage, Louise Cromwell Brooks was a sexually experienced matron, already espousing the liberated values of the newly popular flapper. Her husband, on the contrary, had remarkably less experience in that regard. Indeed, although he was already past forty, there is little evidence to suggest that he had ever known a woman intimately, and considerable reason to believe that he had not. According to one account, this disparity of experience manifested itself almost immediately. On the morning after her wedding, Louise told her brother that while her husband held high rank in the Army, "he's a buck private in the boudoir."[85] Later, after the marriage had been dissolved, Louise often confidentially suggested that MacArthur was less than an effective lover.[86] Admittedly, this information derives from a possibly biased source. On the whole, however, Louise seldom criticized the General after their marriage ended and, in fact, maintained "the greatest respect and admiration for him."[87] More to the point, this information would be of little concern to an evaluation of MacArthur's place in history if there were not reason to believe that this difficulty partly explains his behavior during the next few years of his life, particularly in the Philippines. If that is true, then an analysis of the causes and effects of this sexual problem is important.

Douglas MacArthur's close attachment to his mother probably began at the time of Malcolm's death and increased during their years together in Milwaukee when he was a late adolescent. One task of youth, inevitably, must include sexual separation from the parent of the opposite sex. If MacArthur did not successfully separate himself from his mother, as clearly he did not, part of his attraction to Louise in 1921 may have been due to her similarity to Pinkie. This fact, coupled with his own sexual inexperience, would have complicated their physical relationship. Some of the characteristics which drew the General to his wife may have been those most like his mother. His culture and his own nature would have denied him a satisfactory physical solution to this problem. The marriage, already under stress, could not then survive the added strain. When the MacArthurs returned to the Washington area, his mother's proximity could only have exacerbated these tensions. This reality, coupled with his characteristic inability to maintain an extended conflict with his mother, led to the divorce. Undoubtedly at some level, MacArthur was deeply sensitive to this failure.[88] His response to the situation was most evident after his return to the Philippines in the fall of 1928, nearly a year after Louise's departure.

Ordered to assume command of the Philippine Department, the military administrative organization for the entire archipelago, MacArthur returned to Manila in October 1928. Finally, he had achieved a significant position of power in the Islands, and was determined to use it to carry out some of the programs he had earlier advocated. One of these involved upgrading the Philippine Scouts. During the first few months of MacArthur's command, the War Department finally increased the Scouts' pay and arranged for them to be retired equitably after thirty years' service. Encouraged by these events, MacAr-

thur reported a marked increase in morale and efficiency, noting
that "there was a marked decrease from last year in the propor-
tionate numbers of Philippine Scout enlisted men convicted by
courts-martial." Moreover, he went on, the training and recruitment programs for this arm of the military were progressing
significantly.[89] These developments both reflected and enhanced his standing with the Filipinos who served under him.

The rest of the military picture was not so optimistic. In
Washington, these years saw frequent revisions of the Orange
Plan, each attempting to readjust military reality to the changing
international scene. Each change widened the distance between
the real military needs in the Philippines and the actual amount
of men and matériel that the United States was willing to provide.[90] As Major General Fred Sladen, one of MacArthur's immediate predecessors, put it: "there isn't any plan, and you
won't get any money, so go to it and do the best you can."[91]
MacArthur's reports, couched in more formal tones, were filled
with notations concerning matériel which was deteriorating and
"should be replaced." With the decline in the domestic economic situation in the United States following the stock market
crash in October 1929, affairs only got worse. Soon, the General
Staff was reduced to suggesting that a Philippine militia might
be organized to bolster the diminished American garrison.[92]
MacArthur, frustrated by these events, considered this suggestion seriously.

Despite these setbacks, the general tone of MacArthur's
reports from these years suggested a satisfaction with his command. As always, he encouraged athletic competition among his
troops. "In addition," he reported, "contests with the U.S.
Asiatic Fleet and civilian teams . . . have generally been favorable for the army teams and individual participants have done
much towards upholding a high state of esprit and morale."[93]
His overall effectiveness was confirmed when Colonel Louis J.
Van Schaick, of the Inspector General's department, concluded
his annual inspection for 1929. Commenting on the need to
replace "old and obsolescent" property, the delay (sometimes
of one to three years) in receiving requisitioned supplies, the
inefficiency of the War Department in supplying only a few

airplanes and no spare parts, and the inadequate housing for the troops, Van Schaick recommended that "Major General Douglas MacArthur's fine grasp of the economic problems involved in the administration of this command and his prompt and energetic steps already inaugurated to carry out the policy of the Secretary of War in safeguarding the Government's interests and get [*sic*] value received for the Army appropriations be noted on his efficiency record."[94]

Later that year, MacArthur's optimistic assessment of his command was confirmed during the annual Division maneuvers. He reported

> The maneuver was held in the Lingayen Gulf area, next to the Manila Bay area, the most critical of all. The Field Artillery and the Cavalry marched from Camp Stotsenburg. Upon arrival in the area, dispositions were made to repel a hostile landing, the command was inspected by the Department Commander, was released to the Division Commander, and returned home by marching. The supply was excellent, the weather suitable, and there were no untoward events. The preparedness of the Philippine Division for field service is highly satisfactory.[95]

In contrast to many other observers, he continued to hold this attitude for almost thirteen years.

Although busy with his responsibilities as department commander, MacArthur did not neglect what he understood as his political interests during these years. The untimely death of his friend, Leonard Wood, left the General with no direct link with the American colonial government. Wood's replacement, Henry L. Stimson, arrived in March 1928, and although he remained only one year, the six months that he and MacArthur shared in the Islands laid the foundation for their later relationship during World War II. The two men had met in the War Department in 1913 and again in France in 1919.[96] Now, however, they had their first real opportunity to size each other up.

At the time when he accepted President Coolidge's invitation to become governor general of the Philippines, Henry Stimson had already had a full career. Believing that his professional activities were nearly at an end, the former Secretary of War agreed to a brief tenure in the Islands partly because he thought it would provide pleasant memories, and partly because he had a longstanding interest in the future of the colony. As one historian suggested, Stimson's attitudes toward the Islands were "inspired by fin-de-siècle expansionism and empowered with his own experience and conviction [; his] arguments were the last, most generous eloquence of American empire."[97] This attitude was perhaps best reflected in Stimson's recollection of a conversation he had with President Hoover after his return from the Philippines.

> I also had a short talk with him [Hoover] on the Philippine question on which we do not stand on the same grounds. He is sorry we ever went in. I told him that I was greatly scandalized at our going in when we did go in, but my subsequent experience in the Philippines had changed my views, so that I now thought we had on hand a task which we could not drop, and I was in favor of our permanent holding to that task provided that we could do it with the consent of the Filipinos. I asked him whether he really believed that the United States was not enough of a governmental power and did not have enough of constitutional freedom to evolve relationships to another country like the Philippines similar to the relationship of England to the British Commonwealth of Nations. He did not deny that we could do that. . . . But he simply said, "Well, that's the white man's burden." I said, "Yes, that's what it comes down to and I believe in assuming it. I believe it would be better for the world and better for us.[98]

Although he shared the long-range goals of his predecessor, Stimson understood the delicate diplomacy that was required better than had Wood. Consequently, he was able to accomplish a great deal during his brief period in Manila, including a program to encourage new cooperation between the executive and legislative factions.[99] He smoothed the ruffled feathers of Quezon, Osmeña, and Roxas, and, in the process, made Douglas MacArthur's political position more secure than it had been during his last tour.

Nevertheless, the relationship between the two men did not start well. Stimson liked MacArthur's immediate predecessor,

General William Lassiter, who, Stimson believed, would be very helpful to him. Consequently, when he heard of MacArthur's appointment, he wired Frank McIntyre, chief of the Bureau of Insular Affairs, to suggest that it be cancelled. Contacting MacArthur, the bureau found that "he had already shipped his property and disposed of his home and any change would cause him great inconvenience and financial loss." Also, the bureau noted, "the orders have been announced, much publicity given to his going on foreign service and any delay beyond that already provided would subject him to comment and criticism that might be embarrassing to him and to the War Department."[100] MacArthur relieved Lassiter on October 1, 1928.

Once settled into the routine of command, MacArthur took an active interest in the political situation. He renewed his friendship with Quezon, and felt freer, this time, to sympathize with the Filipino's advocacy of independence. In fact, he even incorporated this attitude into his official reports, explaining that the few examples of anti-American sentiment in the Islands were "developments of the ever recurring 'immediate independence' issue, resurrected periodically by aspiring politicians. A vigorous presentation of this issue, to the voters, is difficult without indulging in attacks on the American Government."[101] While this was still a careful statement, it represented an impressive change of attitude if measured against the American position during the Wood years. MacArthur's further involvement in the political issues of the Philippines was reflected in a report concerning the right of the Philippine government to tax purchases made in the Islands by the United States government. Arguing that the Jones Law had left this issue unclear, he recommended that the "entire subject be given present consideration, and . . . that the entire scope of Section 11 of the Jones Law, in so far as it grants to the Philippine Government the power to tax, be definitely settled." He further advised, "if this be once accomplished, it will remove permanently a constant source of irritation and controversy between the military and civil governments in the Philippine Islands."[102] While this issue did concern the military, it was of a nature generally handled by the Judge

Advocate General's office. MacArthur's investigation and recommendation were just one more example of his ever-widening
involvement in nonmilitary issues.

By the end of 1928, Stimson and MacArthur had worked out
the difficulties between them, and the Governor General offered
his "sincere thanks and appreciation for all the many acts of
assistance and kindliness which have been rendered . . . to the
Government."[103] Three months later, Stimson left Manila to
assume the office of Secretary of State in the Hoover administration. Convinced that the relationship was sound, MacArthur,
who sent "a guard of honor consisting of the entire battalion of
31st Infantry," to the pier as a sendoff, now considered Stimson
an ally.[104] In the months to come, he would have reason to
question this assumption.

During the early months of 1929, the friendship with Quezon took on new importance for the General. After Stimson's
impending departure became known, official Manila anxiously
awaited word concerning the appointment of his successor.
Most Filipinos preferred that one of their own be given the
position, and argued that such a step would indicate goodwill in
the United States concerning the question of independence.
Nevertheless, even Manuel Quezon, who naturally expected that
he would be chosen in this event, realized that the possibility was
unlikely. Consequently, he and his fellow legislators contented
themselves with efforts to influence the choice of an American
for the office. Since Hoover was intent upon maintaining the
calm that Stimson had established in the Islands, their opinions
were considered seriously. As March stretched into April, and
then May, a decision still had not been reached. Several candidates vied for the position including General Frank McCoy, who
had served in the Wood administration, and Vice Governor
Eugene Gilmore, who acted as chief administrator after Stimson's departure. Stimson supported Silas Strawn, a diplomat of
longstanding Asian experience. Only one other contender came
under serious discussion—the commanding officer of the Philippine Department, Douglas MacArthur.[105]

MacArthur's acceptance by the Philippine leaders, and particularly Manuel Quezon, was based in part upon recognition of

his longstanding support of social equality.[106] This unusual attitude on the part of an American military officer, coupled with his interest and experience in the Islands, led Quezon to single the General out for special attention and friendship in the twenties. MacArthur, always fearful that Washington would somehow frustrate his desire to become chief of staff of the Army as it had his father's, decided, once again, that an acceptable alternative career might be forged in Manila. Stimson's departure provided just such an opportunity. With this in mind, he promised Quezon that if the Senate President would back his candidacy for governor general, "he would execute a policy under the Jones Law, of full party responsibility and would recommend changes in the Organic Act [Jones Law] that would be acceptable to us [the Filipinos."][107] Although Quezon was drawn to this idea, backing MacArthur placed him in a difficult position. He had long contended that members of the American military establishment were unsuitable for the position of governor general because such appointments might remind the people of the hated Spanish generals who had also served in that position. His experience with Leonard Wood had only reconfirmed this opinion. Nonetheless, he supported his friend's interest as best he could, mentioning his name frequently in lists of acceptable candidates. He could not, however, stress his support for the General without seeming to contradict his earlier position.

Clearly, Quezon's caution was not satisfactory to MacArthur. As early as the end of March 1929, the General argued this point with his friend and urged further action on the part of the Senate President. In a "Personal and Confidential" letter, MacArthur outlined a suggested plan of attack. After arguing that Quezon's objection to McCoy had given him at least temporary control of the situation, he urged further action in the form of a radiogram to Secretary of State Stimson. Fearful that Quezon might understate the case, MacArthur suggested the exact wording that Quezon should use.

I have carefully canvassed all shades of Filipino thought with reference to the appointment of a new Governor-General. In all circles, political, industrial and labor, I find an almost unanimous agreement on General MacArthur. I know of no man who so thoroughly commands the confidence both of the American people and the Filipinoes [*sic*]. His appointment would be a master stroke of statesmanship and diplomacy. It would not only insure harmonious cooperation but would give promise of constructive accomplishments which would transcend anything which these Islands have ever known. I solicit your cooperation in pressing these views upon the President. I am confident that General MacArthur's great interest in Philippine affairs would cause him to consent to retiring from active military service to accept this great national duty. Please regard this radiogram as absolutely confidential except for the President himself.

The General went on to point out that his position in the Army, with fifteen years more of active duty, probably prevented Washington from considering him, since "none in the United States and few in the Philippines would believe for a moment that I would be willing to leave the Army just as I was about to become its head." Assuring Quezon that his "personal interests in this matter are a minimum," MacArthur ended the letter.

There is no indication that Quezon ever sent the radiogram, or that Stimson seriously considered MacArthur for governor general. A month later, on April 30, the General once again approached Quezon. Advising him that "a powerful junta . . . is trying to influence the selection," he urged the Senate President to repeat the wire to Stimson and to make sure that the representatives of the Philippine government in Washington were doing all they could in his behalf. Again, Quezon left no record of a response. Two weeks later, he wrote the General to inform him of the selection of former Secretary of War Dwight Davis for the post. MacArthur responded almost immediately, once again illustrating his marvelous capacity for bathos.

I recall the incident connected with the death of Stonewall Jackson wherein one of his officers—bloody and disheveled, from the tragic field of Chancellorsville stood for the last time before his dead Chief and gave utterance to those epic words:

"If you should meet today with Caesar, tell him we still make war."

Great Captains ride to ultimate victory over minor defeats.

Your confidence and unflinching loyalty to me in our adventure will always remain one of my greatest memories and inspirations.[108]

On one level, it is difficult to explain MacArthur's attempt to become governor general. And, indeed, analysts of the incident have usually argued that he was not serious.[109] Manila observers, however, getting wind of the General's interest, more clearly assessed his long-range goals. A report from Manila printed in the *New York Times* that spring argued that "according to close friends, General MacArthur has his eyes on the White House for eight or twelve years hence, via a successful administration as Governor General for four years and then four years in a Cabinet post, either as Secretary of State or Secretary of War."[110] This assertion was not as farfetched as it seemed. Indeed, the political path in the article was exactly the one followed by William Howard Taft only thirty years earlier, and this example was never far from MacArthur's mind. In addition, although he seemed sure of the appointment as chief of staff in his correspondence with Quezon, his confidence may have contained an element of bravado. Always fearful that Washington would somehow interfere with his advancement, he correctly understood that there was some opposition to his appointment. In July 1929, Chief of Staff Summerall cabled MacArthur to inform him that President Hoover hoped to appoint him chief of engineers. MacArthur believed, however, that this assignment would only hinder his chances to become chief of staff, and turned down the offer. Advised by his Adjutant General, Colonel Edward Brown, that he had destroyed his chances for further advancement, MacArthur settled back to await the outcome. Nevertheless, he undoubtedly had some fears that this might be true.

As Chief of Staff Summerall's term drew to a close, the debate in Washington over the selection of his successor heightened. Summerall and President Hoover seemed to favor MacArthur. But the new Secretary of War, Patrick Hurley, and General

John Pershing, who retained considerable influence over the Army after his retirement, remained unconvinced. The argument continued through the first half of 1930. Finally the President prevailed, and MacArthur's appointment was announced. He was ordered back to Washington to assume his new responsibilities by October 1930.[111]

Although the General had once again achieved a desired goal, there is reason to believe that he faced this new situation with a certain amount of ambivalence. In his own words, he admitted to a certain reluctance. "I did not want to return to Washington, even though it meant the four stars of a general, and my first inclination was to try to beg off." Not surprisingly, his mother intervened: ". . . my mother . . . sensed what was in my mind and cabled me to accept. She said my father would be ashamed if I showed timidity. That settled it."[112] Although he attributed his feelings to a realization of the difficulties any officer in that position would encounter during the Depression, other factors contributed to his uncertainty. He continued to believe that he had always been most successful when in command of troops in the field. The achievements of the past two years confirmed this opinion. In addition, he could not help but question the effect of this assignment on his long-range career. In 1930, Douglas MacArthur was only fifty years old. At the end of his term as chief of staff, he would still be only fifty-four, with eleven more years to serve before retirement. Memories of his father's position in 1907 undoubtedly reminded him that, within the military establishment, there would be no opportunity for further advancement. His only other option, political appointment, had not usually followed retirement as chief of staff and, indeed, might be more likely from the springboard of office in the Philippines. All of these considerations, and one more, played havoc with MacArthur's composure during the last summer in Manila.

As a result of his recent separation from his wife Louise, Douglas MacArthur returned to the Philippines in 1928, probably unsure of his abilities to achieve a satisfactory relationship with any woman. Clearly, strong white women who resembled his mother only frustrated his needs. Establishing bachelor quarters in Manila which he shared with four junior officers, he described his friends as "a gay and lively group, . . . a source of constant pleasure to me."[113] In their company, his off-duty hours soon were taken up with trips to the fights, polo games, and vaudeville shows he had always enjoyed. These distractions undoubtedly allayed some of his reaction when the newspapers in the Philippines carried word of his final divorce from Louise. Still, something was missing. Attracted by what he described in another context as "the moonbeam delicacy of its [the Philippines] lovely women,"[114] MacArthur determined once again to attempt a romantic liaison. This time, however, he would choose a less threatening object for his attention. With this in mind, he began to look carefully at the beautiful Philippine women. Sometime in 1929 his eyes settled on an attractive choice, and while attending a fight at the Olympic Stadium in Manila, he sent T. J. Davis, his aide, to deliver a note to Isabel Rosario Cooper, an exquisite young woman seated in another part of the stands.[115]

Known in the entertainment world both as "Dimples," and Elizabeth Cooper, Isabel, at the time she met MacArthur, was already established as a popular vaudeville star in Manila. Of Philippine and Scottish parentage, she was short and delicate, and by all accounts, very beautiful. Soon she was seeing MacArthur regularly. Often, his chauffeured car would appear at Isabel's home on Herron Street in the Paco district of Manila. The General would alight, enter and spend an hour or so with the young lady. Sometimes they would share a drink she laughingly called "the Douglas," made of crushed mango, Spanish brandy, and crushed ice. He saw her frequently, and the relationship was not long a secret from Manila gossips. MacArthur did not seem to mind. Nonetheless, his friendship with Isabel complicated his life.

Already drawn to a life in the Islands where he sometimes believed he could achieve the fame so necessary to him without being forced to confront official Washington, Manila now held an added attraction. Moreover, his continued devotion to Isabel, even after he finally decided to return to Washington, suggested that the relationship was more successful than his earlier attempt with Louise. Isabel, small, soft-spoken, and of another race, offered no threat to his masculinity. More importantly, her somewhat checkered past categorized her in his mind in an entirely different light from his mother and his former wife. Perhaps with her he achieved the sexual success that had escaped him for so long. Certainly, her presence became very important to him—so important that he risked a great deal to insure her companionship back in the states.[116]

When, in the fall of 1930, he finally decided to accept the appointment as chief of staff, MacArthur presented Isabel with a jade and diamond ring, and made careful arrangements for her to follow him to the United States. En route to San Francisco, he wrote her regularly.[117] Not surprisingly, the letters reflected the General's longstanding romanticism and were filled with assurances of his continuing devotion, both for now and forever. More noteworthy, however, was his uncharacteristic emphasis on the social aspect of his trip, and the good times he foresaw after they had been reunited. MacArthur seemed fearful that Isabel would not follow him to the States, and spent a great deal of space urging that she prepare with care and allow nothing to interfere with her departure. Between the lines of passionate prose, there was an underlying insecurity—certainly not unusual in May–December affairs, but nonetheless significant as an indicator of the trauma the new Chief of Staff was now experiencing. Another measure of the depth of his involvement with Isabel can be seen in his lack of caution in the letters. Although he was careful not to be too specific, he nevertheless signed one of the letters with his first name, urged her to wire him at 9th Corps Headquarters in San Francisco if anything went wrong, and pinpointed the time and place of their reunion at the Jersey City pier on December 9. Apparently the meeting went smoothly, because although Douglas MacArthur would be stationed in Washington and live at Fort Myer with his mother, he arranged for Isabel to be near his office at the State, War, and

Navy Building in an apartment in the Hotel Chastleton on Sixteenth Street. Obviously, their relationship was very important to the General.

Douglas MacArthur perhaps never fully understood the role the Islands, and Isabel, played in his life. Certainly, he left no comment in that regard. Nevertheless, his continual enchantment with the Philippines, and his sustained desire to return there, suggested more than just a responsible assumption of the colonial burden. He was devoted to the Philippines and the Filipinos. His family tradition and his personal success there provided part of the answer. It is also possible that the continued efforts of the tiny nation to achieve independence triggered a sympathetic reaction in MacArthur who, at some level, had long fought the same battle. Other reasons, admittedly more speculative and difficult to prove, may stem from what another historian, speaking of the British empire, has described as "the export of surplus emotional energy."[118] MacArthur, deeply imbued with Victorian values, and perhaps additionally confused in his sexual identity because of his intense and complex relationship with his mother, seemed unable to relate successfully to women in his own world. His choice of profession, and his preference for service in the colonial empire may have partially reflected a rejection of that world, and particularly the proper women who peopled it.[119] The Islands offered a dual haven. There the colonial administrators could reaffirm their masculinity in an environment which still offered a degree of physical danger. There, also, they could escape the infinitely more threatening control of the wives and mothers they left behind, while fulfilling their need for sexual release and companionship through liaisons with members of the alien race. For MacArthur, there was one more advantage. Both of these goals could be achieved in a realm of which his parents had originally approved. Whatever guilts his relationship with Isabel engendered were lessened by this awareness.

To whatever degree these considerations were a factor in MacArthur's attitudes in the late 1920s, certainly he valued Isabel highly. Since his career goals in the Islands had been thwarted, and could at present only be realized back in the metropolis, he chose, as a consequence, to bring back with him that part of the empire he deemed most precious. By this decision, because it flaunted conventional morality and the discretion required of a high government official, he risked all that he had spent years trying to achieve. Once again, the contradictory forces at work in Douglas MacArthur's nature threatened his destruction.

(5)

The Last Years
Before the War

... as the Military Adviser I will forge for
you a weapon which will spell the safety
of your nation from brutal aggression
until the end of time.
Douglas MacArthur to Manuel Quezon,
June 1, 1935[1]

IN THE TWELVE YEARS between 1930, when he returned to the
United States to become Chief of Staff of the Army, and 1942,
when he left Corregidor to take charge of the Allied forces in the
Southwest Pacific Area in World War II, Douglas MacArthur
seemed finally to have achieved his lifelong goals. He served as
Military Adviser to two American Presidents and the new President of the Philippine Commonwealth. He traveled around the
world inspecting the armies of the great powers. In his public
statements, he addressed the defense issues of the day with
vigor, and even in the antimilitaristic climate of the early thirties,
his views were respected in most quarters. After 1936 as Field
Marshal of the newly organized Philippine Army, he achieved a
distinction previously unknown to any representative of the
American military establishment. From one vantage point, it
appeared that the scion of the MacArthur warrior heritage was
upholding the family tradition.

And yet, as always, there were problems. His army, weakened by cut-backs in the twenties and the even more severe
retrenchment of the early Depression, commanded little respect
from the rest of the world. At home, the disillusionment growing out of World War I still shaped the attitudes of many Americans. Forced by his official position to confront these problems,

MacArthur managed to offend nearly everyone before his tenure as Chief of Staff ended. His personal life was no more satisfactory. His plans for a continued relationship with Isabel were unsuccessful and almost led to professional scandal. Saved from these problems by the opportunity to return to the Philippines, he immediately faced almost insurmountable difficulties heightened by the incongruity of his position as Field Marshal of a virtually barefoot, peasant army. In these years, his desperate desire for success led him to assume more than he should have, and to promise more than he could deliver. Given an opportunity to fulfill many of his goals, the General tried instead to fulfill them all, with little regard for the difficulties and personalities involved. Perhaps his personal ambivalence influenced his decisions in this regard. As a result, he failed.

When MacArthur left Manila in mid-September, 1930, his Filipino friends gave him a grand sendoff. At a banquet held in his honor at the Manila Hotel, he was assured by Manuel Quezon and the other Filipino leaders of their continued devotion and respect.[2] Uncertain of what lay ahead, the new Chief of Staff was undoubtedly comforted by the knowledge that here, at least, he would always be welcomed. It was a thought to which he often returned in the difficult years in Washington.

Sworn in as Chief of Staff on November 21, 1930, MacArthur immediately began to familiarize himself with his new responsibilities. He was determined to make the most of these years, and set out at once to bring new efficiency to what he saw as a sadly neglected institution. The United States Army, which at this point ranked seventeenth in strength of personnel internationally, was, in one historian's assessment, "less ready to function as a fighting force than at any time in its history."[3] Although the National Defense Act of 1920 provided the basis for the necessary reorganization and growth, the isolationist tendencies of the twenties and the subsequent economic crisis after 1929 precluded real improvement. Indeed, MacArthur found that for most of his years in Washington, his major responsibility as Chief of Staff was mainly to fight vigorously to hold onto what he had in the face of continued budget reductions. Consequently, the reforms that he achieved were limited largely to changes in internal structure and to reallocation of already existing funds. Within these narrow limitations, his desire to reorganize and modernize his woefully inadequate forces met with little success.

For the first two years of his term, General MacArthur, now breveted to four stars, was encouraged by the cooperation of the Hoover administration. Although increasingly unable to support the Army's continued demand for more funds, Hoover was at least personally impressed by MacArthur's efforts. In addition, the two men, so opposite in style, shared deeply held political convictions. The friendship which developed between them was to last for the rest of their lives and was certainly buttressed in later years by their joint belief that both had been ill-judged during this period.

Another source of encouragement came from Secretary of State Henry Stimson. Although their immediate realms seldom overlapped, MacArthur appreciated Stimson's internationalist stand, and particularly supported the Secretary's position regarding Japanese aggression in Manchuria. Although they might disagree concerning the ultimate results of nonrecognition, both believed that the United States in the twentieth century could not reject its international responsibilities, no matter how pressing the economic situation at home. Their shared frustration during this period grew out of their inability to find an affordable solution to these economic and diplomatic problems. Joining them in their quandary, Secretary of War Patrick J. Hurley also came to appreciate the talents of his Chief of Staff. Although he had approved MacArthur's original appointment somewhat doubtfully, Hurley soon learned to rely on the General's longer experience in military matters.[4] This support, coupled with the predictable backing of other conservatives like John Callan O'Laughlin, editor of the *Army and Navy Journal,* and George Van Horn Moseley, who served as MacArthur's deputy chief of staff during this period, helped to balance the country's overall negativism toward the military for MacArthur.

The major problem facing the Army was also the major problem facing the nation: the budget crisis. As a result, one of MacArthur's primary duties was to shape an expenditure plan each year, defend it in Congress, and then learn to live with the cutbacks which invariably followed. Within these confines, he established two major policies. His primary concern was that the officers corps, which he believed was an absolute necessity for an expandable army in time of crisis, not be pared down. Secondarily, and as an outgrowth of this initial assumption, he was determined that what little funds were available would be divided equally between all arms of the military. Since some branches, particularly the air and mechanized units, clearly needed more money, he would later be criticized when World War II made the deficiency obvious. But without the advantage of hindsight, it is likely that few Army planners would have handled the depleted resources any more effectively.

The debate over air power, which had raged since World War I and reached a crisis point during the court martial of Billy Mitchell in 1925, continued unabated during MacArthur's years as Chief of Staff. Never fully convinced until World War II of the efficacy of air force units, the General found himself under regular attack from the newly formed Army Air Corps and its leading proponent in Congress, Representative Ross A. Collins. Each year the Chief of Staff recommended balanced distribution of funds to each branch of the Army; each year the Air Corps and its supporters demanded more funds for the research and development of new planes. Usually, MacArthur and his more conservative supporters were successful, and even in 1933 when Roosevelt decided to use the Air Corps for airmail delivery, and eight planes crashed in the first week, few funds were forthcoming. Not until 1935, when the Air Corps was placed directly under the control of its own General Headquarters, did it begin to achieve the autonomy and support it always desired.

MacArthur's position in all this was less than clear. On one hand, he was outspoken regarding what he saw as the essential inequity of allowing the Air Corps more funds than any other branch. Once he even argued that international air disarmament was the only solution to the economic crisis of the thirties.[5] On the other hand, at various times during his years as Chief of Staff, he supported the development of Army torpedo planes and long-range aircraft. After the disastrous airmail crashes, he hoped to review personally Air Corps planes and personnel.[6] Later in the thirties, from his vantage point in Manila, he would plead for more planes and yet de-emphasize the advantage air power would give the Japanese in any potential attack on the Islands. Clearly, his views were in conflict, and it is safe to say only that while he recognized the necessity of upgrading the Air Corps at some level, this goal did not have priority over his basic concern for manpower. This contradiction, which he never publicly acknowledged, was not resolved until his early days in Australia in 1942. Once convinced by his air force chief, George Kenny, he became a firm advocate of air war, and utilized this arm of his forces most effectively. The hard-learned lesson of Corregidor was in the end not lost on the General, but in the early thirties, this usually advanced military planner was more conservative. Whether from necessity or misunderstanding, his position contributed to the comparative weakness of the United States Army Air Corps at the beginning of World War II.

Throughout these early years in Washington, MacArthur's position on general preparedness placed him in direct conflict with the strong pacifist movement of the period. Encouraged by the Kellogg-Briand Pact of 1928, and angered by the findings of the Nye committee, the pacifists argued that any military buildup increased the chance of war. The War Department, with MacArthur as willing spokesman, believed the contrary, that an adequate defense system was the best deterrent. Although his position was not extreme, the General's public statements on the matter resulted in widespread personal attack. When Kirby Page, editor of the religious journal, *The World Tomorrow,* offered MacArthur the opportunity to respond to the results of a poll of ministers which had reflected their heavily anti-war perspective, the General's answer triggered great controversy and at least one threat on his life. His widely published letter argued that the pacifist attitudes of the ministers would encourage lawlessness and that true religion had historically supported the patriotic goals of the nation. Based on his implication that his adversaries were, therefore, not truly religious, he concluded that "atheism has invariably been accompanied by radicalism, communism, bolshevism, and other enemies of free government." Under the specter of this threat, he concluded: "I confidently believe that a red-blooded and virile humanity which loves peace devotedly, but is willing to die in the defense of the right, is Christian from center to circumference, and will continue to dominate in the future as in the past."[7] This statement, along with his public alliance with Hoover, placed him firmly in the camp of those who feared that the continued economic breakdown might lead to revolution. From this public position, he was shortly faced with the most serious criticism of his career to that point.

By 1931, unemployment in the United States had reached crisis proportions. Many of the unemployed had served in World War I, and they began to agitate for the early payment of the deferred bonus that Congress had voted in 1924. Although Congress authorized half payment in 1931, the veterans were still unsatisfied. When Representative Wright Patman of Texas prepared a bill which would allow the payment of the remainder of the funds, the stage was set for a head-on confrontation in Washington. Hoover, who had vetoed the earlier bill (Congress had overridden the veto), argued that the $2.4 billion required by Patman's plan would place an impossible burden on the already strained economy. The veterans, determined to get what they believed was rightfully theirs, organized their own lobby. In early 1932, as the Patman bill came before Congress, the veterans converged on Washington. Under the loose direction of Walter V. Waters, an Oregon cannery worker and former veteran, they formed the Bonus Expeditionary Force. By June, nearly 22,000 men and their families were encamped in almost two dozen makeshift sites in and around the city. In the weeks to come, they visited their Congressmen during the days, and spent the evenings in camp, promising to stay put until they had their bonus. With few exceptions, the mass demonstration was peaceful. Waters successfully maintained order, and with the cooperation of the Washington Police Superintendent, Pelham D. Glassford, the veterans' needs for food, medical care, and recreational facilities were met.

Most of the Hoover administration, however, perceived the B.E.F. as a threat to national security. The President, beleaguered by critics of his economic recovery programs, and aware of the forthcoming election, became virtually inaccessible. On June 17, the Senate defeated the Patman measure and the tension increased. Although Congress allotted funds to buy tickets for those veterans who wished to return home, only one quarter of the original number took advantage of the offer. A month after the legislation met defeat, nearly 10,000 members of the Bonus Army still remained in Washington. The War Department, acting on the widespread belief that the protest was inspired and directed by subversives, began to prepare for action. Although Hoover remained indecisive, official Washington became outspoken in its dissatisfaction with the visitors. The press urged dispersal, Glassford found it increasingly difficult to maintain order, and Waters, frustrated by the situation, issued more militant plans.

Douglas MacArthur, as Chief of Staff, was responsible for the contingency plans being developed in the War Department. In addition, he, and most of his peers, firmly believed that the whole affair was the result of a Communist conspiracy. As a consequence, he advised Secretary of War Hurley of his views, and added weight to the Administration's opinion that immediate action was necessary. When small groups of B.E.F. demonstrators began to march near the Capitol grounds, the Washington District Commissioners joined the efforts to convince Hoover to do something. By the third week in July, a firm decision was reached and Glassford was ordered to begin evacuating the veterans from the empty federal buildings on Pennsylvania Avenue where some of them had encamped. By August 4, all members of the B.E.F. were to be on their way home. As it turned out, this decision would have widespread political ramifications for everyone involved.

Early on July 28, 1932, the operation began. Glassford and members of his police force arrived at the buildings in question and began a peaceful removal. Shortly afterwards, however, a small group of agitators caused a disruption, hurling bricks at the policemen. The police were able to contain the disturbance, but Glassford decided to check with the District Commissioners before taking further action. When he reported to his superiors, the situation was still under control. The police chief suggested, however, that the rest of the evacuation be postponed until tempers had quieted down. The Commissioners, tense and uncertain of the Administration's wishes, seem to have misunderstood Glassford's advice, and requested that President Hoover send federal troops to the scene. Indeed, before Glassford could return to Pennsylvania Avenue, more trouble broke out, and two veterans were fatally injured. When Hoover heard of this, he finally made up his mind, phoned Hurley, and ordered Army intervention.

What followed is still subject to debate. Hoover later maintained that he had only requested that the troops deal with the veterans in the business district. Hurley and MacArthur always argued that the situation required more extreme action, and that the orders of the President were unclear. As one historian of the event has suggested, "the President quickly lost control over the swiftly moving events," and by nightfall, the federal troops, directed by General Perry L. Miles, had successfully cleared the veterans from the downtown area, forced them across the Anacostia River to their main encampment in the flats beyond, and were preparing for a final confrontation in the camp itself.[8] At 11:15 P.M., the Army units slowly crossed the 11th Street bridge, attacked the remaining B.E.F. members with tear gas grenades, and soon the entire area was in flames. The Bonus veterans finally dispersed, seeking refuge wherever they could find it. Although there were few casualties, the property of the marchers was destroyed, and when the remnants of the B.E.F. departed the city as best they could the next day, they were poorer than when they had begun. President Hoover sent only a brief word to waiting reporters that night: "The President is pleased."[9] If nationwide criticism had not immediately developed, there is little reason to believe that he would ever have changed his opinion.

In the days and weeks which followed, the Chief of Staff became the focus around which much of the ensuing controversy centered. He had insisted on taking the field during the operation, and pictures of him in the press accounts, complete with riding breeches and crop, only highlighted his role. In addition, and contrary to the advice of close assistant Major Dwight D. Eisenhower, MacArthur issued his own account of the affair to reporters. Declaring that "had the President not acted today, . . . had he let it go on another week, I believe that the institutions of our Government would have been severely threatened," the General concluded that "had he [Hoover] not acted with the force and vigor that he did, it would have been a very sad day for the country tomorrow."[10]

As criticism mounted and investigations were made, it became increasingly clear that the General, with tacit support from Hurley, had ignored Hoover's weak attempts to halt the Army action. As MacArthur's biographer later suggested, "once MacArthur was convinced that the affair was a Communist assault against the federal government, he acted with overzealous determination and reckless impulsiveness."[11] Most of his critics at the time were much more vociferous, and the incident did more to diminish MacArthur's public stature than any other event in his career. Coupled with his failure to achieve the Army reforms which he desired, the Bonus Army affair made MacArthur's position in Washington even more unsatisfactory than he had suspected it would be. Faced with an almost certain loss of political support after November 1932, his taste for the metropolis and his position of power within it diminished. Although his conservative friends and fellow officers supported his position, the public outcry wounded the overly sensitive Chief of Staff more than he could ever admit.[12]

By the spring of 1933, MacArthur's position was even less secure. His public reputation had not recovered from the Bonus episode, and in March, the New Deal administration of Franklin D. Roosevelt moved into Washington. No one in the War Department knew what to expect, but the conservative Chief of Staff, who had outspokenly supported Hoover's candidacy, had every reason to believe that his continued service might not be required. In addition, the traditional (although not mandatory) tenure of chief of staff lasted only four years. For the General, this meant that he could expect a new assignment in little more than a year, along with the consequent reduction of rank to two stars. No matter what command he received, it would be less prestigious than his present position. Remembering his father's last years, this prospect could not have been a cheerful one for an officer of his still-burning ambitions. While he was uncomfortable at the center of power, his deep-seated ambivalence and need for continued proof of his own worth denied him the option of gracious retirement.

His personal life was no less dismal. Upon his return from Manila in 1930, he had moved with his mother into the residence of the chief of staff at Fort Myer. Pinkie, now in her eighties, was genuinely ill and consequently unable to enjoy much of the prestige of her son's position. One of the chief rewards of their long effort to achieve this goal was thus denied them. As the Hoover administration packed up to leave Washington and was replaced by the vibrant New Dealers, the opportunity for congenial social life, which the General had occasionally enjoyed, became even more limited. Even the secret alliance with Isabel was no longer satisfactory, and in the dark spring of 1934, his effort to achieve a romantic haven threatened to destroy the professional success that he had originally hoped it would support.

After establishing Isabel in her own apartment near his office, the General soon found that his new responsibilities allowed him little time to spend with her. In his early years in Washington, he traveled extensively, reviewing the troops around the United States, and twice visiting Europe in an official capacity. When in the capital, his filial duties also conflicted with his romantic efforts. Soon Isabel grew restless. Unable to pursue the active social and professional life that she had enjoyed in Manila, she soon began to press the General to allow her more freedom. He financed a trip to Havana, and when she returned, encouraged her to enroll in school. She tried art school for awhile, and later switched to law school where she met a young fellow student who promised to relieve the monotony of her situation. Sometime early in 1934, MacArthur began to realize that the lovely Filipina was perhaps more trouble than she was worth. He abruptly attempted to end the relationship, and wrote a brief note, enclosing tickets for her return to the Islands, and suggesting that she leave Washington immediately. Isabel rejected this offer and began to look around for another means of support. Soon, aided by her new friend from law school, she found the opportunity she was seeking.[13]

MacArthur, at fifty-four, once again found himself threatened from all sides. His professional position was at best shaky, and the future held little promise of improvement. His mother, always the central support upon which his self-image was founded, grew increasingly weak. Now another emotional support was gone. Even the press refused to leave him alone. Particularly tenacious in their attack, Drew Pearson and Robert S. Allen, creators of the widely-read "Washington Merry-Go-Round," continually reminded their readers of the General's "dictatorial" leanings.[14] Feeling himself buffeted by every quarter, the General decided to strike back. Consequently, he filed suit against Pearson, Allen, and the United Features Syndicate, owners of the column. Charging libel, the General requested $1,750,000 in damages.

Pearson and Allen immediately set out to defend themselves. Notifying their network of informants that they needed facts to use against the General, they followed every lead. They did not have to wait long. MacArthur's air power nemesis, Congressman Ross Collins, soon volunteered information to the effect that a lovely Eurasian woman lived in his apartment building and, until recently, had been frequently visited by the Chief of Staff. Pearson began a search for Isabel. Shortly thereafter, her school friend arranged for a meeting with the columnist. Before long, Pearson had MacArthur's letters to Isabel, and was carefully guarding his source of information. When the pretrial hearing convened, Pearson's lawyer, Morris Ernst, quietly let it be known that he intended to call Isabel Cooper as a defense witness. MacArthur's lawyer relayed this information to the

General, and the suit was dropped. As Pearson later recounted, "that was all there was to it."[15] Perhaps this was true for Pearson, but for Douglas MacArthur there was more. He was forced to pay the legal defense fees and $15,000 to Isabel through Pearson in order to retrieve his letters. Pearson, who retained several copies, promised not to use them during the General's lifetime.[16] Isabel moved away from Washington, later married and divorced the fellow student who had helped her deal with MacArthur, and finally settled in Hollywood where she attempted to establish a career. In 1960 she died there as a result of an overdose of barbiturates. According to one source, she spent the last years of her life trying to get someone to believe her story about her relationship with MacArthur.[17]

The General's affair with the actress was now over. Whatever solace she had provided in the Islands could not be sustained back in the States, and MacArthur was left alone to face the uncertainties of the new era in Washington. As it turned out, neither he, nor Roosevelt, knew quite what would happen next, but it was clear that the first move had to be the President's. Roosevelt, who had long considered MacArthur a dangerous political rival, certainly did not want to force his Chief of Staff into open confrontation.[18] Consequently, he asked the General to continue in office until a replacement could be found. Several names were being considered, including Malin Craig, the eventual choice, Hugh J. Drum, and George Simonds, MacArthur's own preference. Supporters of the various candidates pressed their cases before the President, but Roosevelt postponed his decision. Aware of the need for increased military preparedness, he believed that MacArthur's experience in the War Department might be useful in preparing the next budget to be placed before Congress. In addition, he undoubtedly knew that the General would enjoy holding the office of chief of staff longer than the traditional four years.[19] By thus honoring MacArthur, Roosevelt perhaps believed that he was diffusing the General's potential political threat. Certainly, this action postponed that threat until a suitable assignment could be found.

Meanwhile, the two men fenced warily. Although MacArthur was appalled by the New Deal programs, he managed uncharacteristically to keep his opinions to himself—most of the time. He cooperated fully with Roosevelt's plan to use the military to help establish the Civilian Conservation Corps program. Only when the domestic programs threatened to further deplete the military budget did MacArthur fight back. When Roosevelt tried to shave $51,000,000 from the appropriations for 1934, thereby cutting back pensions and manpower allotments, MacArthur could no longer contain himself. With newly appointed Secretary of War George Dern, the General went to the White House. According to his later account, MacArthur and Roosevelt exchanged heated words and the General offered to resign. Roosevelt refused the offer and seemed to agree to the General's demands. As he left, MacArthur, again stricken by "that paralyzing nausea," vomited on the White House steps.[20] Clearly, these two strongwilled men were destined for more such confrontations. Roosevelt became even more interested in finding a suitable new position for his Chief of Staff.

Two possibilities soon developed. MacArthur might be appointed either high commissioner or military adviser to the new Philippine Commonwealth. Each position was more prestigious than the corps command, which normally followed duty as chief of staff. Both pleased the General. For the President, both assignments would serve an additional purpose. In either position, MacArthur would be too far from Washington to exert much influence on domestic political issues.

Even before the end of the Hoover administration, the Depression had provided one more reason, perhaps the deciding one, for the settlement of the issue of Philippine independence. Long a popular measure during Democratic administrations, the issue was once again raised after the 1930 congressional election gave the Democrats a majority in the House of Representatives. Pressure from agricultural lobbies soon convinced both Republicans and Democrats that legislation which granted independence to the Philippines in the near future would diminish one source of import competition sorely felt during these years. As a result, the Hare-Hawes-Cutting Bill passed both houses of the Congress in 1932. The bill provided for a ten-year

Commonwealth period during which the Filipinos would gradually assume full control of their domestic affairs while still under the protection and guidance of the United States in foreign matters and some economic arrangements. President Hoover immediately vetoed the measure, arguing that it allowed the United States to back away from responsibilities assumed earlier.

Although Congress overrode his veto, the bill, which was subject to Philippine approval, was defeated in Manila. Quezon, who had remained in the Islands while Sergio Osmeña and Manuel Roxas guided the bill through the U.S. Congress, was fearful that the successful passage of the bill in Manila would give his political competitors an edge in the Commonwealth presidential elections for which the bill provided. In addition, several of the bill's economic arrangements clearly worked to the disadvantage of the Islands. As a consequence, Quezon convinced the Philippine legislature to defeat the bill, and promised that he would immediately go to Washington to renegotiate independence.

When Quezon arrived in the United States in late 1933, he was faced with an entirely new situation. Many congressional seats had turned over in the recent election, and New Dealers were less than interested in the Philippine question. Those who listened offered little hope that a new bill would provide more advantages for the Filipinos. Quezon, trying to avoid the potentially embarrassing possibility of returning home with even less than his predecessors, finally agreed to the Tydings-McDuffie Bill—exactly the same as Hare-Hawes-Cutting, except for a minor adjustment concerning United States military bases in the Islands. The bill passed Congress, and President Roosevelt signed it into law early in 1934. Shortly thereafter, the Philippine legislature, manipulated adroitly by Quezon, approved its acceptance. Since the act changed almost nothing, Quezon's only real victory was political. But his support of the Tydings-McDuffie Act and his facile ability to shape opinion almost certainly assured his election as first president of the newly established Commonwealth.[21]

Dissatisfied with Tydings-McDuffie, Quezon decided that he must return to Washington to attempt to round up as much support as possible for his new nation. Unable to gain anything but vague generalities from Roosevelt, who, as one historian has suggested, "was always too absorbed in other matters to give the Philippines much thought,"[22] the Filipino leader approached his old friend Douglas MacArthur. If Quezon could not obtain the trade advantages and economic aid he needed from the President, at least the Chief of Staff might be able to help with the issue of Philippine national defense. United States disinterest and Japan's new militancy combined to convince Quezon that he could not leave the defense of his country entirely to other powers. He put his question to the General directly: "Can the Philippine Islands be defended?" The accounts of MacArthur's answer vary widely.

Some sources maintained that the General qualified his answer, but most, including Quezon and the General himself, argued that the advice was clearly positive. "I told him any place could be defended if sufficient men, munitions, and money were available. . . ."[23] Quezon then asked if the General would assume the responsibility for this defense. Again, MacArthur agreed, and his acceptance of the invitation gave him even more confidence. In a letter written in the summer after this meeting, his assessment was emphatic: "The great work involved as your Military Adviser seems to me to transcend in ultimate importance anything else that is conceivable. I am prepared to devote the remainder of my life if necessary to securing a proper defense for the Philippine Nation. No question that confronts it in ultimate analysis is of such importance."[24]

With this encouragement, Quezon set out to make the necessary arrangements for MacArthur's assignment as military adviser. He spoke with Roosevelt and found the President remarkably cooperative. It appeared that MacArthur, Quezon, and Roosevelt had all found a satisfactory solution to their separate problems. The General's career would continue to progress, Quezon's defense system would be directed by the former commander of the United States Army, and one of

Roosevelt's most effective critics would be removed from center stage. All that remained was the paperwork, and Quezon made the arrangements. Working closely with the General, the Philippine leader wrote to Secretary of War Dern to request "the friendly counsel and exclusive use of professionally trained military leaders of wide experience." Pointing to a 1926 act of Congress which authorized the President to assign military advisers to certain foreign countries, he requested that the law be amended to include the Philippine Islands. In cooperation with Senator Millard Tydings and Representative John McDuffie, the initiators of the recently passed Commonwealth Act, the amendment passed. By the end of 1934 the General's appointment as military adviser to the Philippine Commonwealth seemed assured. Over the next few months, MacArthur and Quezon negotiated the "compensation and emoluments" that the 1926 act allowed. By the time the Philippine leader returned to Manila to campaign for the presidency of the Commonwealth, they had agreed that the General would receive a salary of 36,000 pesos ($18,000) per year and personal yearly allowances of 30,000 pesos ($15,000). In addition, MacArthur was to be provided with a seven-room, fully air-conditioned suite atop the Manila Hotel.[25] MacArthur expected to complete his tour as Chief of Staff in mid-1935, and leave shortly thereafter for Manila.[26]

Soon, however, complications developed. MacArthur's departure for the Philippines was postponed until later in 1935. Although there is some evidence to suggest that Roosevelt once again extended his tour as chief of staff in order to have more time to select a replacement, the primary reason for the delay was the postponement of the Commonwealth elections. Quezon believed that the General should not assume his duties until the Philippine leader was assured of his right to make the appointment.[27]

In addition, by mid-1935, the General found that he was under consideration for an even more prestigious position—as high commissioner of the Philippine Commonwealth. This office, which replaced the office of governor general under the new independence act, was to be held briefly by Frank Murphy, then serving as governor general. Since Murphy wanted to return to the States, a successor must be found. With this in mind, Roosevelt broached to Quezon the idea of appointing the General as high commissioner before his return to Manila. Sworn to secrecy, Quezon did not mention the possibility to MacArthur until May 1935, when rumors of the potential assignment were already widespread in the Islands. Then the Philippine leader suggested that MacArthur not commit himself to the position until after he could assess the situation in the Philippines. The General responded in June, declaring that he realized

> fully the high glamour and potential political possibilities in the office of High Commissioner as compared with the relative obscurity of a professional military position but in this instance there is nothing that could tempt me from our agreement. I do not believe that the matter will be seriously broached as I cannot conceive, with my intimate knowledge of what is going on, that it is more than the smoke of camouflage which is so frequently used when political positions are discussed.[28]

Recalling his disappointment in 1929 and his previous conflicts with Roosevelt, MacArthur seemed to discount the whole affair. But the temptation of "high glamour and potential political possibilities" was too much for him. Soon he was in hot pursuit of the appointment. In early September, during a private meeting at Hyde Park, the President raised the issue with the General, and suggested that MacArthur check to see if there was any legal reason why he could not accept the position as high commissioner while remaining on the active list of the Army. On September 9, the General reported to the President that, to his dismay, such prohibitions did exist. Although he did not discount the possibility of special legislation to correct this problem, he carefully assured the President that since "the procurement of necessary legislation might prove an embarrassment for you, . . . your final decision must be based solely upon considerations of your own and, therefore, the Country's welfare."[29] Ten days later, Roosevelt assured the General that he would soon see to the necessary Joint Resolution and that "there is not the slightest embarrassment on my part and I am inclined to hope that there will be little or no trouble on the Hill."[30]

At this point, the possibility of MacArthur's appointment as high commissioner was apparently held in abeyance. The President became involved in other matters, and the General continued his plans to leave for Manila to assume the post of military adviser. Since Murphy had agreed to serve as high commissioner for awhile, no decision was immediately necessary, but there is reason to believe that MacArthur still expected the apppointment after Murphy retired. Indeed, as late as November 1935, he told Mrs. Francis B. Harrison that although the position was "nebulous," he still might accept it and combine the duties of both offices.[31] One year later, when Murphy's tenure was ending, rumors in Washington still raised the possibility of the General's appointment to the office.[32]

Neither Roosevelt nor MacArthur ever fully clarified the nature of the discussion. In his memoirs, the General simply stated that "it was a flattering proposal but involved my retirement from the Army. So I declined, stating that I had started as a soldier and felt that I should end as one."[33] Although contemporary records suggest that there was more to the debate than just this issue, the decision in the mid-thirties may very well have hinged on this problem.[34] In addition, there is evidence to suggest that during his final month in the United States, MacArthur once again had reason to question the sincerity of the President and to decide that the position as military adviser was at least a secure alternative.

While MacArthur's possible appointment as high commissioner was being discussed, the War Department continued to plan for his relief as Chief of Staff and appointment as military adviser to the Philippine Commonwealth. In July 1935, Secretary of War Dern suggested to Roosevelt that although MacArthur was needed in the Philippines by early October, he continue as Chief of Staff *in absentia* until December 15, when Dern, himself, would return from Quezon's inauguration and could recommend a successor. Dern concluded that "the advantage of not inducting a new Chief of Staff until my return is so great as to make me very earnestly recommend this procedure." On July 18, Roosevelt sent a message to Dern agreeing with this arrangement. "I see no reason why you should not tell General MacArthur that the plan meets with my approval so that he can make his plans accordingly."[35] On September 18, one day before Roosevelt promised MacArthur that he would look into the legal arrangements for his appointment as high commissioner, the Adjutant General issued orders to the Chief of Staff assigning him as military adviser. The orders, upon which much of General MacArthur's future plans were based, were broad:

> You are hereby given the greatest latitude and general authorities in carrying out this all important mission. In all cases not specifically covered you will use your own judgment and are empowered to call upon the Department Commander for whatever assistance you may require. Your mission must be accomplished—ways and means are largely left to you. . . .
>
> The limitation of time on foreign service is waived in your case and that of the officers and enlisted men at your headquarters. It is expected that your term of service will be at least seven years and probably much longer. . . .
>
> You will stand relieved from duty on the General Staff and as Chief of Staff on December 15th, 1935.[36]

MacArthur, assuming that his dual role as Chief of Staff and Military Adviser would allow him to equip his office in Manila more effectively, set out to gather his staff, order some equipment, and depart for the Pacific by the end of the month. Roosevelt, however, had other plans. Throughout 1934 and 1935, supporters of the various candidates to succeed MacArthur as chief of staff had urged that the President be careful in his dealings with the General. In April 1935, Hugh Johnson, Roosevelt's former NRA head and a classmate of MacArthur's at West Point, urged the President confidentially that MacArthur's favorite, General George S. Simonds, was "just part of my dear friend Douglas's plan to have somebody in who can be replaced by himself shortly." Roosevelt's response was cryptic: "You are right. I do hope to see you very soon."[37] In September, Johnson again renewed his warning in a wire to Roosevelt at Hyde Park. This time, only ten days before his warm letter to MacArthur encouraging him to expect the appointment as high commissioner, Roosevelt was more explicit in his response. "Very strictly confidential between ourselves, I am going to put in Craig in MacArthur's place when the latter leaves for the Philippines at the end of this month."[38] Contradicting the War Department orders to MacArthur and his own explicit promise to Secretary of War Dern, Roosevelt did exactly that.

MacArthur, with his mother, sister-in-law, and some of the advisory staff, left Washington on October 1. En route to San Francisco, the train was stopped in Wyoming the next day, when the General received a wire from the War Department announcing Craig's appointment. Suddenly he was no longer Chief of Staff but just another Major General in the United States Army. According to one account, he was furious.[39] Quickly recovering, he wired appropriate messages to Roosevelt, Craig, and acting Secretary of War Harry H. Woodring. But he could not help feeling that once again, Washington had tricked him. Undoubtedly, this incident also undermined his confidence that he would receive the support he would need from the United States if he was to achieve his goal in Manila.[40] Whatever Roosevelt promised from now on, the General understandably held suspect. As the last dark days on Corregidor would prove, this attitude had some basis in reality.

Although disappointed at Roosevelt's action, MacArthur still faced his new responsibilities with optimism and personal satisfaction. As always, he was happy to return to the Islands. This time he had ample evidence to support his belief that his future was dim in the United States. But in the Philippines, now on its way to independence, things might be different. This time he meant to stay and thus did not need to worry as much about the effect of his decisions on public opinion in the United States. Although his mother was with him, he still may have believed that once again the Islands would provide an opportunity for a new and even more successful intimate relationship. Certainly, the support and appreciation that most Filipinos now offered him provided a balm for his often wounded and very sensitive self-image. Here, finally, he hoped to work it all out—his inordinate need for challenge, respect, and love might for once be fulfilled.

With more immediate problems at hand, MacArthur embarked on the *President Hoover* from San Francisco to Manila early in October. The trip, which lasted three weeks, provided time for the General to assess his new situation. For many reasons, what he saw was not encouraging. His mother's condition, poor at the outset, grew steadily worse. By the time they reached Manila, there was little hope that she could survive. This development, which MacArthur had apparently not foreseen, required that he spend much of his time on board at her bedside. Only occasionally could he join the festivities of the other members of the group, many of whom were making the trip in order to be present at the inaugural celebration scheduled for November 14.[41] Although deeply concerned about his mother's health, the General found time for occasional walks on deck, and during one of them he met Jean Faircloth, an unmarried, thirty-five-year-old woman en route to visit friends in Shanghai. From all accounts, MacArthur was immediately attracted to the tiny Southerner, who was always cheerful and obviously held him in awe.[42] As he faced the potential loss of his mother, Jean offered what solace she could, and in fact, the rapid development of the relationship may have been hastened by the General's deep insecurity resulting from his mother's condition. Whatever forces were at work, the ties between the two grew stronger, and in spite of his concern for his mother and his dejection at Roosevelt's treatment, MacArthur left Jean in Shanghai strengthened by her promise to come to Manila soon. This prospect made the difficult days and weeks which followed more bearable.

Only two weeks after the gala inauguration of the Philippine Commonwealth and Manuel Quezon as its President, MacArthur faced the greatest emotional upheaval of his life. On December 3, 1935, just five weeks after their arrival in Manila, Mary

Hardy MacArthur died of cerebral thrombosis. Her body was temporarily interred in the U.S. Army morgue until it could be returned to the United States at some future date.[43] Characteristically, the General left little record of his reaction to this event. At the end of his life, he said simply, ". . . our devoted comradeship of so many years came to an end. Of the four of us who had started from the plains of New Mexico, three now were gone, leaving me in my loneliness only a memory of the households we had shared, so filled with graciousness and old-fashioned living."[44]

Contemporary accounts suggest, however, that this loss severely affected MacArthur's ability to work in the next few months. As he himself admitted in a letter to his old friend Cal O'Laughlin less than a week after the death, "My mother's illness synchronizing with the induction of the new nation with a complete system of national defense laid greater pressure upon me than I have ever carried before. . . . Mother's death has been a tremendous blow to me and I am finding the greatest difficulty in recoordinating myself to the changed conditions." A little more than a week later, he wrote again to O'Laughlin, revealing even more of his pain. "My loss has partially stunned me and I find myself groping desperately but futilely. . . . For the first time in my life, I need all the help I can get."[45]

These unusually revealing comments reflected the very real confusion that the General faced. For fifty-five years, Pinkie had served as the foundation of his world. With only a few exceptions, she acted as the main compass point by which he charted both his personal and professional course. Although Douglas had occasionally rejected her advice and sometimes resented the tremendous responsibility she placed upon his shoulders, more frequently he had accepted and internalized her views as his own. Her death made this reaction even more profound. Temporarily, it seemed that there was no one to whom he could turn for the same steady support, and for several months afterwards, the General remained in deep mourning, refusing almost all social invitations.[46] Support and escape came from only two sources—the continued friendship of Jean Faircloth, who was now permanently established in Manila, and from his efforts to build a Philippine army as he had promised Quezon that he would.

Spurred on by the need to escape his grief and by his determination to prove to his critics that it could be done, MacArthur now worked harder than ever to create the citizen army which he had outlined for Quezon in Washington. Long convinced that Philippine national defense could not completely rely on United States aid, Quezon had ordered a study of the problem even before his election as President. Prepared by L. Siguion Reyna, technical adviser to the Philippine Department of Interior, this report was submitted in May 1935. It argued that the Philippines could not support a large army due to the need to use all available funds for the economic readjustment necessary to survive the loss of the favored trade agreements which might end with independence. In addition, the geography of the Islands left them much more vulnerable to attack than were Switzerland and Belgium, the two countries to which the Philippines were most often compared. A navy was out of the question at present because of the expense. Therefore, the report concluded, "all our efforts should be concentrated in organizing our means of defense within the limits of our reduced resources, so as to obtain a maximum efficiency at a minimum cost." This goal would be achieved by building a defense system that consisted of "(a) a sufficient nucleus of regular army, reinforced by (b) reserve corps, and supplemented by (c) a national militia." The study then examined all of the advantages which such a national army would encourage. Besides the discipline and protection it would provide, the new defense organization would buttress the police force, provide trained personnel for building projects, and supply additional education for its members.[47] Since this was essentially the same plan MacArthur had outlined in 1934, the Philippine leader was additionally convinced of its merit.

The next few months were spent laying the groundwork for this Philippine army. In June 1936, President Quezon was ready to present his National Defense Plan, prepared by General MacArthur, to the National Assembly. In many ways, this plan echoed the beliefs and attitudes of Arthur MacArthur thirty-five years earlier. Pointing to the strategic significance of the Islands, his son argued that the Philippines were, "in some respects, the most important . . . section of the great and vaguely defined region known as the Far East."[48] He insisted, just as his father had in 1882, that Western markets in Europe and America were now "too small to absorb the overages that world industry constantly produces." As a consequence, the new East Asian market, resulting from widespread nationalistic impulses, was developing at a particularly opportune time and would be vital to continued Western growth. Despite evidence which clearly argued that the United States was less interested in Philippine development than at any time in the past three and a half decades, MacArthur still believed that its relationship with the Philippine Islands would bode well for both nations. His subsequent plan for Philippine national defense was based on the assumption that the United States valued its connection with the Islands and would continue to offer support when necessary. The definition of this support was, however, the subject of much dispute on both sides of the Pacific. Because the issue was never settled, and because each side misunderstood the expectations of the other, the ultimate results were disastrous.

His statement of purpose continued. Although the Americans had nurtured democratic institutions and encouraged the Filipinos to participate in their domestic government, "it had not been considered desirable to complete or to authorize the Filipinos themselves to maintain strong military forces." Consequently, "in the fundamental obligation of sovereign government, namely, that of providing for the common defense, the Philippines were woefully unprepared for independence." For this reason, the Tydings-McDuffie Act had allowed for the transitional Commonwealth period. Since both Philippine and American interests would be served by insuring the survival of the Islands as a democratic nation, the leaders of both countries had agreed that the aid and advice of the United States were necessary.

A regular force of 930 officers and approximately 10,000 enlisted men would serve as the cadre for the larger reserve. Members of the reserve, or militia, would be responsible to the government for a period of thirty years, ten to a first reserve, ten to a second, and ten to a third. Naturally, the program could not be established all at once, and would require ten years to reach full strength. Each year forty thousand reserve members would be trained, and assigned to a "particular geographical area in which its individual members ordinarily reside." Because the island terrain required a specific type of defense, the emphasis of the training program would be on highly mobile small units, with "a minimum of dependence upon elaborate supply establishments and a maximum utilization of local resources for transportation and subsistence." The ultimate goal of the defense system was "resistance from the water's edge to the furthermost retreat left available."

Air and naval defense would be minimal, limited to simple items affordable to the new nation. Specifically, the General foresaw a small fleet of torpedo boats and some fast bomber planes, supported by as few other tactical aircraft as possible. He promised that "every centavo that can be spared from other equally essential purposes will eventually be invested in the development and maintenance of a bombing fleet of reasonable size." At this point, MacArthur's problem became more obvious. Clearly, with the ₱16,000,000 yearly budget allotted him, there would be few centavos to spare after his manpower requirements were met. The entire report emphasized the goal of national autonomy, but his discussion of the economic arrangements reflected a certain ambiguity. Although somewhat vague, his statement that "the form and size of the defense organism be dictated by probable needs, which may be determined only when there is brought into proper perspective every significant factor of geography, international politics, and commercial relationships," might be interpreted to mean that United States aid might supply some of the missing ingredients for the new defense system. Certainly for the Commonwealth period, both Quezon and MacArthur expected that this would be the case.[49]

The remainder of the report outlined specific details of the training program, which was to begin in January 1937, and the immediate problems that the plan faced. In his summation, the General admitted that "the effectiveness of the whole would be vastly increased if supported by a powerful navy and large air contingents." He remained convinced, however, that "the problem of reducing the Philippine defenses will present to any potential invader such difficult problems as to give pause even to the most ruthless and powerful." He went on to discount invasion by sea because his final force would defend "every foot of shore line in the inhabited islands of the Archipelago." Naval blockade would also be ineffective, he argued, because the Islands would, in the transition period, become more self-sustaining. This was his position in 1936, and he adamantly maintained his view even after assuming command of the United States Army Forces in the Far East (USAFFE) in 1941.

From the outset, many in Manila and Washington for a variety of reasons disagreed with this position. In Washington, many, both in and out of the War Department, pointed out that the plan contradicted War Plan Orange. At the same time that MacArthur was developing his National Defense Plan, military leaders in Washington were reevaluating the United States position in the Pacific. The Army, fully aware that the cutbacks of the twenties and thirties had rendered even the minimal defense as outlined in War Plan Orange impossible, recommended that the United States withdraw entirely from the Philippines and China by 1946. The Navy, fearful that an Alaska-Hawaii-Panama defense perimeter would leave it with a narrower field of activity, recommended postponement of any decision. Faced with this fundamental difference of opinion, the Joint Board agreed to revise Orange to allow for a minimal defense of Manila Bay, and await further developments before changing the plans completely. This time, however, the plan did not allow for reinforcements from the mainland as had earlier versions. Between 1936 and 1938, the Army and Navy continued the debate. Both realized that their forces were inadequate to meet a projected Japanese invasion of the Islands, but believed that national policy prevented them from correcting the deficiency. The dilemma is best described in the words of Louis Morton:

> National policy dictated the defense of an insular position which, in the opinion of the military planners, could not be defended with existing forces. The ORANGE plan of 1938, with the compromise between an offensive and defensive strategy, was merely a reflection of this contradiction between American interests and commitments in the Pacific. The nation would not abandon the Philippines but neither would it grant the Army and Navy funds to ensure their defense. . . . American policy had created a wide gap between objectives and means and forced on its planners a compromise strategy and the virtual abandonment of Guam and the Philippines. Already there was a shift in sentiment, a recognition of the danger ahead, and a disposition to prepare the country's defenses, but the neglect of almost two decades could not be overcome in the three years of peace that remained.[50]

MacArthur, who had participated in earlier discussions of War Plan Orange, certainly understood these difficulties. Yet he seemed never to have accepted the fact that his new responsibilities in the Philippines were for the defense of territory that most planners in Washington did not consider vital. Even Henry Stimson, more aware than most Americans of the Philippines, advised against the Quezon-MacArthur plan.[51] Quezon, however, wanted desperately to believe that his new nation would survive as a democratic stronghold in the Pacific. And MacArthur, who also needed to believe that his new mission was worthwhile, refused to accept the possibility of total United States withdrawal. The Tydings-McDuffie Act notwithstanding, both men continued to believe that the Philippine Army, buttressed in an emergency by aid from the mainland, could render the Islands secure.[52] MacArthur never changed his mind. Quezon, whose fears increased in the face of the continuing criticism, nonetheless in the long run allowed himself to be convinced that his dreams could become a reality.

Planners in the United States were not the only critics of the Philippine Defense System. From the very beginning, Quezon's adversaries in the Philippine Assembly saw a variety of problems in the MacArthur program. Led by Camilio Osias, editor of the *Philippine Forum* and member of the Assembly, they argued that the entire defense plan was unrealistic. Since the nation could not possibly build an adequate defense against Japan, the reasonable alternative, they suggested, was to build no defense at all. Rather, they urged earlier independence, followed by immediate neutralization which, they hoped, would preclude a Japanese invasion in force. Emphasizing their belief that the military build-up would only encourage "a jungle philosophy" and thereby lead to ultimate and extensive destruction, these critics were convinced that the national defense budget would be better spent for education, agricultural adjustment, and other peaceful purposes. They were particularly careful to point out that large salaries were being paid to Quezon's American advisers, and that the most visible of these was his friend General Douglas MacArthur.[53]

Despite the newspaper attacks and legislative debates, most Filipinos readily accepted their popular President's assurances that the defense situation was well in hand. With little experience in foreign affairs, many legislators even held to a kind of blind faith in Providence.[54] Consequently, early in 1937, when Quezon attempted to counteract the criticism and calm the fears in a public statement to the R.O.T.C. units of the University of the Philippines, most of his countrymen were more than willing to believe his assertions. At this time, his support of his Military Adviser, recently elevated to the position of Field Marshal, was unequivocal.

> I do not know enough of the science and art of war to be able to come to any conclusions of my own on this question. All I can say in this regard is that I have sought the opinion of the most competent man to give me advice thereon,—Field Marshal MacArthur. I believe in him and his opinion I accept fully. He told me and he told our people that when our national defense program has reached full fruition that the cost of conquering the Philippines in men and money would incomparably be greater than the possible advantages and benefits derived from its conquest. That's enough for me to go ahead undisturbed with our defense program.[55]

With such support, plans for the Philippine Army envisioned by MacArthur temporarily continued in full force. Within a few months, however, the situation changed.

In 1936, while planning and beginning to implement his new army, MacArthur continued to keep a careful eye on events in Washington. His distrust and disapproval of the Roosevelt administration increased, and although finally not surprised by the results of the 1936 election, he was disappointed at the outcome.[56] When High Commissioner Frank Murphy returned to the States early in 1936, MacArthur's candidacy for the position was once again discussed. Since Murphy refused to reveal his long-range plans, however, an acting High Commissioner was appointed. By this time, MacArthur had decided that for the moment at least, he was no longer interested.[57]

Relieved to have the General out of the way politically, Roosevelt and his advisers in the War Department nevertheless grew concerned over the strong defense posture MacArthur was advocating in the Philippines. As the European situation grew more ominous, the administration increased its attempts to downplay the Japanese threat in the Pacific. As a consequence, MacArthur's often-stated position concerning the need for Philippine defense against that threat was viewed with alarm in Washington. The Japanese had cautiously conveyed their concern in this area to the State Department, and as O'Laughlin warned, "the timidity of Hull and his anxiety to smooth over any ruffling of Japanese feathers" might lead to pressure from the War Department.[58]

As it turned out, O'Laughlin's suspicions were sound, although a trifle late. On August 5, 1936, two days before O'-Laughlin's letter was written, Chief of Staff Craig issued a mild warning to MacArthur. Interestingly, he continued to accept MacArthur's argument that a strong Philippine army would serve the interests of the United States in the event of war in the Far East, and focused his caution toward a more traditional area of concern. "There is much apprehension here, particularly in the State Department, over the present rapid rate at which munitions are being accumulated by the Commonwealth Government. . . . This apprehension," Craig continued, "does not arise from any lack of confidence in the loyalty of Mr. Quezon, but it is felt that we must not be unmindful of the possibility that he may pass out of the picture, or, if he remain, be unable to control a serious disaffection imperiling American sovereignty."[59] Always subject to the influence of their earlier colonial views, both the State and War departments were not quite comfortable with MacArthur's new army. Six weeks later, Secretary of State Hull made the State Department position even clearer in a confidential letter to newly appointed Secretary of War Harry Woodring:

> As you are aware, the future status of the Philippine Islands and the problems arising incident thereto, are inextricably interwoven with some of the most vital problems of our Far Eastern policy. One set of problems cannot be solved without reaching decisions as to others. . . .
>
> Because of their bearing upon these relations and problems, the State Department is obliged to take notice of certain aspects of the steps now being taken toward the creation of the Philippine Military Establishment. The rapidity of accumulation of armament by the Commonwealth Government, the organization of its defense program, and the form of publicity now being given to this program, seem to me to constitute steps which should be taken only after the fullest study and joint consideration by all the Departments of this Government concerned and after a final decision of certain of the fundamental issues by the President. In making this comment I do not refer to the merits either *pro* or *contra* of the armament program of the Commonwealth Government.
>
> Might I suggest, therefore, in the interest of the future relationships of the United States both with the Philippines and with the nations of the Far East, that further steps and plans directed toward building up an independent Phillippine armament not be undertaken without full consideration with this Department, the Philippine High Commissioner, and such other Departments or officials as are directly concerned, and that no further commitments be made until we have had the opportunity to assure ourselves that such plans are not inconsistent with the underlying Far Eastern policies and plans of our Government.[60]

Clearly this position represented an about-face in Washington. As MacArthur's original orders had suggested, in 1934 and 1935, Roosevelt and his advisers were willing to allow the General broad powers in order that he might achieve his goal of an adequate Philippine defense system. By late 1936, however, increased Japanese militancy and the serious European situation had convinced the State Department and the President to exert more caution in the Pacific. As a consequence, MacArthur and Quezon soon sensed that the already questionable support in Washington was being undermined. As a result, they determined to confront the issue on its home ground. With this in mind, the two men, accompanied by several members of their staffs, set out in January 1937 for Washington. Ostensibly, their goal was to attend the swearing-in ceremony of Paul V. McNutt as new High Commissioner of the Philippines. In addition, Quezon hoped to visit Mexico and several European nations to promote future goodwill for his new country. MacArthur would use this opportunity to take his mother's body to Arlington National Cemetery, and to attempt to obtain additional equipment for the Philippine Army. Both men intended to have serious conversations with the President.

En route from Manila, Quezon and his party stopped in Canton and Tokyo, where they were received with full honors. In the United States, however, the reception was strangely cool. After waiting for several days in New York for an invitation from the White House, MacArthur left the party and journeyed to Washington to see what was wrong. Finally the President agreed to see Quezon. Apparently angered by the Filipino leader's frequent public statements during the trip concerning his desire for early independence for the Islands, Roosevelt determined to take a hard line. Although personally involved in the debate only peripherally, the United States President's policy soon became obvious. There would be no early independence, and the hoped-for revision of the Philippine-American trade arrangements would be postponed for study by a Joint Preparatory Committee on Philippine Affairs. Of particular interest to the General was the advice of the State Department's Interdepartmental Committee on the Philippines. In a memorandum to Roosevelt, the committee's chairman, Francis Sayre, suggested that subject to the 1946 independence date, neutralization of the Islands should be arranged at "the earliest practicable date." Further, "full consideration should be given to the present Philippine national defense program and possible modification thereof." This emerging fear in the State Department that Philippine armament threatened the delicate balance in the Pacific conflicted with all previous War Department plans for defense of the Islands. In 1937, for the first time, the State Department views seemed to be the influential factor in Roosevelt's consideration of the issues brought up by Quezon's visit. As a consequence, MacArthur's position in Washington and Manila weakened, and Quezon began to question his earlier support of the General's plan.[61]

For the time being, however, more personal concerns occupied MacArthur. After a brief trip to Mexico with Quezon, he returned to the States in mid-April for his mother's burial in Arlington National Cemetery. In a simple, sparsely attended ceremony, the General finally laid to rest his almost constant companion of the past fifty-seven years. Their parting had been prolonged by his desire to see her buried beside her husband in the United States, and during the period between her death in 1935 and the final interment in 1937, his mourning continued. For the year after her death, her room in the Manila Hotel was kept empty and locked on his orders.[62] Finally, however, he seemed ready to relinquish at least part of their mutual bond. A few days after the burial he acted on this decision in a particularly symbolic way.

On April 30, 1937, Douglas MacArthur and Jean Marie Faircloth were married in a quiet civil ceremony in the New York Municipal Building. They had kept their plans secret from all but a few of the General's closest staff members. Perhaps recalling the publicity surrounding his first matrimonial venture, this time the couple made every effort to avoid the press. The General's only comment for publication was a brief but significant "this is going to last a long time."[63] And he was right. The marriage, from all accounts, was nearly idyllic. Rarely separated, even during World War II, the couple maintained a somewhat formal but obvious devotion for the rest of their lives. Finally, the General had solved whatever problems of intimacy he had faced during the years before his mother's death. A closer examination of Jean Faircloth MacArthur may account for the change.

The new Mrs. MacArthur did not physically resemble either Mary MacArthur or Louise Cromwell Brooks. She was short, small-boned, dark, and, although outgoing and friendly on the surface, essentially very private. She had traveled widely and shared with her new husband a particular fondness for the Philippines. In many ways, however, the tradition from which she sprang and the attitudes that she held were reminiscent of Pinkie. Deeply proud of her southern heritage, she was extremely patriotic and particularly enjoyed the ceremony of Army life. Although thirty-seven at the time of her marriage, her upbringing in Tennessee had been strictly regulated by a grandmother and a devoted "mammy," and she in no way came to the marriage with the worldly experience Louise had. Most importantly, she, as had Douglas's mother, firmly believed that the General was destined for great things and that it was her first duty to see that nothing she could control interfered with this achievement. She was perfectly willing to curtail her social activities in order to be available whenever her husband needed her. Beyond normal endurance, she accompanied him nightly to the western movies that he found so relaxing. She fully agreed that his work in Manila required his sustained attention and, from all evidence, never attempted to persuade him to participate in any activity that made him uncomfortable. In every way, she attempted to supply the support he had previously found only from his mother. In addition, or perhaps because of all these things, their physical relationship appeared successful. In February 1938, their only child, Arthur MacArthur III, was born in Manila. Both parents, seemingly amazed at their good fortune, devoted inordinate amounts of time to his upbringing.[64]

Undoubtedly, the long and mutually rewarding relationship Jean and Douglas MacArthur shared was partially the result of timing. Had they met at an earlier point in their lives, there is no guarantee that the relationship would have developed so successfully. The twenty-year difference in their ages might very well have dampened the General's pursuit or Jean's acceptance of his attentions. Earlier, before she had traveled so widely, Jean might have been less willing to settle into what eventually became a very cloistered way of life, albeit one which existed in the eye of an international storm. Most obvious, however, was the role Mary MacArthur played in the final result. Although the two women never met, in a very real way, Douglas's mother handed over her son's care to Jean. Faced with the chaos engendered by the loss of his mother, MacArthur naturally, and perhaps quite unconsciously, looked for a replacement. That Jean Faircloth was there, remarkably suited to take up the General's cause, was a well-timed accident. As his grief healed, Douglas began to spend the time previously devoted to his mother with his future wife. There can be little doubt that if she had not been available, MacArthur's recovery from his loss would have been less complete. Once again, random circumstance had joined with personal need to result in new adaptive patterns which would sustain both his private and public life. More importantly, with Jean there was no cultural or psychological restraint on Douglas's devotion. Finally, he had found a woman very much like his mother with whom he could enjoy the fullest rewards of intimacy. And with Pinkie gone, there was no one to compete with this wife for his attention.

Shortly after their wedding, the MacArthurs returned to Manila. Almost immediately, events took a turn for the worse. By midsummer, 1937, although the General claimed he was satisfied with the first five-month training program, it was becoming increasingly clear that the Philippine Army was faced with serious problems. As Major Dwight D. Eisenhower and Major James B. Ord, MacArthur's chief of staff and deputy chief of staff respectively, pointed out, although 20,000 reservists had graduated from the first training program as planned, they were inadequately prepared to meet even the basic tests required of them. There were several reasons for this disparity. The primary problem resulted from the defense plan's assumption that the Philippine schools would turn out potentially trainable young men. In reality, these men were often functionally illiterate since education in the distant provinces did not yet measure up to the Manila standards upon which MacArthur had based his plans. As a consequence, much of the brief training time had been spent devising ways to communicate with the trainees in their native dialects, and instilling in them the rudimentary principles of hygiene, barracks living, and the military structure necessary for a modern army. In addition, equipment shortages and inadequate training facilities further complicated the program.[65] The allotted budget of ₱16,000,000 was proving entirely too low and Philippine critics were adamant in their demands that more money not be spent.

At the same time, a new source of conflict developed. Ordered in 1935 to cooperate fully with MacArthur's plans, the Philippine Department of the United States Army had fulfilled his requests for men and matériel in 1936 and early 1937 to its utmost capacity. The General's broad powers were resented in some quarters, however, and by mid-1937, General Lucius R. Holbrook, commanding the Philippine Department, finally began to complain. The new mood in Washington supported his position, and soon the War Department issued an order to MacArthur requiring that henceforth he obtain approval from Washington before transferring further personnel from the Philippine Department to his program. Although cooperation between the two groups continued, the seeds of future tension had been planted.[66]

Engulfed by these problems in Manila, the General was soon forced to face a much more serious complication. In early August he was notified by Chief of Staff Malin Craig that at the end of his two years of foreign service (ending on December 31, 1937), he was to return to the United States for a new assignment to a post or corps command.[67] Since rumors to this effect had been widespread in Washington since June, the announcement did not come as a surprise to MacArthur.[68] Although neither he nor future historians were able to pinpoint the exact cause for the decision, it seemed clear that certain domestic influences shaped Roosevelt's final action. Perhaps Harold Ickes or former high Commissioner Frank Murphy, both longstanding MacArthur critics, had a hand in the affair.[69] Certainly, the State Department's concern over MacArthur's strident defense posture in Manila and its effect on Japanese-American relations was one consideration. Whatever the deciding factors, Roosevelt was determined to settle the problem, and for a time, even hoped that he could terminate the entire advisory office in the Islands.[70] Because the War Department advised him that it was "desirable that there should be as little disturbance as possible in the existing relations between the War Department and the Government of the Commonwealth of the Philippine Islands," however, Roosevelt decided that diminishing the General's official capacity would be sufficient at present.[71]

The General's response to this development was predictable. Rather than return to the United States and assume a lesser command, which as he pointed out "would be as though Secretary Woodring were suddenly assigned to be a Bureau Chief of the War Department or as though President Roosevelt was required to go back to his former functions as Assistant Secretary of the Navy," he would retire. Since his health was failing, he said, and he wanted to make room for younger, more deserving officers, the situation provided him with the opportunity he had been looking for. His future plans were as yet not settled.[72] On October 11, 1937, Craig notified the General that Roosevelt had approved his request for retirement.[73]

In actuality, MacArthur's future plans were quite definite. By the end of November, despite criticism in the National Assembly, Manuel Quezon, now returned from his world tour, obtained a resolution thanking the Military Adviser for his past service to the Commonwealth. The resolution did not, however, include authorization for the continuation of the Military Advisory Office as Quezon had requested. This was achieved on December 31 by executive fiat.[74] From all appearances, very little had changed. Although MacArthur was no longer on the

United States Army active list, his retired status did not preclude recall in case of national emergency. In addition, his loss of status in the War Department had not really changed much either. Since Roosevelt's preemptory decision to cut short his service as Chief of Staff in October 1935, the General's rank had meant little in the way of additional equipment and support for the Philippine Army anyway. From a personal point of view, his salary and benefits were reduced only minimally by the switch from active to retired status. He was still a major general and, more importantly in Manila, still Field Marshal of the Philippine Army. It was a position he intended to maintain for the rest of his life.[75] But his success was dependent upon the backing of Manuel Quezon, and as future events illustrated, the Filipino leader's continued support was very much influenced by Washington's decision.

Almost immediately after MacArthur's retirement new conflicts began to develop. In January 1938, believing that a public demonstration of the progress made by the Philippine Army would spur interest and support for his program, the Military Adviser ordered his closest assistants, Eisenhower and Ord, to begin planning for a huge gathering of the reservists on the outskirts of Manila. Although Eisenhower counseled that the project would cost more than the budget could bear, the General temporarily prevailed. When Quezon heard of the plan, however, he was furious. Faced with increased criticism of the defense system, he did not believe that this was the time for a public exhibition, and in addition, he too agreed that the money involved would be a waste of the scant available funds. He ordered the plan cancelled, and when MacArthur heard of this decision, he denied that he made the original order. Eisenhower and Ord were angered by this falsehood, and, as Eisenhower later recounted, "never again were we on the same warm and cordial terms."[76] Although the future Allied commander remained on the staff of the Military Adviser's office until late in 1939, seeds of their future rivalry and distrust had been sown, and a certain coolness in their relationship could be noted.

That same month, tragedy struck the advisory staff when Major Ord was killed in a plane crash in Baguio. He was replaced shortly by Richard K. Sutherland, who took Ord's place until Eisenhower's transfer and then became chief of staff. Sutherland, described by one fellow officer as "a 'hard' man," served with the General from 1938 until 1946. Efficient and capable, Sutherland lacked Ord's warmth. After he joined the staff, the easy camaraderie of the office, already strained by the conflict over MacArthur's parade plan, was never the same.[77]

The internal strife of these months was matched by increased criticism from outside sources. Japanese advances in China, which had begun in July 1937, encouraged panic and a certain defeatism in the Islands through 1938 and 1939.[78] As these feelings spread, support for MacArthur's program diminished in the National Assembly. As a consequence, the already shaky development of the reserve force suffered new setbacks. Recruitment, which had never reached the annual figure of 40,-000 for which MacArthur planned, was even more difficult to maintain. Supplies, always an uphill battle even during the early years, became harder to stockpile as prices rose in the prewar world market. In addition, MacArthur's newly retired status no longer permitted him to draw from the Philippine Department, and now, as the Department itself tried to upgrade its defense position, the General increasingly found himself vying with the U.S. Army for the same stock of matériel. The Philippine officer corps could not be maintained by the minimal schools established for that purpose. The planned development of the air and naval contingents fell way below expectations. From every angle, the Field Marshal of the Philippine Army found himself disappointed, and under heavy criticism. When in the summer of 1938 Quezon made a quiet trip to Japan without his Military Adviser, even the generally optimistic MacArthur could no longer deny his difficult situation.

Although officially a "vacation," the Filipino leader's trip to Tokyo was suspected by Americans and Filipinos alike as a tentative effort to assess the chances that the Japanese would respect Philippine neutrality, if it could be arranged. Quezon denied it, but his actions after returning to Manila belied his claims. Within a few weeks, he persuaded the National Assembly once again to separate the Philippine Constabulary from the Philippine Army, action which cut back MacArthur's budget still further.

Early in 1939, Quezon once again strongly urged immediate independence, apparently hoping that in that way neutrality could be assured, and as a consequence, that a strong defense would no longer be necessary. In May, he established a Department of National Defense, and although he denied this intention, the act effectively diminished the authority of the Military Adviser's Office. From that point on, MacArthur was required to clear his orders through the new department. Throughout the rest of the year, Quezon continued to work at cross-purposes with MacArthur. Public school military training ended, and the R.O.T.C. program was gradually reduced.[79] When Poland fell in September 1939, the effect on the Filipino leader was profound. Almost immediately, he admitted to the National Assembly that he was now convinced that the Philippines could not be effectively defended either now or "for many years to come." In November, he was even more explicit: "The Philippines could not be defended even if every last Filipino were armed with modern weapons."[80] Clearly the always mercurial Commonwealth President had finally, and completely, reversed his support of the National Defense Plan that he and General MacArthur had devised in 1935; or so it seemed.

The dilemma which faced the Filipino leader at this time was not entirely of his own making. If his temperament contributed to his disparate and contradictory positions concerning national defense, the United States position in regard to the Philippines certainly had done nothing to clarify the situation. Throughout the Philippine-American relationship, domestic political shifts in the United States had alternately promised continued protection or early independence. After the passage of the Tydings-McDuffie Act, these contradictory forces were embodied in the policies of the Roosevelt administration. On the one hand, the deteriorating international situation led the executive branch to deny the early independence that Quezon at times believed was the only way his nation could escape unscathed from the Japanese advance in the Pacific. On the other hand, the economic drain that the Philippine privileged trade arrangements placed on the depression-ridden United States caused the U.S. Congress to refuse extended protection. In the Islands, also, parallel contradictory forces existed. Economic interests accurately feared that United States withdrawal would place impossible strains on the underdeveloped and long-colonialized nation. Political leaders, however, had traditionally derived their electoral support from the issue of immediate independence. They believed, again accurately, that the unsophisticated Filipino electorate would react negatively to the idea of continued dependence. In this quandary, Quezon vacillated. He listened to and supported first one side and then the other. As one scholar has suggested, "unable himself to confer security, unwilling to require sacrifices of those able to make them, Manuel Quezon could do little more with his semi-presidency than to suffer it and enjoy it; to radiate charisma and restrain his own anxiety."[81] In late 1939 these anxieties seemed to have gotten the better of him.

As a result of Quezon's altered views, Douglas MacArthur faced the new decade in a position far less secure than any he had ever known. Not only was his position in the Commonwealth government insecure, but his relationship with the Philippine Department was also strained. Although now commanded by General George Grunert, an old friend of MacArthur's, the Department was increasingly forced into competition with the Philippine Army for both men and matériel. In addition, as the Japanese threat heightened, Grunert was frequently called into conference with Quezon, the new Department of National Defense, and the High Commissioner's Office. Because Quezon was no longer relying so completely on his Military Adviser, MacArthur was often not privy to these meetings. When an old friend from the Islands called this to the attention of the newly appointed Secretary of War, Henry Stimson, he immediately set out to remedy the situation. Soon, General

George Marshall, now Chief of Staff of the U.S. Army, notified Grunert that MacArthur's position and experience might be helpful to him, and advised that from this point forward, further mobilization plans be discussed with the Military Adviser.[82] Grunert made no objection, but the situation deteriorated even further in the light of his frequently voiced suggestions that the Philippine Army be called into service under the Philippine Department and that he, Grunert, be placed in command. While Washington assessed this proposal, MacArthur could not help but wonder if he would soon find himself without any troops at all.

Another area of conflict developed between Quezon and MacArthur when the Filipino President, increasingly frightened by reports of Japanese action in China, attempted to inaugurate civilian mobilization plans. Supported by Grunert and the new High Commissioner, Francis Sayre, Quezon hoped to establish a civilian defense program which would protect his people in the event of a Japanese attack. MacArthur disagreed. Arguing that Washington's position was still unclear concerning the role of the Islands in a Pacific war, he advised the Filipino leader that "until . . . the military concepts of Washington have been determined and communicated it would be premature to attempt civic regimentation of the populace."[83] Again, Quezon listened to both points of view, following first one, and then the other.

Quezon's disillusionment with the defense situation led to continued difficulty with MacArthur. Although certainly much of the problem was the result of Washington's indecision, the Philippine leader naturally felt misled by MacArthur's earlier optimism. By early 1940 his resentment led him to ask Sayre to have the General sent home. Unwilling to put the request into writing as Sayre had asked him to, Quezon chose simply to ignore MacArthur much of the time.[84]

Faced with the reality of his own diminished influence, MacArthur tried at least twice during this period to remedy the situation. As early as July 1939, when High Commissioner Paul V. McNutt returned to Washington to head the Federal Security Administration, the General once again asked to be considered for the office of High Commissioner. Wiring his friend Steve Early, MacArthur asked that he "kindly tell the President confidentially that I would be very glad to have his favorable consideration. At this time I believe that I could render him and our country valuable service in this exposed outpost. Here is the weakest link in our defense system."[85] Roosevelt, who was favorably impressed by Sayre's candidacy for the post, and still uncertain of MacArthur's future value to the United States position in the Far East, did not respond.

In March 1941, when newspaper reports suggested that Sayre might be recalled to the State Department, MacArthur tried once more. In another letter to Early, he reviewed the past five years as Military Adviser to the Commonwealth, and admitted that he had "now completed about everything along that line that is possible." Since that was the case, MacArthur would probably close out his work in the Islands sometime in 1941 and return home. Clearly, another alternative was more attractive to the General, and in lines reminiscent of his 1929 request for the position, he once again asked to be appointed high commissioner.

I hold the complete confidence of the Filipinos, having served here during four different tours, a total period of twelve years. I know local conditions, especially military and naval affairs, as possibly no one else does. From Vladivostok to Singapore I am thoroughly familiar with the most intimate details, political, military and commercial. I have a personal acquaintance with everyone of importance in the Orient and I believe no American holds the friendship and respect of this part of the world more than myself. In the present situation these are assets which the President might utilize in his co-ordination of the Pacific problems. I can respond to any call here or elsewhere. I am in robust health and feel that I was never quite so able to return to the Government in full measure the years of training it has devoted to me.

He closed the plea with a grandiloquent tribute to Roosevelt: "He has proved himself not only our greatest statesman but what to me is even more thrilling, our greatest military strategist."[86] In the light of his earlier comments to O'Laughlin and Moseley, and his later resentment of Roosevelt's World War II military strategies, this statement was undoubtedly dissimulative.

Early passed the letter on to the President, and by the middle of April, Roosevelt had decided on an answer. His aide, General Edwin "Pa" Watson, conveyed the message. Grateful for MacArthur's offer, Roosevelt now believed that the General could serve his purposes in the Far East best in a military capacity. Although vague about which position the General might fill, Watson went on to assure MacArthur that "in all discussions as to the availability of various active and retired officers, your name is always outstanding and most seriously considered."[87] Encouraged by these words, MacArthur postponed his plans to close the Military Mission and settled back to await future developments.

Before long, however, he grew restive. Uncertain concerning his own future position in the war which was now clearly on its way, he once again wrote Early. This time he asked the President to recall him to active duty. When he did not get an immediate response, he made reservations to return to the States and notified Chief of Staff Marshall of his intentions. Whether he was genuinely disillusioned with his prospects or hoped that his action would force Washington to make a decision is not clear.[88] Whatever his purpose, however, the results were better than he had expected. In late June, the Chief of Staff informed MacArthur that while no official decision had yet been reached, both Secretary of War Stimson and Marshall believed that he was "the logical selection for the Army Commander in the Far East should the situation approach a crisis."[89] Marshall asked that MacArthur keep this information to himself for the present.

General MacArthur did not have to keep his secret for long. By the end of June 1941, the situation in Europe had relieved Japan of its concern about Russian interference in the Pacific, and convinced its military planners that they might now put their proposed southern mission into effect. The increased mobilization in Japan led the War Department finally to seize the initiative in the Philippines. On July 24, Japanese troops moved into South Indo-China. Two days later, the United States froze Japan's assets in the United States and closed the Panama Canal to its trade. At the same time, Roosevelt placed the Philippine Army under United States control, and named Douglas MacArthur as commanding general of the United States Army Forces in the Far East.[90]

Almost immediately, Manuel Quezon reversed his position of the last two years. After personally congratulating the General on his new appointment, the Philippine President assured him, in a warm and friendly letter written on July 27, that he was "fully confident that you will attain in this difficult assignment the same success that has crowned your every endeavor in the past."[91] Clearly, Washington's confidence in MacArthur inspired Quezon as the General's service as Military Adviser had not been able to. Not privy to the confusion in Washington, the Commonwealth leader quite naturally expected that now the Roosevelt administration was firmly committed to a build-up in the Pacific. As a result, he threw the weight of his government behind MacArthur's efforts. The General, delighted with his new position and the widespread support that the majority of the Filipinos immediately expressed, renewed his efforts in the tremendous task before him. Seemingly, he harbored no grudges and accepted Quezon's new attitude without question.

The next few months were filled with activity. With the Philippine Department now under his control, MacArthur consolidated his staff and equipment as best he could. Still short-handed and undersupplied, he nonetheless established a competent headquarters staff led by Sutherland as Chief of Staff and Richard Marshall as Deputy Chief of Staff. Sidney Huff, previously in charge of the naval contingent of the Philippine defense program, and LeGrande Diller became MacArthur's aides. The personnel section (G-1) was headed by Charles Stivers, intelligence (G-2) by Charles Willoughby, operations and training (G-3) by Constant Irwin, and supply (G-4) by Lewis Beebe. To command his air force, the General requested Lewis Brereton, who arrived in early November.[92] George Grunert, still officially in command of the Philippine Department during the first few months after MacArthur's appointment, was recalled to the United States in October, and MacArthur assumed his duties as well.

At that point, the General, although more convinced of Japan's potential threat, was optimistic. Voicing this feeling to his friend Cal O'Laughlin, he assessed the new situation: "President Roosevelt's action . . . completely changed the picture and an immediate and universal feeling of confidence and assurance resulted. . . . The spontaneous transition was one of the most inspirational events that I have ever known. The reaction throughout the Netherlands East Indies, Malaya, and China, was one of complete jubilation. It was the sign they had been waiting for. Tokyo was dumbfounded and depressed." Although marked "Personal," MacArthur may have hoped that O'Laughlin would pass his views onto his readers in the *Army and Navy Journal.* With this in mind, he went on to review his achievements to date. His new army, which would contain nearly 200,-000 men, was to be "organized into eleven divisions and divided into three Force Commands." Although the arrangements for reinduction and for housing and equipment were still in process, the General was "confident that we can successfully resist any effort that may be made against us." Part of his attitude was based on the "splendid support" the War Department was supplying. Concluding with the comment that "no field commander could have received better support from a Chief of Staff than I have from Marshall," MacArthur promised his "most loyal and devoted service."[93] Believing that there would be no Japanese attack until spring, and that Washington would be able to deliver what it was now promising, the General's confidence was restored. Almost immediately, he was given reason to reassess his position.

Planners in Washington, faced with worsening crises both in Europe and the Pacific, spent 1940 and 1941 revising and reversing their war plans. When, in the fall of 1941, they reached tentative agreement in Rainbow-5, the plan which replaced War Plan Orange, the ultimate strategy for the Pacific was still vague.

Only two decisions appeared definite. The Asian front was to be secondary until the war in Europe could be brought under control, and then Japan, somehow, "would be brought to her knees."[94] Once again, they decided that the first line of defense in the Pacific would be the Alaska-Hawaii-Panama perimeter, and the Philippines would, at best, be strengthened only in order to hold the vital Manila and Subic bays of Luzon.

When MacArthur received word of Rainbow-5 in October 1941, he was furious. He immediately sent off a message to Washington in an attempt to reverse the decision. He argued that his now-activated army was capable of more than this minimal defense, and that, in any event, the bays could not be held if the rest of the archipelago was allowed to fall to Japan. He wanted permission to defend all the Islands, and pointed out in addition that not only was his plan tactically possible, but morally imperative in the face of the United States relationship to the Philippines. Marshall, whose sympathies at this time ran along the same lines, tentatively agreed, and in late November, Rainbow was altered to allow MacArthur to proceed as he wished.

Once again, a failure in communications, coupled with what planners on both sides of the Pacific wanted to believe, led to misunderstanding. In Manila, MacArthur continued to issue optimistic reports concerning his progress and potential. In Washington, Stimson, Marshall, and Eisenhower, all sympathetic to the vulnerability of the Philippines, accepted MacArthur's assessments and, within the limitations the European situation forced upon them, tried to fulfill the General's needs. Unfortunately, the U.S. war machine was simply not geared up to what world events required, and the supplies and personnel promised to MacArthur had still not arrived by the first of December 1941. In addition, although the USAFFE headquarters worked around the clock, the mobilization of the Philippine Army did not progress at the pace suggested by MacArthur's statements. Although officers previously assigned to the Philippine Department were now in command, they faced the same problems of the earlier years. Language differences and previous training levels still posed almost insurmountable problems. Communications to and from the various outposts and the main center of command in Manila were often inadequate, and air fields and defense emplacements developed slowly. Equipment shortages continued, and the G-4 problems were now multiplied as more recruits had to be fed, housed, and clothed.

The more basic problem, however, was an outgrowth of MacArthur's determination to defend the entire archipelago at the beaches. Since the Philippine coastline was longer than that of the entire United States, the USAFFE forces, even at full strength, would have been entirely inadequate to meet this demand. MacArthur's plan was partially based on his assumption that the Japanese would attack at predictable points. In this he was remarkably accurate, but the timing of the attack, coupled with the still-unprepared condition of the defense forces and the uncooperative attitude of the U.S. Navy, obviated the value of his judgment. The tragedy of the situation lay in the fact that until early in 1942, no one in a position of power was willing to face this reality. As D. Clayton James has argued, MacArthur's "overconfidence and unjustified optimism as to the abilities of himself, his staff, and the untried Filipino soldiers unfortunately became a contagion which ultimately affected even the War Department and the Joint Army and Navy Board."[95] As a result, the last few months of 1941 were filled with essentially fruitless attempts on both sides of the Pacific to bolster the Philippine defense after two decades of neglect.

On December 8, 1941, only a few hours after their surprise attack on the United States forces at Pearl Harbor, the Japanese began their onslaught on the Philippines.[96] Although the Pacific commanders had been warned that a Japanese attack was imminent, no one was prepared for the way it came. As a consequence, communications were less than effective, and although Naval Commander Hart received word of the Pearl Harbor attack through official channels, MacArthur's headquarters was notified only after news of the event was received from a California radio station. By dawn, the headquarters staff had rallied, and was busy trying to understand the news and its possible effect on its position. The next few hours were filled with uncertainty and confusion. MacArthur, apparently believing that the Japanese forces had suffered losses in the Hawaiian strike, hesitated to act without clear instructions from Washington. Closeting himself in his office, he conveyed his somewhat contradictory decisions through Sutherland. As a result, the hours before noon in Manila were spent indecisively.

By then, it was too late. For reasons never completely explained, most of Brereton's precious B-17 bombers and P-40 fighters were caught on the ground at Clark Field, and totally destroyed by the first two waves of Japanese bombers, which began their attack at 12:15.[97] This, coupled with the destruction at Pearl Harbor, rendered Rainbow-5, with its plan to keep communications open in the western Pacific, totally impracticable. For all intents and purposes, the Philippines, and the USAFFE forces stationed there, were now completely isolated from the additional supplies and personnel they would need to defend their position. From December 8, 1941, until May 6, 1942, when General Wainwright surrendered the Filipino and American troops to the Imperial Army of Japan, the tragic story in the Philippines was shaped by the denial and then gradual acceptance of this truth, both in Washington and Corregidor.

Almost immediately after the Japanese bombers left Formosa on the morning of December 8, Japanese forces landed on the northern islands of the archipelago. By Christmas, they were firmly entrenched at six strategic points in the Islands. MacArthur's plan to defend at the beaches had collapsed, and he reluctantly returned to the original Orange and Rainbow plans for a defense of Manila Bay maintained largely by troops on Bataan and Corregidor. On December 24, the General declared Manila an open city and moved his headquarters, along with some members of the High Commissioner's Office, and representatives of the Commonwealth government to Fort Mills on Corregidor. By the first week in January the drastically reduced USAFFE forces completed their retreat onto the Bataan peninsula. Although they were inadequately supplied and sheltered, they turned to face the enemy. With little news from the outside world, their rations cut again and again, these men struggled valiantly until, weakened by tropical disease and malnutrition, they could fight no more.[98] Gradually, the troops, and their commanders on Corregidor, recognized the inevitability of defeat. The men grew bitter and lost hope. Their leaders on the Rock, provided in some cases with the possibility of rescue, struggled as best they could to adjust the situation.

The move to Corregidor on December 24 required severe readjustment for all those involved. MacArthur, accompanied by his wife, small son, and the child's nurse, settled into a cottage near the opening to Malinta Tunnel. When the bombs began to hit the small island after December 29, he still refused to spend any more time than necessary in the dark and narrow laterals which provided shelter, hospital space, and headquarters for most of the others. Needing room for the long hours of pacing during which he seemed to do his best thinking, the General characteristically refused to be cowed by the steady bombardment.[99]

The situation was grim, and despite a steady flow of demands and requests from USAFFE, Washington seemed unable to offer much help. In fact, by the first of 1942, it was becoming increasingly clear that with the best intentions, the War Department simply could not hope to rescue the Philippines.[100] When, on January 1, 1942, a message underlining this reality was received from Washington, the leaders on Corregidor met to assess its meaning and to decide on their next move.

The wire advised that if at all possible, President Quezon be removed from Corregidor to the United States where he could set up a government in exile and rally support for the "redemption of the islands."[101] For the first time, Chief of Staff Marshall had put into words Washington's growing assumption that the Philippines would not be immediately reinforced, but might fall and then be rescued at some later date. The reaction at Fort Mills was heated. After conferring with Sutherland, Marshall, Huff, and Willoughby, the General called Quezon, and later, High Commissioner Sayre, to the headquarters. Their response, drafted at this time, stated that removal of the seriously ill

Filipino President was too dangerous to undertake.[102] In addition, MacArthur argued, Quezon's evacuation would weaken Filipino support for the American effort. Instead, since the USAFFE forces could probably hold out for another three months, that time should be spent in a stronger effort on the part of the United States and Great Britain to aid the entire Southwest Pacific Area. The wire ended with a request for a broader statement of United States policy and an assurance to Marshall that Sayre concurred in this assessment.

The General and his staff were cut off from most news of the world situation, and could not accept Washington's failure to reinforce the garrison. Their isolation, coupled with MacArthur's longstanding distrust of Roosevelt and the military establishment in Washington, encouraged resentment and disaffection at Fort Mills. Deeply sensitive to his own inability to aid his men on Bataan, the General refused, with rare exception, to visit the front lines. Although certainly not a reflection of any fear on his part, as both his past and future bravery would attest, this hesitancy resulted in increasing disenchantment among the men. Soon there were songs about "Dugout Doug," and the USAFFE leader felt even more oppressed. Always sure of his rapport with the troops in other command situations, this new development added one more reason for MacArthur's growing desperation. Throughout his long career, his need for external confirmation of his own value had always been a vital factor in his behavior. Now, feeling unsupported by his men or his government, the General's frustration reached its limits. As a result, he allowed himself to become involved in an exchange with Manuel Quezon which, if it had been widely known, could have destroyed the image that he had worked so long to build. Once again, the Philippines offered Douglas MacArthur solace and support not available from any other source. As was the case at the time of his affair with Isabel Cooper, he may have been willing to risk his future place in history for immediate evidence of his value as a man and a leader.

Two days after the January 1 meeting and dispatch, Manuel Quezon issued an executive order which, in its grandiose wording and the reward it conveyed, supplied MacArthur with the reassurance he needed so desperately, and much more. The statement of gratitude offering "recompense and reward" from the Filipino people as represented by their President began by reviewing the accomplishments of the Military Mission after 1935. It referred to the present "magnificent defense" of the Islands, and then went on to offer the highest praise to the General and his staff: "They stand as the outpost of victory of individual freedom and liberty over slavery and tyranny in the mighty struggle that engulfs the world. Win or lose, live or die, no men have ever carried a heavier burden or weightier responsibility with greater resolution and determination. The record of their services is interwoven forever into the national fate of our people."

As concrete proof of the regard that the Filipinos held for the Military Mission, Quezon presented Douglas MacArthur, Richard K. Sutherland, Richard J. Marshall, and Sidney L. Huff with $640,000 in U.S. currency.[103] Seldom, if ever, have American military officers received such evidence of high esteem.

Although issued on January 3, the transfer of funds for which Executive Order #1 provided was not undertaken until mid-February. In the interim, the suspicions generated by Chief of Staff Marshall's January 1 message were confirmed. The Japanese continued their invasion of the Islands, and by their regular bombing, emphasized their total control of the air. A puppet government was established in Manila, consisting primarily of members of the Commonwealth government who had not joined Quezon on Corregidor.[104] Despite USAFEE propaganda efforts, Japanese statements to the Filipino people concerning the advantage of cooperation with the Greater East Asia Co-Prosperity Sphere seemed to be taking effect. In Washington, the War Department faced at least momentary defeats on every front, and its continued efforts to reinforce the Philippine garrison failed again and again. On Corregidor, MacArthur, Quezon, and High Commissioner Sayre followed these developments as best they could, and grew increasingly discouraged.[105]

By early February Quezon could no longer stand the enforced inactivity of Corregidor, especially in the face of rumors from Manila of Japanese atrocities and repeated wires from Washington urging his evacuation. Since his removal to Fort Mills in December, he had argued insistently that he might best serve his people by returning to Manila. Now, realizing that the Filipino expectations of aid from the United States would not be fulfilled, he brought increasing pressure to bear on Sayre and MacArthur. If the United States could not, or would not, aid his people, then he wanted immediate neutralization of the Islands. Perhaps then the Japanese would withdraw their forces and he could return to Manila. Although he remained loyal to MacArthur, Quezon was by now deeply resentful of what he saw as American rejection. He stated his position most poignantly in a memorandum to MacArthur on February 7. "I wonder if those men [of the Philippine Army] knew that help is not coming within a reasonable time and that they are only being used to gain time in other fronts. [*sic*] I wonder, I repeat, how long their morale and will to fight would last."[106]

The next day, the USAFFE Commander and the President of the Philippines decided to make one last desperate attempt to force Washington into action. Directing his message to President Roosevelt, Quezon argued at length for the neutralization of the Philippines and the subsequent withdrawal of both American and Japanese troops. Pointing out that "while enjoying security itself, the United States has in effect condemned the sixteen millions of Filipinos to practical destruction in order to effect a certain delay," he concluded that "under the circumstances we should take steps to preserve the Philippines and the Filipinos from further destruction." The remaining paragraphs of Quezon's message outlined the legal basis for such action, and were followed by a message from MacArthur. Assuring Roosevelt that High Commissioner Sayre agreed with Quezon's plan, the General went on to assess the present military picture. He explained that "the temper of the Filipinos is one of almost violent resentment against the United States. Every one of them expected help and when it has not been forthcoming they believe they have been betrayed in favor of others."[107] Although

he placed the final decision in Roosevelt's hands, it was clear
that MacArthur approved of the Filipino leader's suggestion.

The reaction in Washington was immediate. Stimson, Marshall, and Roosevelt conferred on the morning of February 9
and agreed that a strong response was in order. The result was
Roosevelt's often quoted order "emphatically deny[ing] the
possibility of this government's agreement to the political aspects of President Quezon's proposal." While he was willing to
grant MacArthur permission to surrender "the Filipino elements of the defending forces," if necessary, the President insisted that the United States soldiers continue to fight because
"it [was] mandatory that there be established once and for all in
the minds of all peoples complete evidence that the American
determination and indomitable will to win carrie[d] on down to
the last unit."[108]

The next three days were filled with indecision on Corregidor and increased concern in Washington. According to one
source, Quezon threatened to resign and return to Manila.[109]
Persuaded that this action might lead to abuse of his family by
the Japanese, the Filipino President finally gave in. On February
11, MacArthur wired Washington that Quezon would not act in
contradiction to Roosevelt's order, and that evacuation of members of the Commonwealth government and the High Commis-
soner's Office would be attempted immediately. Although
grateful that Jean and Arthur had been offered a chance to
escape as well, "they and I have decided that they will share the
fate of the garrison." Finally, he attempted to correct the impression his earlier message had left that his forces were disloyal. "My statement regarding collapse applied only to the
civilian populace. There has never been the slightest wavering
among the troops. I count upon them equally with the Americans to hold steadfast to the end."[110] Despite Quezon's assessment of the seventh, and reports from the front to the contrary,
MacArthur was now determined that the world should believe
that his garrison stood ready to shoulder the responsibilities it
had been given.

Although these statements continued to convey a picture of
a beleaguered general determined to lead his forces to unavoid-

able defeat in the service of his country, other evidence suggested that the story was not so simple. MacArthur, who as early as February 4 had been advised that he might eventually be evacuated to another area in the Southwest Pacific,[111] was still deeply resentful of Roosevelt's decision against neutralization. Admittedly, there was a certain tragic grandeur implicit in his situation. Nonetheless, dissatisfied that what might be his last engagement would be a defeat and uncertain of any possible future assignment or of his evacuation from the Islands, the General decided to accept Quezon's earlier offered reward. Therefore, on February 15, completely convinced that Washington would not rescue his garrison, MacArthur wired the War Department regarding Executive Order #1.[112] On February 19, after assuring officials of the bank that "the original radiogram was shown to the President of the United States and to the Secretary of War and they were informed of the action taken," the exchange was completed, and shortly thereafter, the War Department relayed this information to Quezon.[113] On the twentieth, the Filipino leader was evacuated to the southern islands.

As a result of this exchange, Douglas MacArthur was enriched by $500,000, his Chief of Staff Richard K. Sutherland by $75,000, his Deputy Chief of Staff Richard J. Marshall, Jr., by $45,000, and his aide, Sidney L. Huff, by $20,000. Although their eventual evacuation from Corregidor was still not assured, MacArthur undoubtedly was aware that Roosevelt intended to order him out of the Philippines before the situation became much worse. Despite his public statements concerning his intention to remain with the garrison, he could not refuse a direct order, and both he and the War Department in Washington were aware of this fact. As a consequence, he, and the members of his staff who shared in the reward, would face the rest of the war and their lives afterward secure in the knowledge that they had substantial nest eggs in their personal bank accounts. Since none of them (except Sutherland) left any retrievable record of this event, their ultimate reasons for accepting the money must remain a mystery. It is possible that they felt justified in accepting it based on the 1935 law which had allowed them to accept "compensation and emoluments" as military advisers to the Philippine Commonwealth. On the other hand, the situation had changed in July 1941, when the military advisory staff was called back to active service in USAFFE. In this light, acceptance of the gift placed them in jeopardy on the basis of the Army Regulation that "every member of the Military Establishment, when subject to military law, is bound to refrain from . . . acceptance by an officer of a substantial loan or gift or any emolument from a person or firm with whom it is the officer's duty as an agent of the government to carry on negotiations."[114] Since, with one exception, none of the officers involved made any effort to make public the exchange, it is probably safe to say that they understood that their action was at best questionable.[115]

If greed, resentment, and a need for reassurance explained the acceptance of the money, it is still necessary to examine Quezon's reasons for offering it. Perhaps, in January when the original document was issued, the Filipino leader believed that this sum would convince MacArthur to use his influence in Washington to insure relief for the Philippines. When it became clear that the General could not achieve this goal, Quezon may have decided that some of the suffering of his people could at least be temporarily eased. Certainly, as D. Clayton James has argued, "some of MacArthur's reactions and behavior in early 1942 are hard to comprehend apart from the context of his personal ties and devotion to the Philippine nation and its president, Quezon." Much needed food was often left in local provinces, further diminishing the scant USAFFE stores in Bataan. In addition, bombing schedules were often revised on the advice of the Commonwealth President.[116] Perhaps MacArthur's "personal ties and devotion" were reinforced by the half million dollars given him by Quezon.

If this is true, then Quezon's motives and actions become understandable within the context of Philippine culture. Filipino social relationships have always been based on a strong sense of personal and familial loyalty, with a clear awareness that this loyalty requires a reciprocal response. As David Joel Steinberg has described it, "Central to Filipino values has been the sense of debt felt by each individual to the network of people who surround and help him. No Filipino dares to ignore this social obligation, called *utang na loob* (an internal debt of gratitude), for fear of being liable to the accusation of *walang hiya* (shamelessness)."[117]

Utang na loob, felt most strongly within extended family units, could be extended to nonfamily members through *compadrazgo,* a ritual which resembled the Roman Catholic concept of godparenthood, but drew additionally from the earlier Malay tradition of blood compacts. Finally, while the sense of *utang na loob* was strongest within personal relationships, it nonetheless was also considered relevant in a broader context. As a result, the United States, as benevolent colonizer, at some level assumed the role of *compadre*/protector, a participant in *utang na loob* and subject to great discredit if it fell into *walang hiya.* Thus, when Quezon suggested that his countrymen should fight valiantly along with the United States in what would become World War II, he promised that "it will give us an opportunity, before we finally sever the ties that bind us with the United States in 1946, to show the American people that our gratitude to the American flag for all the manifest blessings it has brought us is so deep-seated we are willing and ready to lay down our fortunes and our lives in its defense."[118]

Douglas MacArthur, who saw himself and encouraged the Filipinos to view him as the personification of the United States in the Pacific, entered into a *utang na loob* relationship with Quezon and his countrymen on many levels. He was not only the representative of the powerful American government which seemingly held the Philippine future in its hands and had every reason to be grateful for the Filipino sacrifice, but he was also linked to Quezon personally through the ties of *compadrazgo,* which had been established when the President and his wife served as young Arthur's godparents in 1938. Certainly in Manuel Quezon's eyes, the constraints of *utang na loob* must have seemed valid at this time, doubly insured by the national sacrifice of his people on the battlefield, and the monetary gift of gratitude conveyed to Douglas MacArthur by Executive Order

#1. If the United States could not or would not immediately reciprocate, surely eventual strategic decisions would not reflect its *walang hiya*. In the meantime, the General's ability to temporarily ease the plight of the Filipinos lessened his country's shame in Quezon's opinion. Ironically, while the Philippine leader's offer of the money can be justified once this aspect of Philippine culture is understood, the mores of MacArthur's country defined its acceptance as dishonorable.

One final question remains to be answered. If, as the evidence indicates, both Roosevelt and Stimson were aware of this exchange, what persuaded them to allow it? Again the records provide no answers, but it is possible that the war leaders believed that their approval would help to convince MacArthur and Quezon to continue the struggle against the Japanese. Dwight Eisenhower, at the time serving as deputy chief of the War Plans Division of the War Department in Washington, recorded evidence in his diary which would seem to substantiate this argument. On January 19, 1942, Eisenhower commented that "in many ways MacArthur is as big a baby as ever. But we've got to keep him fighting." On February 3, Eisenhower noted that it "looks like MacArthur is losing his nerve. I'm hoping that his yelps are just his way of spurring us on, but he is always an uncertain factor." On February 8, in response to a long radiogram from Corregidor, General Eisenhower wrote "today another long wail from Quezon. . . . I *think* he wants to give up." [Emphasis his.][119] Since Eisenhower and Marshall worked closely together during this period, there is reason to believe that they may have shared this fear and that Marshall then conveyed these impressions to the President and the Secretary of War. Certainly, in the face of worldwide Allied defeats at that time, and influenced by the attitude of Eisenhower and Marshall, Roosevelt and Stimson could have agreed that such a decision was a small price to pay to insure that somewhere in the world Allied forces, if not victorious, were at least illustrating "determination and indomitable will."

That MacArthur's peers in Washington may have questioned the propriety of his acceptance of the gift was also suggested by Eisenhower's attitudes and actions. Shortly after he arrived in Washington in the spring of 1942, Manuel Quezon attempted to present a similar "recompense and reward" to Eisenhower for his service in the Philippines "between November 15, 1935 and December 1939," and, no doubt, to establish a *utang na loob* relationship with the now well-placed Brigadier General. In a Memorandum for Record dated June 20, 1942, the future President of the United States explained his response to the offer:

> I carefully explained to the President [Quezon] that I deeply appreciated his thought and was grateful for his expressions of gratitude, but that *it was inadvisable and even impossible for me to accept a material reward for the services performed.* [Emphasis his.]
>
> I explained that while I understood this to be unquestionably legal, and that the President's motives were of the highest, the danger of misapprehension or misunderstanding on the part of some individual might operate to destroy whatever usefulness I may have to the allied cause in the present War. My government has entrusted me with important tasks, carrying grave responsibility. We agreed that the only matter that is now important is for everyone to do his best in the War effort, and any gossip on such a matter might reflect upon the Army and the War Department.
>
> In view of the representations I made, the President accepted my explanations and stated *that the matter was ended once and for all.* [Emphasis his.]
>
> He then said he wanted to do something that could not possibly embarrass me. It developed that this plan was to present to me, in official form, the citation he had written to accompany the honorarium he had in mind. I stated that I now [*sic*] only had no objection but that I would be highly honored in the receipt of a commendation from him, which, I explained would be supplementary to the flattering citation he gave me 2 years ago. I told him that such a citation would be of great and more lasting value to me and my family than any amount of money his government could possibly present to me.
>
> The matter was dropped on this basis, with the President stating that he honestly believed that in the same circumstances he would probably have given the same answer that I did. He obviously accepted my decision without resentment and without

loss of face—this latter point was one that had given me tremendous concern. To refuse a gift from anyone raised in the Far East, especially if a point of ethics has to be plead, is quite apt to develop into a serious personal matter. I'm certain that President Quezon feels I did the right thing and that he has respect for my decision.[120]

Whatever rationalizations and conflicts in attitudes surrounded the exchange process, it is clear that by the end of February, Quezon was safely on his way to an area where he would be less tempted to give way to the Japanese. By this time, too, MacArthur had been ordered to Australia and was planning for his final departure from the Philippines. The military situation in the Islands continued to deteriorate, but after remaining on Corregidor long enough to establish a new chain of command, he arranged for his family and several members of his staff, including Sutherland, Marshall, and Huff, to be removed from Fort Mills on March 12, 1942.[121]

Gathered at Corregidor's South Dock, the small group prepared to board the four PT boats which would attempt their evacuation. Undoubtedly relieved to be going, the departing party still hated to leave those remaining to their now obvious fate. All the farewells were emotional, and perhaps somewhat guilt-ridden. None of those involved, however, agonized more that night than Douglas MacArthur. His recollection of the event, even after more than twenty years, still conveyed the intensity of his feelings and revealed more, perhaps, then he planned.

On the dock I could see the men staring at me. . . . I must have looked gaunt and ghastly standing there in my old war-stained clothes—no bemedaled commander of inspiring presence. What a change had taken place in that once-beautiful spot! . . . The desperate scene showed only a black mass of destruction. . . . It was as though the dead were passing by the stench of destruction. . . . I raised my cap in farewell salute, and I could feel my face go white, feel a sudden, convulsive twitch in the muscles of my face. . . . I stepped aboard PT-41. "You may cast off, Buck," I said, "when you are ready."[122]

(6)

The Return

I was tasting to the last acid dregs the
bitterness of a devastated and beloved
home.

Douglas MacArthur
Reminiscences, 286.

ON MAY 6, 1942, Lieutenant General Jonathan M. Wainwright
surrendered the last American and Filipino troops under his
command to Japanese Lieutenant General Masaharu Homma.[1]
Although supported by Washington, this decision was criticized
harshly by MacArthur, who had hoped that the U.S. Forces in
the Philippines (USFIP) troops could hold out until he could
rally Allied support for an early rescue of the archipelago.[2]
Despite the optimism with which he had faced his reassignment
to Australia and his appointment as Supreme Commander of the
Southwest Pacific Area in late March, the General was now
forced to accept the reality of a long and difficult battle before
he could fulfill his promise to return to the Philippines and to
redeem his country's honor in the eyes of the Filipinos now held
hostage there.

Having been unable to forge the weapon which would "spell
the safety of [their] nation from brutal aggression until the end
of time," he spent the next two and a half years in an attempt
to remedy what he believed, at some level, to be his personal
failure. It was a bloody and grueling task, and one which often
seemed impossible. But in the Philippines he had known opportunity and freedom which had largely escaped him elsewhere.
The tropical beauty of the archipelago had provided a fertile
backdrop for his romantic imagination. In contrast to his other
acquaintances, the Filipinos had for long periods of time bolstered his often uncertain self-image. These were gifts he was

determined to repay and so, at the first public opportunity, he promised, "I shall return."[3]

MacArthur determined to return to the Philippines and to resume his life there after the war. Much of his planning and strategy during the war years was shaped by this firmly held intention. Indeed, the very strength of his will, in direct conflict with other American military advisers, helped to achieve the liberation of the Philippines before the attack on Japan. Nonetheless, his plans for continued service in the Islands were not to be fulfilled. A larger stage beckoned, and his Philippine sanctuary had been transformed by war into a quagmire of uncertainty, pain, and political intrigue. His efforts to shape the developing nation's future met with criticism. As a consequence, he withdrew. To understand this determined approach and subsequent withdrawal, a closer examination of the period is necessary.

As Commander in Chief (CinCSWPA) of the Southwest Pacific Area, MacArthur spent the thirty-one months between his departure from Corregidor in March 1942 and his return to Leyte in October 1944 painstakingly recovering, both publicly and privately, from the Philippine debacle. As the most visible of the American military commanders, and as the result of a well-organized public relations effort, the General often seemed to be regrouping the Allied forces in the Pacific single-handedly. By May 1942, the Japanese surge began to slow as a result of the Battle of the Coral Sea. Midway, in early June, made the reversal much more definite. The Guadalcanal campaign began in late summer, and although the long and bitter struggle was not over until February 1943, Allied momentum now clearly presaged the war's outcome. The Battle of the Bismarck Sea, the long struggle in the New Guinea jungles, and the "leap-frog" strategy, which worked so well in the Pacific islands, all encouraged Western planners to look forward to the long-awaited invasion of Japan. By mid-1944, when Allied approaches both to the west (in the Marianas) and the south (in northwestern New Guinea) of the Philippines seemed guaranteed, Washington stepped up its efforts to map out the remainder of the war. The ultimate goal was an invasion of Japan; the strategic debate centered around finding the most effective route to that end.[4]

Although MacArthur in these years consistently maintained that it was both militarily and politically necessary to reconquer the Philippines before the invasion of Japan could begin, by early 1944 the U.S. Joint Chiefs of Staff were questioning this wisdom and suggesting that Formosa might prove to be a more effective base from which to launch the air bombardment preliminary to the main attack on the home islands. By early June, heartened by Allied progress in the Pacific, the Joint Chiefs requested that both Fleet Admiral Chester W. Nimitz and General MacArthur submit their reactions to this possibility. For the two American military leaders, so often at odds, the big debate was on. It would continue throughout the summer, reach a high point in a July meeting at Pearl Harbor with Roosevelt, and be conclusively resolved only two weeks before the final plans were to be put into operation.[5]

The ultimate decision to recapture the archipelago represented a turning point in the consistent concern for the Islands which had marked MacArthur's absence of more than two years from that area. Upon his arrival in Australia in March 1942, his insistence upon an early return frequently reached the level of obsession. The surrender of the USFIP troops and his realization of the inadequacy of the SWPA forces at his command in those early months forced him to reevaluate his timing. But the Philippine rescue was always in the forefront of his planning during 1943 and early 1944. During these months, he maintained close communication with Manuel Quezon's government-in-exile in Washington. In addition, contact with the Fil-American guerrilla forces was established quickly and often provided intelligence reports which contributed much to the invasion plans.[6] Finally, and on a much more negative plane, reports of the puppet government established by the Japanese and made up of many of the prewar Filipino governing elite irritated the American leaders and encouraged their determination to reassert Western hegemony over the Islands.

Of these three sources of communication, MacArthur's continuing relationship with Manuel Quezon was certainly the most important. Throughout the war, until the Philippine leader's death in August 1944, the two corresponded regularly, sent personal emissaries to each other, and consulted frequently regarding the most effective ways to insure continued American interest in the liberation of the Islands.[7] Both men realized that Washington intended to keep the promise made in early 1942, but both believed that this intention was not a high priority with either Roosevelt or the Joint Chiefs. Their goal, therefore, was to draw attention to the Philippine situation whenever possible through public statements in the press—a method which both used with particular efficiency. Their steady efforts to attract Roosevelt's personal attention met with less success. Throughout the war, Quezon found himself on the outskirts of power, a situation which he resented deeply, and one which increased his empathy for his former Field Marshal.

During these final two years of his life, the always mercurial Philippine President had periods of confidence during which he reaffirmed his faith in the colonizing power under which he had served all of his public career. At such times, he issued shortwave messages to his people in attempts to instill a parallel optimism in them.[8] More frequently, however, and increasingly as his health failed and he lost hope of returning to his homeland, Quezon questioned the strength of the American commitment to his country. As he outlined in a letter in early 1944, sent through MacArthur, to his friend Thomas Confesor,

> When I followed General MacArthur to Australia at his invitation
> I did it under the impression that General MacArthur was to have
> there the forces he needed for the speedy reconquest of the Philippines. Upon arriving in Australia I realized how mistaken I was
> [. T]hen I came to Washington in the hope that I might secure the
> force that General MacArthur needed. Once here I found out that
> it had been decided to give first consideration to the European war
> and neither General MacArthur nor I could do anything to change
> this decision.[9]

The frustration evident in this account was the major force motivating the Filipino leader's efforts in the United States capital. It shaped his own understanding of the war, and, more importantly, it influenced his messages to MacArthur in the Southwest Pacific. To the General who had long believed that Washington was always apt to thwart his efforts and ambitions, Quezon's attitude only provided additional supporting evidence. The distance between them seemed only to secure the friendship which had seen, over its long lifetime, several bad moments. Their vision followed a parallel and mutually reinforcing course. Both firmly believed that their bravery and loyalty were receiving less than their due in the Allied centers of power. As Quezon's health deteriorated, MacArthur became more and more concerned that the Philippine President might not live to accompany him when he returned to the Islands, and this concern provided yet one more support to the now primary relationship that the two enjoyed. By the time of the Filipino leader's death, the bonds created by the shared dangers and common goals of the early 1940s and buttressed by *utang na loob* were stronger than they had been throughout the entire forty-year period during which they had known each other.[10]

Concurrent with Quezon's growing disillusionment, guerrilla reports and Japanese propaganda continued to describe a situation developing in Manila which threatened to make the Allied liberation efforts more difficult. As early as January 1942, while Quezon and MacArthur were still on Corregidor, the Japanese had begun to establish an occupation government composed of members of the Commonwealth government remaining in Manila. Headed originally by Jorge Vargas, Quezon's former secretary, this Executive Commission was required to serve as a liaison between the Japanese and their Filipino captives. Asserting their wish to incorporate the Philippines into the Greater East Asia Co-Prosperity Sphere, the occupation leaders offered early independence to the Filipinos in exchange for their cooperation. Gradually, most of the prewar Commonwealth government officials agreed to participate in this effort, maintaining privately that their collaboration was necessary in order to alleviate the harsh treatment the Japanese would otherwise have imposed.

Although guerrilla intelligence supported this argument to some degree, news of Filipino cooperation with the enemy made the American picture of the loyal outpost in the Pacific more difficult to sustain. When, in October 1943, José P. Laurel was inaugurated president of the puppet republic, and a year later this government declared war against the United States and Great Britain, critics in Washington urged that these collaborators be severely punished after the war. Although both MacArthur and Quezon argued consistently that the Filipinos involved were motivated by various purposes and that decisions as to their ultimate fate would have to be reached after individual consideration, both men were troubled by the turn of events. Better than most, they understood the complexity of the situation. Nonetheless, their need, on both public and private levels, to sustain a vision of Philippine loyalty to the Allied cause made the collaboration of their compadres a matter of great concern.

As a consequence, MacArthur was particularly careful to emphasize in his public reports a picture of the vast majority of the Filipinos fully supporting the United States, and led reluctantly by a government carefully treading the fine line between treason and necessity. Certainly there was much that was true in this vision, and certainly its public acceptance was necessary if he was to receive the support he would need for the liberation attempt. Undoubtedly, however, his firm insistence on this perspective reflected a personal need as well. If his efforts to achieve redemption of the Islands were to be meaningful, the worthiness of the goal must not be suspect. For a man whose conscious definitions of right and wrong usually tended toward the absolute, the ambiguity inherent in the problem of collaboration introduced a factor that he would have preferred to ignore.[11]

Throughout the period preceding MacArthur's return to the Islands the war wrought significant changes in the Philippine situation. By mid-1944, it was obvious that Manuel Quezon would be unable to resume control of the Commonwealth gov-

ernment once it was reestablished. His successor, Sergio Osmeña, would undoubtedly introduce a new tone to the postwar
governing process—a tone certainly less familiar and perhaps
uncomfortable to MacArthur.[12] Moreover, many of the General's friends in the Manila elite were now making choices of
allegiance which blurred the clear-cut support that he had always confidently expected from them. The loyalty of the masses
to the American cause was still unquestioned, but the war-
induced suffering to which they were most subject might change
this reality as well. During the long hours of lonely pacing at the
various command posts of 1942, 1943, and 1944, an awareness
of these changes must undoubtedly have infringed upon the
General's usually optimistic outlook.

Other changes were occurring as well, not the least of which
involved the enhancement of Douglas MacArthur's public image. Always popular with the press, MacArthur's adroit handling
of news coverage after he assumed command of the USAFFE
forces in mid-1941 had already called American public attention
to his position before the beginning of the war. With the full
cooperation of the War Department during the fall of the Philippines, MacArthur's heroic public statements and tragic predica-
ment provided the most noteworthy symbol of resistance
available in the dark early months of the conflict. By the time the
Allied situation in the Pacific improved in May 1942, the noble
profile of the Commander in Chief of SWPA was a familiar
image in American newspapers, and "MacArthur's Army," with
the help of an evergrowing public relations organization,
seemed often to be singlehandedly winning the war. Perhaps
never unmindful of the possibility of higher accolades, the General did not seem to object when a serious "MacArthur for
President" drive began to develop in mid-1943. Although the
carefully orchestrated groundswell fell apart by the spring of
1944, the seed had been planted in the ever-ambitious leader's
mind, and continued to germinate there throughout the rest of
his public career.[13]

Although he later denied any interest in political office,
there is reason to believe that these statements were not wholly

sincere. Certainly, if his hopes in this area were temporarily diminished, his thoughts concerning the presidency must have reminded him that there was a possibility that his familiar nemesis in the White House, Franklin Roosevelt, might soon be replaced. Noting at the time of their Pearl Harbor meeting that "physically he [Roosevelt] was just a shell of the man I had known,"[14] the General undoubtedly expected that there would soon be a changing of the guard in Washington. He could not have predicted Harry Truman's ascension to the presidency, but surely he expected a shift in this arena. This too must have added to his growing awareness that despite his personal wishes, the world as he had known it before 1941 would never again exist.

On October 3, 1944, the Joint Chiefs of Staff issued the final order for the invasion of the Philippines. Seventeen days later, on October 20, the first of more than two hundred thousand American troops secured beachheads near the town of Tacloban on Leyte Gulf.[15] The Commander in Chief of SWPA, on board the *Nashville,* watched his careful plans unfold successfully with relief and what one observer characterized as "dignified good humor."[16] That he was pleased to have begun his long-postponed return was clearly evident. As soon as possible, he and some of his staff walked ashore through the knee-deep water of Red Beach to proclaim formally the fulfillment of his dramatic promise of 1942.[17]

Accompanied by President Osmeña, MacArthur delivered a carefully prepared statement to the Filipino people.

> People of the Philippines: I have returned. By the grace of Almighty God, our forces stand again on Philippine soil—soil consecrated in the blood of our two peoples. We have come, dedicated and committed to the task of destroying every vestige of enemy control over your daily lives, and of restoring upon a foundation of indestructible strength, the liberties of your people. . . .
>
> The hour of your redemption is here. . . .
>
> Rally to me. Let the indomitable spirit of Bataan and Corregidor lead on. As the lines of battle roll forward to bring you within

the zone of operations, rise and strike. Strike at every favorable opportunity. For your homes and hearths, strike! For future generations of your sons and daughters, strike! In the name of your sacred dead, strike! Let no heart be faint. Let every arm be steeled. The guidance of Divine God points the way. Follow in His name to the Holy Grail of righteous victory.[18]

Once again, at some level, the experience of Arthur MacArthur at Missionary Ridge was joined to that of his son in a cry for loyal support and superior effort to achieve the victory that he envisioned so clearly and needed so desperately if his self-esteem was to be sustained.

While the early phases of the invasion progressed smoothly, this did not assure an easy victory in the rest of the Philippine venture. The Japanese, under the command of recently arrived General Tomoyuki Yamashita, were convinced that they must hold out as long as possible in the archipelago in order to forestall the forthcoming Allied invasion of the home islands. Correctly learning from MacArthur's 1942 error, the Japanese commanders did not attempt significant opposition at the beaches, but withdrew into the interior for a "resistance in depth."[19] As a consequence of this decision, Allied operations on Leyte were painfully slow and costly. The rain, which seemed always to haunt American efforts in the Philippines, appeared on schedule when, on October 28, the first of three typhoons moved across the battlefields, slowing necessary airfield construction and creating incessant difficulties for the infantry. At the same time, Japanese kamikaze introduced a terrifying new element to the always irrational battle experience.

In the face of these difficulties, MacArthur was forced to postpone his planned invasion of Luzon at Lingayen Gulf until early January. On January 9, the massive preassault naval bombardment began, and once again the Japanese offered little resistance. By early afternoon, MacArthur and his staff were once again wading ashore, this time just south of San Fabian. The General now felt confident that, although delayed, the final push for Manila was well underway. Soon his long-heralded return would be complete.

Although MacArthur tried desperately to reach Manila in time for his sixty-fifth birthday on January 26, the struggle across the plains of Luzon lasted the entire first month of 1945. His armies, pitted against the Japanese, vied frantically with each other to be the first to reach the city. Entering the northern Manila suburbs on February 3, parts of the 1st Cavalry Division won the race, but soon discovered that the Battle of Manila would be as long and difficult as the other phases of the liberation had been. This fact surprised not only the advance troops, but their commander in chief as well. In the words of the comprehensive Army history: "Every command in the theater, from MacArthur's headquarters on down, hoped—if it did not actually anticipate—that the city could be cleared quickly and without much damage. GHQ SWPA had even laid plans for a great victory parade, à la Champs Elysées, that the theater commander in person was to lead through the city."[20]

The Americans had assumed that the Japanese would remove the major portion of their defenses to the countryside. They soon learned instead that almost 17,000 naval troops, under the command of Rear Admiral Sanji Iwabuchi, had elected to make a final stand in the city. In combination with nearly 4000 members of the Japanese army who had been caught in the Allied encirclement, these forces waged an urban guerrilla and block-by-block defense of terrifying proportions. As one scholar has noted, "with their concrete fortifications, ample supply of weapons and ammunition, and fanatical determination to fight to the last, Iwabuchi's defenders were prepared to make the capture of Manila a bloody, time-consuming ordeal for MacArthur's forces."[21]

The Japanese decision resulted in a month-long fierce battle waged primarily in the southern portion of the city—the area of Intramuros, Fort Santiago, Fort McKinley, Neilson Field, and many of the prewar government structures. The outcome was predictable in that the superior American forces ultimately achieved their goal, but for everyone involved, and particularly for the Filipinos caught in the crossfire, the price was overwhelming. By the end of February, more than 100,000 Filipino civilians had been killed, and a major portion of their city laid waste. Although MacArthur, hoping to save civilian lives, had forbidden aerial attacks on Manila, massive artillery bombardment literally tore the ancient earthquake-resistant stones of the Walled City from their foundations. Nothing remained of the sturdy government structures but piles of rubble. In comparison to the human costs, however, this destruction of property was the least important. As D. Clayton James has rightly assessed,

> The greatest tragedy, however, was that for each American or Japanese soldier killed in the fighting for the city, at least six Filipino residents of Manila—men, women, and children—died as hapless victims of fires, shellings, stray bullets, grenades, or atrocities. The great city, once known as "the Pearl of the Orient," lay devastated, with much of the downtown area in shambles and the transportation, sewage, water, and electrical systems paralyzed.[22]

Douglas MacArthur, as had his father Arthur MacArthur nearly half a century before, faced a mammoth task of restoration as head of one of the most destructive, albeit well-intentioned, armies of "liberation" the world had ever seen.

On a personal level, the vast destruction was brought home to the General when, on February 23, he was finally able to enter the area around the Manila Hotel where the MacArthurs had lived for the six years before the war. After examining the ruins of the Army-Navy Club nearby—his first home in the Islands back in 1904—he carefully entered the nearly destroyed hotel. Almost everything was missing or ruined. The broken pieces of two vases which had been given to his father by the Emperor of Japan in 1905 lay scattered around the corpse of a Japanese colonel in one of the doorways. The nearly 8000 volumes in the library of which he had been so proud had been ravaged. Everything he saw confirmed the message he had sent to his wife on the eighteenth while the battle for this area still raged: "Commissioner's house and hotel were destroyed this afternoon. Do not be too distressed over their loss. It was a fitting end for our soldier home."[23] Just as he had expected the elusive "Fan" of long ago to adjust to the necessary sacrifices demanded by his fantasized military life, so now he assumed that Jean would accept the tragic forfeiture that this very real war required. This time he was not mistaken. Predictably, she soon returned to Manila, picked up the pieces of their life together there, and cheerfully made the best of it.

If Jean adjusted quickly to the changed circumstances of her life, there is reason to suspect that her husband did not. Even before the devastation of Manila, the General suffered periods of depression in the early weeks of the Philippine action.[24] Certainly, much of this can be attributed to his separation from Jean and Arthur—the longest they had ever known. Moreover, the unexpected Japanese defense of Manila and the costly human sacrifice it required must have weighed upon his usual optimism. But there was yet one more reason for the change in MacArthur's attitude during these months. Expecting that his return to the Islands would be greeted by a great outpouring of gratitude and welcome, he was at first not disappointed. The guerrillas who met the American forces in the Leyte action were warm and enthusiastic. But as his troops struggled through Mindoro and particularly after their arrival in Manila, another mood was obvious in the behavior of many Filipinos. As one observer has noted:

> The majority of the people had not been enhanced in spirit by war, but had suffered spiritual erosion; they were prey to cynicism, corruption, and a philosophy of *agaw-buhay:* "snatch-life." This damage to the moral fiber of the Philippines, as well as material destruction there, is in part traceable to American military unpreparedness. Any account of the American years in the Philippines must include this vast debit item.[25]

The internees at Santo Tomas and the Old Bilibid Prison had gratefully welcomed their liberators, but many Filipinos were both physically and morally exhausted by the long years of the Japanese occupation and the terrible battle for the liberation of Manila. The optimism with which they had greeted the promise of independence in the thirties was gone, and with it went a part of their warm support for the Americans who had promised to insure its rewards. First among these Americans was, of course, Douglas MacArthur, and he was not insensitive to this shift. As his public image had grown in the eyes of the larger world, it had in some ways diminished in the Islands where he had always before felt secure and appreciated. Although there would be no grand parade, insofar as the Filipinos had the emotional strength to respond, they celebrated his return—but often there was simply no reserve enthusiasm left.

The General's understanding of this change was most clearly illustrated on February 27 when he spoke at a ceremony at Malacanang Palace which marked the resumption of the Commonwealth government throughout the Philippines. Delivering what seemed almost a plea for vindication, MacArthur paused frequently to recover his composure as he recounted the past three years of Fil-American history:

> More than three years have elapsed—years of bitterness, struggle and sacrifice—since I withdrew our forces and installations from this beautiful city. . . . Much that I sought to preserve has been unnecessarily destroyed by his [the Japanese] desperate action at bay. . . .
>
> Then we were but a small force struggling to stem the advance of overwhelming hordes treacherously hurled against us behind the mask of professed friendship and international good will. That struggle was not in vain! . . . My country has kept the faith!

Describing the efforts of his army, he went on to outline the tasks which lay before the Filipinos, to call for their consecration to those necessities, and to formally turn over the reins of government to the Commonwealth. This accomplished, he began to discuss the situation in Manila: "Your capital city, cruelly punished though it be, has regained its rightful place—Citadel of Democracy in the East. Your indomitable. . . ." but he could not go on. After a long pause, he concluded briefly with a request that those present join him in the Lord's Prayer, and left almost immediately thereafter. As he later explained, "to others it might have seemed my moment of victory and monumental personal acclaim, but to me it seemed only the culmination of a panorama of physical and spiritual disaster."[26] Certainly this

statement partially explained his abrupt breakdown and departure. Nevertheless, his difficulty in delivering the entire speech
and his failure at this particular point as he discussed the reality
of Manila revealed his awareness that "the Citadel of Democracy
in the East," where he had hoped to live out the remainder of
his life, could never again be the supportive context that it had
been in years past.

In addition to the discomfort that MacArthur felt with regard to the changing attitude in Manila, his position as Supreme
Commander of the American military government in the Philippines was made more difficult when he finally was forced to deal
with the twin problems of civil administration and collaboration.
He had hoped to transfer both problems to Sergio Osmeña's
Commonwealth government when he precipitately restored
sovereignty to the civilian administration both at Tacloban in
October and at Manila in late February. Although this hasty
transfer could be justified in light of the necessity to prepare his
military command for the still-planned invasion of Japan,
MacArthur's other actions during the early months of 1945 complicated his attempt. Maintaining a firm intention to separate
civil and military concerns as soon as possible, he nonetheless insisted on making statements and decisions which weakened Osmeña's already impossible position. As one observer
argues:

> Confusing, perhaps intentionally, the importance of a civilian gov-
> ernment's control of its own military forces with the complex
> dependence of the Commonwealth government on American sup-
> port (entirely a military dependence, while the Philippines was a
> combat area), MacArthur abandoned the messy problems of re-
> construction to the fiction which was the Commonwealth govern-
> ment. Osmeña had no staff, no money, and no room for
> maneuver.... [MacArthur] seems to have taken the glory for him-
> self while avoiding sullying his hands with the thorny problems of
> reconstruction. He foisted upon Osmeña the myriad problems of
> governing a devasted [sic], bankrupt, and divided land with only
> the semblance of a government.[27]

In reality, however, many of MacArthur's actions during this period after the recapture of Manila did indeed "sully" the principled position he defined in his public statements. By restoring responsibility to the Commonwealth Government, he created a situation whereby President Osmeña would be blamed for breakdowns in the delivery of relief shipments from the United States, misunderstandings concerning backpay for the guerrillas, and the confused bureaucratic tangle which resulted as prewar and wartime administrators struggled to resume their place in the government. This latter problem, growing out of the whole issue of collaboration, was perhaps the most troublesome.

That most of the prewar governing elite left behind in Manila in 1942 had eventually cooperated with the Japanese was an undeniable fact. The degree to which each participant had aided the enemy was more in dispute. Most difficult of all, however, was the question of motivation. How much of the collaboration had been the result of a genuine attempt to alleviate the harsh oppression of the Filipino people by the Japanese? How much had been an effort to secure personal safety or to achieve other goals of self-interest? Even the collaborators themselves could probably not have answered these questions conclusively. Yet it was precisely these questions which faced both the military authority headed by MacArthur and the Commonwealth government of Osmeña.

In Washington, the issue had always seemed clear. Roosevelt, his Secretary of the Interior, Harold Ickes, and most other American officials saw collaboration as a clear-cut offense, punishable as treason. Throughout the war they had promised a purge of the collaborationists as soon as the liberation was accomplished. While perhaps impractical in view of the fact that the collaborators provided the only body of trained leaders available to the Commonwealth government after the war, this solution at least avoided the difficulty of deciding issues of individual motivation. In the opinion of these observers in Washington, all collaborators should be forced out of the government, and then at a later date, the specific circumstances in each case would be examined by the courts.

A great gap existed, however, between Washington's wartime theory and the reality in Manila in the early spring of 1945. Not unlike the situation facing the victorious Northern government after the American Civil War, the returning Commonwealth officials, if they followed this policy, would have been forced to remove and imprison men with whom they had served in the long years of the colonial period; men, as one scholar has explained, with whom they "were interlocked personally by reciprocal bonds predating the war."[28] Osmeña, whose sons were possible collaborators, reacted indecisively, and was encouraged in his uncertainty by the fact that no plans had been developed in the United States to implement the purge. Moreover, MacArthur's position concerning the collaborationist issue did nothing to clarify Osmeña's responsibility.

Throughout the war, MacArthur had seemed to take the Philippine cooperation with the Japanese as a personal affront. At the time of the reinvasion of the Islands, he had issued a clear-cut decree stating that the collaborators would be removed from office and held captive until after the war. At that time, they were to be turned over to the Philippine government for final judgment. By this act, as in so many others of this period, he neatly placed the major problem back at Osmeña's feet. While this tactic made the ultimate resolution of the issue much more problematic, its impact was minimal compared to another widely publicized decision made by MacArthur later in the spring.

As the Japanese in central Luzon gradually submitted to the American onslaught in February and March, 1945, their commanders, accompanied by the leading members of the Philippine collaborationist government, retreated into the mountainous reaches of Benguet province. In late March, President Laurel and a few companions were flown to Japan. The other members of the wartime government were left in Baguio and allowed to "escape" as best they could. By early April, small groups of these officials began to make their way toward the American lines. One of those escaping was Manuel Roxas, an officer in the American Army, and General MacArthur's longtime friend.

A member in good standing of the prewar oligarchy, Roxas had served in the Philippine Senate for many years and had known MacArthur at least since the 1920s.[29] Secretary of Finance in the 1941 Philippine Council of State, he had been appointed lieutenant colonel on MacArthur's staff to serve as liaison officer to Quezon after the Japanese attack. As acting Philippine Treasurer on Corregidor in February 1942, he had witnessed the enactment of Executive Order #1 whereby Quezon had awarded $640,000 to MacArthur, Sutherland, Huff, and Marshall, and had signed MacArthur's receipt when the General returned the Philippine pesos he had been given to hold as security until the transfer in the United States could be confirmed. Roxas had been instrumental in persuading Quezon to go into exile in Washington, and had remained behind after the departure of the other members of the Commonwealth government in order to act in Quezon's behalf and to oversee the destruction of Commonwealth bullion reserves in Manila Bay.[30]

During the months after MacArthur's departure from Fort Mills, Roxas had escaped to Mindanao, but had ultimately fallen into Japanese hands. After narrowly escaping execution, he was able to remain inactive for much of the war by claiming poor health. Finally, however, the Japanese insisted that he participate in the Laurel government, and in late 1944 he briefly accepted a position as "food czar."[31] Although his efforts in this capacity were short-lived, Roxas was among those taken to Baguio when the Battle of Manila began.

Throughout their long acquaintance, both MacArthur and Quezon had found Roxas's personality more compatible than Osmeña's, and throughout the war both remained convinced of his loyalty to the Allied cause. From Washington Quezon frequently requested information regarding Roxas's safety, and when rumors suggested that the Japanese were going to force Roxas to accept the presidency of the 1943 occupation-sponsored republic, the Commonwealth President insisted that attempts be made to spirit his friend out of the Islands. Although a complex plan was devised to achieve this goal, it failed and MacArthur subsequently decided that the idea was too dangerous.[32] Part of Quezon's concern undoubtedly stemmed from his fear that if Roxas were given the opportunity, he would replace the now absent president in the hearts of the Filipino people. On the other hand, there seems to have been a genuine regard for his heir apparent's safety on Quezon's part, and an absolute conviction that Roxas would do nothing which in the long run would harm the future of the Philippine nation. When word reached Quezon of Roxas's capture by the Japanese, his response clearly revealed his position.

> The news that Roxas has fallen into the hands of the enemy is the worst news I can receive from the Philippines. I am afraid that after his insistent refusal to be President, the Japanese have murdered him. If so, he is the greatest loss that the Filipino people have suffered in this war. He can't be replaced. I regret more than I can say that I did not order him to come with me to Australia. But he insisted that he felt it his duty to remain in the Philippines, and in the belief that Mindanao would never surrender, I let him stay. Oh! I am proud of him! He will go down in history as one of our greatest national heroes.[33]

In late April 1945, then, when Roxas and four other members of the collaborationist cabinet escaped to Sixth Army Headquarters at San Fernando, Pampanga, MacArthur reacted to the news quickly. Although the officers to whom Roxas and his companions had surrendered confined the five men as they had been instructed, a phone call from Roxas to General Sutherland at MacArthur's headquarters in Manila quickly reversed this decision. In a statement to the press MacArthur announced that "among those freed is Brigadier General Manuel Roxas, former speaker of the Assembly. Four members of the Philippine collaborationist cabinet have been captured. They will be confined for the duration of the war as a matter of military security and then turned over to the government of the Philippines for trial and judgment."[34]

By distinguishing Roxas's position from that of the other members of the collaborationist government, MacArthur set a precedent which would later obfuscate the entire collaboration

issue. Maintaining that he knew that Roxas had cooperated with
the Japanese for the good of his nation, MacArthur shifted the
Allied collaborationist policy from one which dealt with behavior to one which was forced to deal with motivation. From that
point onward, Osmeña had to consider the individual reasons
for each collaborator's wartime action. Since each man would
obviously argue that his motivation was altruistic, very few could
justifiably be condemned. The American General, while on the
one hand attempting to separate civil and military issues as early
as possible, had by this action involved himself irretrievably in
postwar Philippine politics.

Undoubtedly, MacArthur's actions in this instance were influenced by his awareness of Quezon's earlier judgment of
Roxas, as well as his own prewar acquaintance with the Filipino
leader. Moreover, his belief, shared by Quezon, that Roxas was
a more dynamic, and therefore a more suitable, leader for the
Philippines than was Osmeña encouraged his decision. Perhaps
additional weight resulted from Roxas's involvement in the exchange brought about by Executive Order #1. In later years,
the General always argued that his decision regarding Roxas was
based on Roxas's guerrilla activity during the war, and the fact
that as a member of the U.S. Army, Roxas's situation was
unique.[35] MacArthur's motivation, like that of the collaborators,
can perhaps never fully be understood. That his action blurred
the issue of collaboration and thereby allowed the wartime oligarchy gradually to resume power and, headed by Roxas, to
defeat Osmeña in the 1946 election is an indisputable fact.

Reaction to MacArthur's decision was vehement both in
Washington and in Manila. Led by the outspoken Harold Ickes,
officials in the United States, struggling to move forward in the
wake of President Roosevelt's sudden death, were harsh in their
criticism. In Manila, Roxas took immediate advantage of the
situation to resign his military commission and begin to reassert
his control over Philippine politics. The other collaborators
were quick to point to his situation as precedent for decisions
regarding their own circumstances. Osmeña, caught in the middle, understood that if he fought Roxas's supporters on this
issue, he would waste time and talent necessary to postwar re-

covery. By not fighting, however, he allowed Roxas's faction to mount an ultimately successful campaign against his own position as President. Exhausted by the insoluble nature of the question, he gradually gave up the fight.

Other issues of civil administration involved MacArthur during this period. Despite his disclaimers, there can be little doubt that his influence on public opinion, as well as his interference in the Osmeña government, affected many of the decisions which would shape the post-independence relationship between the United States and the Philippine Republic. When he insisted that the 1941 Philippine Congress be reconvened in 1945, he was, as he argued, helping the civilian arm of government resume its responsibilities. Since many of its members were collaborators, however, he was at the same time helping to create a situation in which Filipinos would thereafter be confused as to what constituted loyalty in their public officials.

In lieu of a comprehensive directive from Washington, the General developed his own department of civil affairs to be implemented after the invasion. While he announced that Osmeña was in charge, it was often these Philippine Civil Affairs Units which had the authority and capacity to solve day-to-day problems. As in Europe at the same time, it was often the men and women on the scene at the fighting's end who made the decisions, established the precedents, and gained the power which would be used later on. In the Philippines, those on the scene were almost always members of MacArthur's forces rather than Osmeña's government.

In addition to the power which adhered to the military government in this inadvertent fashion, MacArthur insisted that his position as the sovereign American authority in the Philippines in this period remain unchallenged. Even before his return to the Islands, he had made clear his opinion that the Interior Department's plan to send a high commissioner to the Philippines along with Osmeña was ill-advised. In September 1944, he sent a statement of policy to the War Department in which he stated:

Throughout the military period, the Commonwealth Government operates under my supreme authority. It would hardly seem advisable for the High Commissioner's Office to be placed in a similar role. It would appear preferable that the High Commissioner should not be introduced into the local scene until he can assume his primary function as the personal representative of the President of the United States and thereby be the senior American official present.[36]

According to a memorandum prepared by the War Department for Roosevelt's Chief of Staff General Watson, Secretary of War Stimson agreed with MacArthur's position. Arguing that "neither General MacArthur's authority nor the standing of Osmeña should be diluted by the intervention of any other person," Stimson further suggested that "if the President should insist on the appointment of a High Commissioner that General MacArthur should be that man." Stimson went on to say, however, that he believed that this appointment "would be a mistake as it would confer unnecessary authority on General MacArthur as well as introduce the unpopular idea of a military governor."[37] Attempting to avoid a direct confrontation between MacArthur and his most adamant critic, Secretary of Interior Harold Ickes, the War Department seems to have persuaded Roosevelt to postpone the appointment for the time being.

The issue did not come up for serious discussion again until February 1945. At that time, in response to a query by Secretary of War Stimson, MacArthur repeated his position, reminding Stimson that

> Our history is replete with examples of friction resulting from lack of cooperation and from confusion caused by the reestablishment of civil functionaries prematuraly [*sic*] while our troops were still in active campaign. Coordination in order to attain a maximum effort against the enemy is difficult enough when it involves only the two agencies of the War Department and the Philippine Government. To inject into this scene the Interior Department in the person of the High Commissioner cannot fail to bring about deterioration of existing conditions and to prejudice the mustering of our full offensive potentiality. . . .[38]

Once again reminded of his father's experience in the Philippines at the turn of the century, MacArthur seemed determined that he would not be placed in the same position. His power would remain absolute so long as he remained in Manila. Not until Japan had been defeated would the Truman administration in Washington appoint a high commissioner to the Philippines. By that time, MacArthur knew that his departure from the Islands was imminent.

Clearly MacArthur's influence undermined the attempts of the Osmeña government to implement some of Washington's policies regarding the Philippines. Moreover, by attempting to oversee both military affairs and civilian reconstruction without help from a high commissioner's office, he undoubtedly weakened the efficiency of the rehabilitation efforts, and in the process, Osmeña's standing with his people. These realities notwithstanding, the General's actions really only helped to replace one faction of the prewar governing elite with another faction from the same class. More important to the future of the Islands after independence in 1946 was the fact that no real restructuring of power occurred in this period. Given the opportunity to adjust the wide disparities of income and control which had existed in the Philippines throughout the entire colonial period, the American government instead encouraged prewar economic arrangements to continue along the same lines. By insisting that American economic interests in the Philippines be given parity with those of Filipinos after independence in return for U.S. reconstruction aid, officials in Washington, supported by Roxas's government in Manila, eased the immediate situation but insured long-range dislocations and extensive popular unrest for the new nation.[39] While MacArthur was often in conflict with planners in Washington during this period, his identification with the prewar oligarchy was such that he never questioned these decisions. He believed instead that the old friends in Manila who shared his own conservative views concerning arrangements of power were unquestionably the ones who should continue in control of the government.

As the issues in the debate concerning Philippine-American relations after independence became more clearly defined, MacArthur found himself increasingly criticized. Not only did the Ickes faction in Washington continue its attack, but progressive Filipinos began to raise questions concerning the wisdom of his position. Fearing that their wartime sacrifice was not fully appreciated by the new administration in Washington, they argued for more aid and, in some cases, for a change in the economic relationships now being devised in the U.S. Congress under the Bell Act. Since both Roxas and Osmeña seemed powerless to change Washington's stand on these issues, the upcoming election between the two held very little promise of a solution. As this reality became clear, some groups in the Philippines increased their efforts to change the situation by force, and although this movement would not fully develop until after MacArthur's departure to Japan, its implications nonetheless disturbed him.[40]

Although MacArthur had always seen Washington as an adversary, these new developments in the Islands caused him to revise his opinion of his Philippine sanctuary. Not only was his alliance with Roxas and the Manila elite more frequently assaulted, but his insistence on his own power and control was increasingly seen as unnecessary. More unbearably, rumors began to spread concerning MacArthur's personal financial alliances with members of the Manila oligarchy. It was even suggested that some of his decisions concerning rescue operations, and, indeed, his very support of the Bell Trade Act, hinged on these relationships. MacArthur later denied these suggestions in a statement to the press.

My attention has been called to statements recently made that I have large business and commercial interests in the Philippines and that I had associations with industrial leaders engaged in large enterprises with political backgrounds and implications.

I possess no property or land holdings there. My only Philippine belongings are some shares of mining stock bought on the stock exchange as investment many years before the war. . . .

I have never had the slightest contact with political life in the Philippines and have remained aloof from all activities there outside of military ones.[41]

This statement, issued after his arrival in Tokyo, is clearly more than a denial of questionable economic practices. While these accusations against his personal honor undoubtedly infuriated the General, they were perhaps without foundation and therefore he could convince himself of their unimportance. The criticisms of his official position as a representative of the United States in the Philippines were another matter. No matter how frequently he issued statements to the contrary, he faced growing disapproval of his public involvement in civil matters. If he did not personally involve himself in the economic arrangements of his friends in Manila, there could be no question that he had professionally involved himself in their political machinations. While he might be able to rationalize his activity as necessary to the next phase of his military campaign, this stance became more and more difficult to maintain. As a result, the opportunity to leave the Philippines for a more important role on the world's stage began to look increasingly inviting.

As early as March 1945, MacArthur had received the first hint from Roosevelt that he would lead the Allied invasion of Japan. Although he discounted the likelihood of this assignment, he was clearly intrigued by its possibilities.[42] On April 3, the decision was made official when MacArthur was appointed commander in chief of United States Army Forces, Pacific (AF-PAC), and given control over all American Army and Army Air Forces in the Pacific.[43] From that moment on, much of his energy went into the planning for this momentous undertaking. As the situation in the Philippines became more complex and as the General became the target of more and more obloquy, this venture—the culmination of his efforts of the past four years—undoubtedly began to seem a possible escape route. If he could not achieve his goals in the Philippines as he had planned since 1935, he would insure his place in history in this larger and more important arena.

In the next four months, planning progressed for the Allied invasion. Although command conflicts continued as they had throughout the entire war, target dates were set for early fall, and the General became more and more involved in this final task. On August 6, the situation changed abruptly when an atomic bomb was dropped on Hiroshima. Three days later Nagasaki also became a target for the new terror. Although not informed of the potential attack until just before it occurred, and judging this drastic action to be unnecessary, MacArthur joined in the Allied celebration of the war's end. Before he had time to question his own next step, he received word from President Truman of his appointment as supreme commander for the Allied Powers (SCAP). In this official capacity, he would not only assume responsibility for the Japanese occupation, but would also preside at the Japanese surrender ceremony.[44] No greater opportunity could have come his way.

In the two weeks between V-J day, when MacArthur received word of his next assignment, and August 30, when he arrived in Japan, much of his attention was diverted from the Philippine situation to the larger issues in the entire Pacific. As a result, planners in Washington took steps to reassert their control in Manila. Almost immediately, Truman appointed Paul McNutt high commissioner to the Philippines. Ickes, who had long recommended this action, was delighted.

> I said to the President that now that MacArthur had been given a bigger theater in which to operate he might no longer object to a High Commissioner. Truman interrupted to say in entire good nature that I couldn't blame on him the appointment of MacArthur as the chief commander in the Far East Area. I replied that I agreed with him thoroughly. Politically, he couldn't do anything else. That blame is due to Roosevelt. I remarked that Roosevelt had made a mistake in taking MacArthur away from the Philippines; that he should have left MacArthur to clean up his own mess and taken Wainwright out. Truman agreed, saying that Wainwright was a better soldier. He knows, as do others, that the Philippine campaign under MacArthur was a fiasco.[45]

Despite the private attitude of Ickes, and perhaps that of Truman, most of the world now looked upon Douglas MacArthur as a very important figure. From 1945 to 1951, his efforts to liberalize the Japanese nation, widely publicized through the auspices of his now extensive public relations department, and enhanced by his virtually total control of the occupation certainly validated this judgment. In this period he was able to avoid many of the difficulties with which he had been faced in the Philippines. As he had stated earlier, progressive attitudes on the part of the United States in this effort "will make us the greatest influence on the future development of Asia. If we exert that influence in an imperialistic manner, or for the sole purpose of commercial advantage, then we shall lose our golden opportunity; but if our influence and our strength are expressed in terms of essential liberalism we shall have the friendship and cooperation of the Asiatic people far into the future."[46]

Once again, the General drew upon the attitudes and policies of his father who, in his 1907 address to the Wisconsin Bankers Association, had argued for progressive "tuitionates" in the Pacific. Seasoning this advice with his own long experience in the Philippines, MacArthur determined that this, his last chance for glory, would not be clouded by the mistakes of his final period in the Philippines.

Douglas MacArthur left the Philippines in late August 1945, and returned only once during his remaining years in the Pacific for a brief visit in July 1946 to participate in the inauguration of the now independent Republic.[47] Despite his attempt to glorify the occasion in his public statements that day, he could not help but recognize the continuing misery present all around him in the city. In the words of one commentator,

Manila was a quagmire in the rainy season; and in the hot season the red dust above the city, thrown up by heavy army traffic, made it look from a distance, afire. The city was full of jerry-built shelters, and its hasty bazaars were full of gimcrack goods. Soldiers, sailors, and peddlers jammed its sidewalks; whores and pimps and pickpockets, confidence men and influence mongers; ex-guerrillas still in jungle uniform, and throngs of common men and women,

tired and unemployed. To one observer who had loved the old
city, the new Manila looked like a carnival in hell.[48]

No matter how optimistic his public statements were that day,
the General could not help but be aware of the devastation
around him. Never again could this city, or these Islands, provide the safe shelter and bolstering influence that they had given
to him so generously in his earlier years. This was a loss from
which, despite his future achievements, Douglas MacArthur
would never fully recover.

Epilogue

ON JULY 3, 1961, retired General of the Army Douglas MacArthur and his wife Jean returned one last time to the Philippine Islands. During the next nine days they would help to celebrate the fifteenth anniversary of the nation's independence as personal emissaries of United States President John F. Kennedy. Described by the General as "a sentimental journey,"[1] the trip at one level provided an opportunity for a grateful nation to reward one of its greatest heroes.

Honored at the many sites of his previous adventures in the archipelago, the MacArthurs visited the scenes of his World War II victories at Tacloban and Lingayen. At Iloilo City, he once again recalled his first assignment there in 1903. The MacArthur Highway from Lingayen to Manila was formally dedicated at this time, and the General received honorary degrees from two Philippine universities.[2] In his response to the greeting of Philippine President Carlos P. Garcia at Balagbag Airport, MacArthur characteristically assessed the meaning of this last visit.

I have returned. . . . I am once again in this land that I have known so well and amongst these people that I have loved so well. . . .

When your distinguished President invited me to come once again to these friendly shores, I felt as though I were at last really coming home, for it was here I lived my greatest moments and it is of here I have my greatest memories.

. . . in spite [of] my long absence, you have in all your broad land no more loyal and devoted Filipino. . . . I thank you with my full heart for this opportunity to renew old ties and old friendships and I anticipate the next few days as amongst the happiest of my life.[3]

On the surface, the visit seemed to be a fitting coda to the long and often happy MacArthur experience in the Philippines.

And yet, reflections of the pain and anger which had developed in the last years of the General's tenure in the Islands were obvious. Antagonisms rooted in the early years of the Commonwealth and nurtured by the trauma of the war and the postwar conflicts between the Philippines and the United States were now more clearly defined. Critics voiced resentment at the honors bestowed on MacArthur. As Teodoro F. Valencia argued in a previsit column in the *Manila Times:*

We are relieved to know that no special session [of the Legislature] will be held for General MacArthur. If the special session had been held, it would have created the wrong impression in the United States that Filipinos actually give all credit to the USA for their liberation and independence. . . . Even now, we are already taken for granted by the USA. Idolatry for MacArthur at this time would encourage American policymakers to put the Philippines in the general category of furniture to be moved about at will.

True enough the American armed forces helped liberate the Philippines but it took Filipinos three years of guerrilla action to enable MacArthur to come back with the ease and confidence that he did. The Philippines that America liberated was American territory and it may be presumed they did not do it for the Filipinos only but more to redeem American prestige or perhaps to use the Philippines as a staging area for the onward march towards Japan.[4]

Even more extreme in his rejection of MacArthur's hero status was Ignacio P. Lacsina:

All this ballyhoo about MacArthur as some sort of "hero" to be venerated by the Filipino people is utterly nauseating. History shows that MacArthur never regarded the Filipinos as anything more than expendable pawns in his bloody game of chess with the Japanese during the last war.

When the Japanese needed to be stalled some place in order that preparations might be made to save such valuable American allies as the Australians from being engulfed by the mighty Japanese war tide, MacArthur decided on Bataan and Corregidor. To make the gullible Filipinos stick to their posts, he ordered his propaganda corps to spread the rumors that aid was forthcoming.

When a staging area was needed for the invasion of the Japanese mainland, MacArthur proposed the Philippines. Threatening to quit if he did not have his way, he was able to secure the reluctant approval of the late President Roosevelt who entertained serious fears that the Philippine campaign might prove too costly to the Filipinos. Roosevelt was right. For greater destruction in terms of Filipino life and property was suffered during MacArthur's "return" than during the Japanese invasion and the whole period of the occupation.[5]

Although admittedly representing only one faction of Philippine opinion in the early sixties, and certainly attributing more foresight to Roosevelt and more cynicism to MacArthur than was really the case, this interpretation is significant because it convincingly revealed that many Filipinos no longer viewed Douglas MacArthur, nor the country he symbolized, as a benefactor. As a result, the General's postwar decision to leave the Islands once and for all is more easily understood.

Almost from the very beginning of American involvement in the Philippines Douglas MacArthur was an active participant. Indeed, long before the colonial empire became a reality, his father, Arthur MacArthur, had foreseen its potential importance. His assumptions, stated so clearly in the early 1880s, were more firmly fixed during the years in which he served in the Islands both as military commander and governor. His experience in battle and in the political realm convinced Arthur MacArthur that the Filipinos were both equal adversaries in conflict and viable leaders of an eventually independent nation. For a long time he stood alone among the American military leaders of his generation in this assessment. Nonetheless, his

strongly held opinions in this regard exerted a substantial influence upon the developing attitudes of his son, Douglas MacArthur. Because the younger man so completely patterned his own
beliefs after the opinions of his father throughout his life, their
agreement concerning the Philippines and the Filipinos, as one
of their first shared professional concerns, has special significance.

If, of course, this shared concern had been an isolated one,
its importance would have been minimal. But this was not the
case. Because Douglas MacArthur's first professional experience was also in the Philippines, and because he returned there
again and again at various stages of his career, the Islands
became one of the primary factors which shaped his entire view
of the world, and through that view is revealed the broader
canvas of MacArthur's personality and motivation. Each sojourn
there added additional experience he would use in other arenas.
In addition, his father's special interest helped to define the
Philippines as an appropriate place within which the younger
MacArthur could work out the tensions and anxieties inspired
by his early experiences and the enormous expectations that his
family imposed upon him.

MacArthur's first year in the Islands, in 1903–1904, provided the earliest level of this experience. Because he found
danger in his provincial adventures there, and met that danger
with success, the Islands became for him the frontier he had
dreamed of during his childhood. Since he was born too late to
succeed militarily in the American West, the Philippines provided him with a second chance. In addition, during this first
year, the months in Manila provided opportunities for him to
succeed within the bureaucracy of the increasingly modernized
American military establishment. The world for which he had
prepared as a child was changing. No longer could success be
attained entirely through battle. By the turn of the century military success of the sort to which Douglas MacArthur aspired
required an understanding of command relationships and polit-
ical-military power. In his staff experience in Manila he achieved
promotion and special recognition from future American and
Filipino leaders. His success in the capital, coupled with his

earlier, more conventional adventures in Panay, allowed him to define the Philippines as a locale within which he could fulfill his nineteenth-century romantic visions of military life as well as the less exciting but equally necessary relationships of power required by the twentieth century.

This year, followed almost immediately by the reconfirming experience of the Oriental tour he shared with his parents, defined for MacArthur the realities of the various colonial relationships of Southeast Asia. He concluded this part of his life with the firm conviction that he understood the Philippines in the neo-imperialist context of the period. This understanding continued to shape his view of his own responsibilities in that world for the rest of his life. Thereafter, with each return to the Islands until 1945, his longstanding ambitions were spurred by the place which he continued to define as important, and therefore increasingly appropriate for his success.

In the second period, between 1922 and 1925, the Philippines once again fulfilled his expectations. Arriving there as the result of what he perceived as unfair treatment in Washington, he was able to face the somewhat muted danger of the Philippine mutiny with great success. More importantly, he established a relationship with Leonard Wood which helped him to attain his next promotion. In addition, he very carefully continued to maintain his friendship with Manuel Quezon in a situation which often required the reticence and diplomacy he had been unable to acquire in the periods between these two Philippine assignments. Once again, the Philippines had provided a setting for success which seemed to escape him elsewhere.

In 1928, returning to the Islands in a position of considerable importance, he found solace, which helped him to recover from the personal failure of his first marriage, and professional encouragement from Quezon, which, although it did not lead to his appointment as governor general, certainly did not hinder his subsequent assignment as chief of staff. In both the more securely cemented alliance with the Filipino leader and the personal relationship with Isabel Cooper, MacArthur once again bolstered his somewhat weakened self-image during an assignment in the archipelago.

As Chief of Staff between 1930 and 1935, MacArthur met with uneven success. Both the economic and political situations in the United States frustrated his plans, and his response to the Bonus Expeditionary Force tarnished his public image. His career ascent seemed likely to diminish when he returned to regular military duty at the end of his service in the War Department. His personal security, so long founded on the support he derived from his mother's strong personality and ambitions for him, seemed destined to collapse with her now predictable demise. Once again the Philippines offered an opportunity which might allow him to escape these realities. As Military Adviser to the new Philippine Commonwealth, he could continue to exert substantial influence on an area of the world that he sincerely believed was vital to America in the polarizing international situation. In addition, the friendship and respect that the Filipinos had always provided might give him the personal support he would need so desperately once his mother was gone. Although the threat to peace and its disruption in the Pacific during MacArthur's last years in the Philippines between 1935 and 1942 made his tenure there less successful than his other tours of duty, he nonetheless achieved in his own mind some of the goals so necessary to both his professional and personal stability. As Field Marshal of the Philippine Army, and later as Commanding General of the USAFFE forces, he was rescued from the early retirement which would almost certainly have occurred in the United States. As successful husband and father, he acquired a new lease on his personal life at an age when achievements of this sort seemed unlikely. Again, the Philippines fulfilled central needs for the General.

Although the international situation beyond the Philippine realm forced MacArthur's departure in 1942, his carefully planned return to the Islands shaped much of the wartime strategy of 1943 and 1944. There was every indication that he wanted to live out his final years in the archipelago until his sudden assignment as Supreme Commander for the Allied Powers in Japan in August 1945. Greater opportunities called, and the Philippine haven to which he had so often returned had been altered almost beyond recognition by the war. With a relief which he rationalized as the call to greater duty and responsibility, he moved on. Except for two brief ceremonial visits, he never again returned to the now-changed island nation.

His final disillusionment with the Philippines does nothing to negate the importance of the Islands for Douglas MacArthur's earlier personal and public development. During the first sixty years of his life, MacArthur was shaped by many forces. Certainly paramount among these were the familial influences and traumas brought about by his brother's death, his own sensitivity, and his intensely close relationship with his mother. While these early experiences undoubtedly laid the foundation for MacArthur's basic personality structure, his adult responses cannot completely be explained on the basis of this understanding alone. The tensions and anxieties which first developed in his youth engendered defenses and responses which met with varying degrees of success. Those successful responses were then incorporated into his future patterns of adaptation. Thus, to reach an understanding of Douglas MacArthur, in the broadest sense, it is necessary to isolate those developmental strategies which worked best for him. One of these was undoubtedly a periodic retreat to the island haven which from the outset had provided him with a structure which supported his psychic needs.

MacArthur's early anxiety, inspired by Malcolm's loss, forced him for the rest of his life to substantiate his autonomy within the confines of his now-exaggerated need for parental protection and approval. Since his family saw the Philippines as a suitable arena for his professional development, the Islands were soon defined by Douglas as a place where he could test himself with less threat than he perceived in the rest of the world. His experiences there, particularly during his first three tours, confirmed his earliest perceptions. There he could meet danger, both physical and political, with success. His early understanding of the Philippines as a place of safe success combined with the frequent opportunities his career provided for him to return there. As a result, the Islands eventually became the one place which offered the security of a home, in its truest sense, while also providing a convenient staging ground for his next attempts at success in the outside world.

In a partial and developmental biography such as this it is necessary to consider both the basic personality structure of the individual and the various situations to which he returned regularly. These regularly recurring incidents and environments must be selected for careful analysis in order to identify the patterns which developed within them and which, then, shaped and influenced the larger career. For Douglas MacArthur, the Philippines provided such an environment. At the beginning of his career, after his first major success in World War I, before his highest professional achievement as Chief of Staff, and again at the peak of his worldwide success, MacArthur returned to the Philippines. There both professionally and personally he established and re-established the patterns which, when transferred to other places, would define his life. There he first tested the bravery which would bring such acclaim in World War I. There he practiced the political expertise which led to his rapid advancement in the military establishment of the twenties and early thirties. There, as Military Adviser to a new nation, he believed that he had reached the pinnacle of power available to him at the time. There, also, he first achieved a personal intimacy, which may later, under more satisfactory conditions, have encouraged his successful second marriage. On both private and public levels, the Philippine Islands provided an environment and experience that Douglas MacArthur incorporated into the other arenas of his long life. And when, in 1944 and 1945, the Philippines no longer provided that haven and support, he left it willingly, indeed abandoned it as quickly as possible, ready now to stride on to the larger stage for which history better remembers him.

In the minds of many, Douglas MacArthur has taken on an aura of heroism well beyond the capacity of any human being to sustain. His own attempts at creating this myth, coupled with the efforts of some of those who knew him, have encouraged this vision. As the historical perspective broadens, however, a reassessment is possible and, indeed, necessary, if the General is to take his true place in history. As a biographer of another hero has argued, "By stripping him of his flesh-and-blood traits and enshrining him as a flawless deity, the myth-makers have denied him something to which he's entitled: his right to be remembered as a human being."[6]

This study has not meant to denigrate the greatness which rightfully adheres to Douglas MacArthur. Instead, it has attempted to examine a dimension of the man usually disregarded, yet common to all. Public action is always on one level inextricably linked to private needs. By accepting the rewards of public office, a leader relinquishes his or her right to deny observers access to the inner springs of motivation which shape this public action. It is the historian's duty to lay bare such private concerns to the fullest extent possible in order to encourage greater understanding and appreciation of the advantages and burdens of leadership in both those who assume its mantle, and those who follow.

Notes

For publication purposes, many of the notes originally attached to this work have been cut. Interested readers and scholars in the field are referred to Carol M. Petillo, "Douglas MacArthur: The Philippine Years" (Ph.D. dissertation, Rutgers University, 1979).

Key to Abbreviations in Notes

DDEL	Dwight D. Eisenhower Library
LC	Library of Congress
MMBA	MacArthur Memorial Bureau of Archives
NA	National Archives
NNFN	Natural Resources Branch
NNG	General Archives Branch
NNMM	Modern Military Branch
NNMO	Navy and Old Army Branch
OCMH	Office of the Center of Military History
PNL	Philippine National Library
FDRL	Franklin D. Roosevelt Library
USAMHI	United States Army Military History Institute
USMA	United States Military Academy
UP	University of the Philippines
VF	Vargas Foundation
YUL	Yale University Library

Chapter One: The Early Years

1. John Gunther, *The Riddle of MacArthur, Japan, Korea and the Far East* (New York, 1950), 32. Earlier, in 1942, in a letter to the chairman of the committee dedicating a memorial commemorating his father's birthplace, the General stated unequivocally: "Of all men I have known my father was the one I most

respected and admired." MacArthur to Moriarity, 9–8–42, Folder #6, RG 26, MMBA.

2. The choice of names in the MacArthur family is confusing. It is helpful to remember that the grandfather (Arthur), father (Arthur, Jr.), eldest brother (Arthur II), and son (Arthur III) of General Douglas MacArthur shared the same first name.

3. The details of family background which follow have been drawn from Douglas MacArthur, *Reminiscences* (New York, 1964), 7–25; D. Clayton James, *The Years of MacArthur* (2 vols. Boston, 1970–75), I, 7–31; Frazier Hunt, *The Untold Story of Douglas MacArthur* (New York, 1954), 3–12; and Conklin Mann, "Some Ancestral Lines of General Douglas MacArthur," *The New York Genealogical and Biographical Record,* LXXIII (July, 1942), 167–172.

4. Operations Report of Lt. E. K. Holton, January 1863, quoted in James, *Years,* I, 14.

5. MacArthur, *Reminiscences,* 12–13. For a more objective description of the event but one which still emphasizes the importance of Arthur MacArthur, Jr.'s part in the battle, see James, *Years,* I, 14–15. It is interesting to note that the Congressional Medal of Honor given to MacArthur for this action was not awarded until 1890 when he himself was serving in the Adjutant General's Office in Washington and that the first published appearance of the Missionary Ridge adventure bearing a resemblance to Douglas MacArthur's later account did not appear until 1900 when Arthur MacArthur, Jr.'s friend, Major J. A. Watrous, USA, recounted it in an article entitled "How the Boy Won: General MacArthur's First Victory," *Saturday Evening Post,* February 24, 1900. I am indebted to Dr. Henry I. Tragle, a specialist in early MacArthur and Hardy family history, for this information. Tragle to author, October 15, 1979.

6. John Hersey, *Men of Bataan* (New York, 1943), 45; and William Manchester, *American Caesar* (Boston, 1978), 16.

7. 228.03 Permanent HRC 201 file for Arthur MacArthur, Jr., OCMH.

8. Mann, "Some Ancestral Lines," 172.

9. Russell F. Weigley, *History of the United States Army* (New York, 1967), 265–292; and William A. Ganoe, *The History of the United States Army* (rev. ed., New York, 1942), 298–354.

10. Arthur MacArthur, Jr.'s assignments are documented in 228.03 Permanent HRC 201 file, OCMH. See also "History of the 13th U.S. Infantry," RG 15, MMBA.

11. Philippe Régis de Trobriand, *Military Life in Dakota: The Journal of Philippe Régis de Trobriand,* trans. and ed. Lucile M. Kane (St. Paul, 1951); and James, *Years,* I, 20–21.

12. MacArthur to Randall, Oct. 10, 1866, in AGO #5551 (Arthur MacArthur, Jr., Appointment, Commission and Personal File), NNMO, NA.

13. Arthur MacArthur, Sr., to A. W. Randall, Sept. 20, 1866, and March 15, 1867; Arthur MacArthur, Jr., to AG, December 6, 1867, May 27, 1870, and July 24, 1874, in AGO #5551, NNMO, NA.

14. This outline of the early years of Mary Hardy MacArthur is drawn from information found in the "Hardy Family File," Norfolk Public Library, Norfolk Va.; Hardy family correspondence, deeds, and wills found in "Documents Donated by the General Public," RG 15, MMBA; and MacArthur, *Reminiscences,* 19.

15. Although Douglas and his mother later tended to refer to the Hardy soldiers as Confederate heroes, their careers seem to have been without dis-

tinction during the war. One Hardy fought with the VMI cadets at the Battle of New Market, but another had been expelled from the same school before the war for drunkenness.

16. Letters written by Mrs. Elizabeth Pierce Hardy, Thomas's widow, in the years preceding her death in 1881, reflect this hardship and mention a struggle between Charles Hardy, his father's executor, and Thomas, Jr., apparently the family ne'er-do-well, in connection with money from their father's estate. See, particularly, "Mother" to "Missy" (Mary Hardy MacArthur's sister), April 30, 1877, RG 15, MMBA.

17. All the letters which have survived from these years reflect the resentment and dissatisfaction which Mrs. Hardy held toward her children. She felt neglected, and believed that she should have been more careful concerning their early upbringing. See "Mother" to "Missie," letters written between April 1877 and June 1878, RG 15, MMBA.

18. For an astute and helpful discussion of the realities faced by military wives in the Southwest during this period, see Frances M. A. Roe, *Army Letters from an Officer's Wife* (New York, 1909), passim.

19. Eleanor P. Cushman to Douglas MacArthur, May 10, 1944, RG 10, MMBA.

20. For a description of Arthur MacArthur during the Fort Wingate years, see Edward Brown to Douglas MacArthur, Oct. 16, 1937, RG 1, MMBA. Brown, who served as schoolmaster at Fort Wingate in 1882, remembered that the Captain "never frequented their [the other officers] club room or took much part in their social affairs." He also made an interesting comparison between MacArthur and Adna Chaffee, serving as Captain of Cavalry at Wingate at the time. Chaffee, "rough and profane," apparently achieved a loyal response from his men different from their respect for MacArthur. This contrast became more obvious in the later careers of the two men (see chapter three).

21. Although in later years Douglas always referred to his brother, Arthur, with respect, there is no evidence to suggest that the two ever developed a close relationship. This can probably be accounted for by the fact that Arthur II left home when Douglas was only thirteen, just at the time when the difference in their ages would have begun to matter less. In addition, we may speculate that Arthur II, given an earlier opportunity to develop a relationship with his father, may have had a special position with the Captain. Douglas, on the other hand, always belonged to Pinkie.

22. The significant fact that all the MacArthur boys were ill during this period is mentioned in wires from Arthur MacArthur, Jr., to AG, April 9 and 13, 1883, AGO #5551, NNMO, NA. For evidence supporting the idea that the MacArthurs went East regarding settlement of the Hardy estate, see Arthur MacArthur, Jr., to AG, September 15, 1882, AGO #5551, NNMO, NA.

23. Much of the insight reflected in this discussion grows out of A. C. Cain, I. Fast, and M. E. Erickson, "Children's Disturbed Reactions to the Death of a Sibling," *American Journal of Orthopsychiatry,* 34 (1964), 741–752. See also George H. Pollock, "Childhood Parent and Sibling Loss in Adult Patients," *Archives General Psychiatry,* 7 (1962), 295–305.

24. Readers familiar with the work of Erik Erikson will recognize the phase which I have described as Erikson's third psychosocial developmental phase: "Initiative vs. guilt." Freudian theory categorizes this developmental phase as the first oedipal stage. Conflict at this stage in Douglas's life may also have

confused his nascent sexual identity, but there is no evidence to support this contention for these years. The question of sexual adjustment will be raised again later in this chapter and in chapters four and five. (See Introduction for a more complete discussion of the Eriksonian model and my use of it in this study.)

25. George H. Pollock, "On Mourning, Immortality, and Utopia," *Journal of American Psychoanalytic Association,* Vol. 23 (2) (1975), 334–362.

26. The belief in certain great men that they have been chosen by destiny is not uncommon. Both Isaac Newton, who survived premature birth, and John Wesley, who escaped a family fire, seem to have been influenced by this attitude. See Robert L. Moore, "Justification Without Joy: Psychohistorical Reflections on John Wesley's Childhood and Conversion," *History of Childhood Quarterly: The Journal of Psychohistory,* II, nr. 1 (Summer, 1974), 31–52; and Frank E. Manuel, *A Portrait of Isaac Newton* (Cambridge, 1968).

27. Her determination to limit her family is evident when she clearly stated that "I am glad to tell you I am not in family way. My pessary is sure I believe." This active choice of a birth-control device reflects a forcefulness of will which, while not uncommon for Pinkie, was less than usual for women of that time period. She probably would have had to make the arrangements for obtaining the device while on one of her trips East, and might have had to visit several doctors before finding one who would supply her with the pessary. That she had gone to these lengths confirms the strength of her decision to escape the fate her mother suffered, and the forthrightness with which she approached her goals. I am grateful to Professor James Reed for a discussion which helped me to understand the realities of late nineteenth-century contraception.

28. "Pink" to "My Precious Sister," May 11, 1884, RG 15, MMBA.

29. MacArthur, *Reminiscences,* 20.

30. Added support of the argument that the adjustment to Malcolm's death was never completely achieved satisfactorily for Douglas may be found in the fact that when he returned in 1951 to Norfolk for the dedication of a memorial to his mother on the site of Riveredge, he was invited to visit his brother's grave in Cedar Grove Cemetery, nearby. He adamantly refused. Although he later arranged for a new gravestone to be placed at the site, he never could bring himself to view the burial place. Conversation with archivist, January 1977, MMBA, and letter from Dr. Henry I. Tragle to author, May 10, 1978, in which he states that Frank Blackford, special feature writer for the *Virginian-Pilot,* accompanied the MacArthurs during this 1951 visit to Norfolk and was "especially puzzled by the fact that MacArthur flatly refused to visit Malcolm's grave in Cedar Grove Cemetery."

31. MacArthur, *Reminiscences,* 20.

32. Pictures of the MacArthur family, c. 1885, showing Douglas in curls and costume are preserved in the MacArthur Archives in Norfolk. Although little boys often did not have their first haircut before school age in the late nineteenth century, the difficulties and incongruities of this attire in a dusty fort in the New Mexico wildlands attested to Pinkie's determination in this regard.

33. MacArthur, *Reminiscences,* 20.

34. MacArthur, *Reminiscences,* 21–22; and James, *Years,* I, 27–28.

35. For a discussion of the increased importance of schooling in adolescent development in the late nineteenth century, see Joseph F. Kett, *Rites of Passage, Adolescence in America 1790 to the Present* (New York, 1977), 144–211.

36. MacArthur, *Reminiscences,* 22.

37. Ibid.

38. Kelton to MacArthur, n.d., quoted in James, *Years,* I, 29.

39. Information concerning Douglas MacArthur's years at the West Texas Military Academy is derived from "Annual Catalogues of the West Texas Military Academy," 1893–1898, RG 15, MMBA.

40. MacArthur, *Reminiscences,* 23; in addition, the "Annual Catalogues" confirm MacArthur's high academic standing in his four years at the academy. See also James, *Years,* I, 645, n.18.

41. For a perceptive discussion of the developing awareness of this group in connection with the teenage years, see Kett, *Rites of Passage,* 215–243. Kett explains that while working-class youths were still expected by their subculture to mature earlier, the prolongation of educational preparation for young people of the middle and upper classes allowed these years to take on more significance. Middle-class youths at this age were no longer faced with the immediate necessity to become self-supporting. Obversely, their status in these years also lacked the confirmation that society still reserved for its fully producing members. These conflicting tendencies resulted in heightened stress for the individuals going through this developmental phase, but also provided them with a culturally sanctioned period of time during which they could evaluate and define their future place in the world. This time period was not unlike the one reflected in Erik Erikson's concept of a moratorium. See Erik H. Erikson, "Ego Identity and the Psychosocial Moratorium," in Helen Witmer and Ruth Kotinsky, *New Perspectives for Research* (Washington, D.C., 1956), 5.

42. See D. Clayton James in *Years,* I, 58–62, for the detail from which I have extracted the information pertinent to the following discussion.

43. MacArthur, *Reminiscences,* 23.

44. Again, it should be clear that much of this discussion is based on Erikson's continuing definition of the tasks involved in the fifth stage of his developmental model, most commonly referred to as the identity crisis. Although this theory is exemplified in many of Erikson's own writings, I have found most helpful a clarification provided by Helen L. Witmer, "Delinquency and the Adolescent Crisis," in *Facts and Facets,* No. 11 (Washington, D.C., 1960), and quoted and further explained in Henry I. Maier, *Three Theories of Child Development* (New York, 1965), 58–60. The argument made by Erikson and clarified by Witmer and Maier suggests that seven tasks must be successfully accomplished before identity formation is complete for this phase. They include the successful use of time, the establishment of more self-certainty, the assumption of a self-satisfying role within one's culture, development of the ability to work in appropriate arenas, definition of an adequate sexual identity, the nurturing of leadership skills, and the assumption of ideals and values which help the individual to understand a world which is perceived as increasingly complex. While this model is by no means the only way to understand the growth which occurs during the adolescent years, it does, I believe, clarify some of the issues of the period.

For a discussion of the increased passivity of the generation of which Douglas MacArthur was a member, see Kett, *Rites of Passage,* 174–211.

45. MacArthur, *Reminiscences,* 23.

46. Although it is impossible to document, based on the sources available from these years, this failure to separate himself successfully from his mother may also have affected his establishment of a mature sexual identity. Certainly, everything we know about his later attempts at sexual intimacy with women seems to substantiate the existence of a problem in this area (see chapters four

and five). In Freudian and neo-Freudian terms, the argument might be put forth that the genital phase of his development had been disrupted by Malcolm's death when MacArthur was three. This disruption may have led to a failure on Douglas's part to accept the impossibility of his mother as a sexual object. Later, as an adolescent, he was once again faced with the necessity of establishing a personally viable and socially acceptable sexual separation from his mother. He may have failed again, but this time successfully sublimated the energy generated by this unresolved conflict into his academic and extracurricular achievements. Certainly there must be no attempt to reduce the sources of MacArthur's remarkable success to any one determinant. This interpretation should, then, be considered as a possible explanation of one of the many influences, both internal and external, which propelled him onward.

47. Quoted in Manchester, *American Caesar,* 44.

48. MacArthur, *Reminiscences,* 24.

49. Ibid.

50. Both James, *Years,* I, 64–65, and Manchester, *American Caesar,* 47–48, suggest that it was at this point that Douglas began to develop a more extensive interest in the young ladies available to him in Milwaukee. Their argument is apparently based on a misreading of an earlier source (Clark Lee and Richard Henschel, *Douglas MacArthur* [New York, 1952], 46–47) which, upon closer examination, states that the love poetry MacArthur wrote to one of the sisters of his friend, Billy Mitchell, was produced after his return from duty in Asia in 1906. This apparently minor point becomes significant to my later argument in chapter four.

51. Interestingly, their last months at the Plankinton House were interrupted one night by a fire in the wing of the hotel they occupied. The two barely escaped. It is possible that this brush with danger convinced Douglas and Pinkie even further that they had been saved for a purpose. At any rate, the shared escape could only have served to increase their mutual devotion. See James, *Years,* I, 64.

52. MacArthur, *Reminiscences,* 32.

53. For a detailed discussion of MacArthur's hazing, and the reality of his later testimony, see James, *Years,* I, 68–71, and 646, n.4. The complete account of the West Point years that James provides (I, 67–84) is the basis for the following summary. Since these years are well documented in all the MacArthur studies, it is not my intention to review them to any great extent. Only those points significant to my argument will be examined.

54. Douglas MacArthur File, USMA Archives.

55. Although not as tall as he often appeared in photographs, Douglas MacArthur, at nearly 5'11" was taller than average for that period. In later years, he encouraged this impression by occasionally advising photographers to shoot from below eye-level. Conversation with archivist, January 1977, MMBA.

56. Charles Burton Marshall, "The Very Image of a General," in *The Washington Post,* October 11, 1970.

Chapter Two: The First MacArthur in the Philippines

1. This brief summary of Philippine history has been drawn largely from Teodoro A. Agoncillo and Milagros C. Guerrero, *History of the Filipino People* (Quezon City, P.I., 1977), 1–244.

2. Leon Wolff, *Little Brown Brother* (Makati, P.I., 1960), 66–88.

3. Weigley, *History*, 265–312, and 313–344.

4. Superintendent's Letter Book, 1901, #12, 6, USMA Archives.

5. "Cadet Record of Douglas MacArthur, USMA Class of 1903," Special Collection, Douglas MacArthur File, USMA.

6. Hunt, *Untold Story*, 34.

7. See A. MacArthur to W. H. Taft, Feb. 4, 1905, War Dept., and Grant to MacArthur, June 10, 1883, War Dept., Historical Record, G-2, War Dept. Corr.: "Accounts, etc., Maj. Gen. MacArthur, Military Observer, Jap. Army, Russo-Jap. War.," (hereafter cited as AHF), NNMO, NA.

8. Charles B. Elliott, *The Philippines to the End of the Military Regime* (Indianapolis, 1916), 485.

9. See Volunteer Record, Arthur MacArthur, Jr., March 7, 1882, 2, AGO #5551, NNMO, NA; and Weigley, *History*, 281.

10. See Walter LaFeber, *The New Empire* (Ithaca, 1963), 80–85.

11. It is interesting to note that not all of the MacArthurs were as happy with the General's assignment. When the orders arrived in June, Mary MacArthur wired Adjutant General Henry C. Corbin to plead that he change her husband's orders to "anything else but this [the Philippines]." Since Mrs. MacArthur's ambitions for her husband were longstanding, this curious request can probably best be explained by the fact that most Americans were convinced that the important engagements of the Spanish-American War would occur in Cuba, for which Arthur MacArthur had originally seemed destined. By August, however, when news of the General's advancement to major general of Volunteers arrived, her wire to Corbin of "a thousand thanks" reflected satisfied acceptance of the turn of events which would place the head of the MacArthur clan as close to the pinnacle of power as he would ever be. See wire from Mary MacArthur to H. C. Corbin, June 12, 1898, and August 27, 1898, AGO #5551, NNMO, NA; and James, *Years*, I, 31.

12. The following account of the Philippine aspect of the Spanish-American War and the Philippine-American Revolution which followed is drawn from *Correspondence Relating to the War With Spain* ... (2 vols., Washington, D.C., 1902), II, 633 and passim; William T. Sexton, *Soldiers in the Sun* (Harrisburg, Pa., 1939) entire; Uldarico S. Baclagon, *Philippine Campaig* (Manila, 1952), and *Military History of the Philippines* (Manila, 1975), entir See also John Morgan Gates, *Schoolbooks and Krags* (Westport, Ct., 1973), entire; Walter Millis, *The Martial Spirit* (Boston, 1931), entire; Wolff, *Little Brown Brother*, entire; James, *Years*, I, 31–40; and MacArthur, *Reminiscences*, 25–31.

13. See David Yancey Thomas, *A History of Military Government in Newly Acquired Territory of the United States* (New York, 1904), 283 and passim; Elliott, *The Philippines*, 433–434; and Gates, *Schoolbooks*, 57.

14. Wolff, *Little Brown Brother*, 136, 180.

15. Compton to Brothers of Psy Upsilon, December 14, 1898, RG 20, MMBA.

16. See "History of the Philippine Scouts, 1899–1934," compiled by Charles H. Franklin, U.S.A., in AGO 314.73 (5–1–35), NNMO, NA.

17. See U.S. Congress, Senate, "Affairs in the Philippine Islands," Hearings Before the Committee on the Philippines of the U.S. Senate, 57th Congress, 1st Sess., 1902 (hereafter cited as Sen. Doc. #331). MacArthur's testimony begins April 7, 1902, Pt. II, 861, and continues, with interruptions, through the end of this section, concluding on May 2, 1902.

18. Gates, *Schoolbooks*, 57; and *Correspondence*, 557.

19. The accounts and assessments of the Philippine-American Revolution which follow have been drawn largely from Sexton, *Soldiers in the Sun*, 97 and passim, supported by Millis, *The Martial Spirit*, Gates, *Schoolbooks*, and Wolff, *Little Brown Brother*, throughout. In the 1899 effort, MacArthur insisted that Aguinaldo must be captured alive so that the mythmaking advantage of a dead hero would not further encourage the revolutionary thrust.

20. These claims, widely publicized in the United States by the Anti-Imperialist League, led to the 1902 Senate Hearings on Affairs in the Philippines at which Arthur MacArthur and William Howard Taft testified. Since that time, historians have emphasized either the vigor of the American tactics or their moderation in the face of insurgent atrocities. These interpretations seem to depend largely on which revisionist phase was current at the time of publication of the studies. See, for example, Sexton, *Soldiers in the Sun*, 240–242, which stresses the good judgment of the Americans, and Wolff, *Little Brown Brother*, 304–308, which emphasizes just the opposite.

21. The "feud" between Arthur MacArthur and William Howard Taft has long interested historians, partly due to the fame of their sons, partly because Taft's major biographer, Henry F. Pringle, stressed the point in an entertaining, if inaccurate, manner. See Henry F. Pringle, *The Life and Times of William Howard Taft* (2 vols., New York, 1939), I, 167–169. The Taft papers in the Library of Congress contain many complaints concerning the difficulties of working with Arthur MacArthur, while MacArthur chose to remain silent on the issue. The account which follows is taken largely from two more recent, and more detailed, accounts: Rowland T. Berthoff, "Taft and MacArthur, 1900–1901: A Study in Civil-Military Relations," *World Politics*, Vol. 5, # 2 (Jan., 1953); and Ralph Eldin Minger, "Taft, MacArthur, and the Establishment of Civil Government in the Philippines," *The Ohio Historical Quarterly*, Vol. 70, No. 4 (Oct., 1961). See also Ralph Eldin Minger, *William Howard Taft and United States Foreign Policy: The Apprenticeship Years, 1900–1908* (Urbana, Chicago & London, 1975), 42–50.

22. Elliott, *The Philippines*, 521, n.54.

23. Gates, *Schoolbooks*, 106.

24. There can be little doubt that MacArthur, as the highest ranking commissioned officer in the U.S. Army in that period, hoped for the appointment as chief of staff. For correspondence supporting this hope, see Beach to MacArthur, Jan. 13, 1906, AHF, NNMO, NA.

25. Sen. Doc. #331, Pt. II, 1918.

26. For an example of this difference of opinion, see Taft's assessment of the Filipinos in Sen. Doc. #331, Pt. I, 77.

27. Although this attitude is obvious throughout MacArthur's testimony, it is particularly interesting in his discussion of his relationship with Aguinaldo, who was captured during the last months of MacArthur's tenure in the Islands. See Sen. Doc. #331, Pt. II, 1410, and 1948–1949.

28. Again and again MacArthur's relatively advanced racial attitudes were evident, particularly in his indignant response to a question asking him to compare the Filipinos "with the negro." Sen. Doc. #331, Pt. II, 877.

29. Sen. Doc. #331, Pt. II, 894–895.

30. Sen. Doc. #331, Pt. II, 867.

31. See *Report on National Defense in the Philippines* (Manila, 1936), in which Douglas MacArthur reflected much of his father's attitude in 1902. Particularly significant is his argument that "the problem of reducing the Philippine de-

fenses will present to any potential invader such difficult problems as to give pause even to the most ruthless and powerful," 41. (For a more complete discussion of the 1936 Report, see chapter five.)

32. James, *Years,* I, 68.

33. For examples of Arthur MacArthur's clear appreciation of this romantic nature, see Sen. Doc. #331, Pt. II, 1383 and 1898.

34. Agoncillo, *History,* 280–298.

35. The information for this account of the period between 1901 and 1903 is drawn from Agoncillo, *History,* 280–298; and Lewis E. Gleeck, Jr., *The Manila Americans (1901–1964)* (Manila, 1977), 1–49.

36. A full analysis of this period is in Peter W. Stanley, *A Nation in the Making* (Cambridge, Mass., 1974), 51–178.

37. Gleeck, *Manila,* 13–14.

38. Many of the American churches and clubs in Manila were founded during this period, and contemporary accounts suggest that one of their primary goals was a desire to control the excesses of the newly discharged volunteers. See Gleeck, *Manila,* 11.

39. For a complete history of the Army-Navy Club, see Lewis E. Gleeck, Jr., "American Club Life in Old Manila," *Bulletin of American Historical Collection,* Vol. III, #4 (Oct. 1975).

40. Walter Robb, one of the early schoolteachers who later became editor of the *Journal of the American Chamber of Commerce,* and a reliable observer of Manila for many years, provided this account of the evening activity on the Luneta, quoted in Gleeck, *Manila,* 7.

41. Mrs. William Howard Taft, *Recollections of Full Years* (New York, 1914), 108–111; and Charles P. Taft, "Charlie-Baby Taft in the Philippines, 1900–1903," *Bulletin of American Historical Collection,* Vol. II, #3, (July, 1974). See also McMaster Diary, entry for July 31, 1899, Spanish-American War Survey, USAMHI.

Chapter Three: First Assignments

1. Gates, *Schoolbooks,* 286–287.

2. Telford to Farman, March 22, 1942, File "USMA Class of 1903," Douglas MacArthur Special Collection, USMA Archives.

3. The description of the arrival of the *Sherman* has been drawn from the many accounts of travelers of the period, both civil and military, who kept records of their trip and first impressions of Manila. See particularly the William and Grace Paulding Papers, the Charles Gerhardt Papers, and the Fred Arnold Papers, USAMHI; Mary H. Fee, *A Woman's Impressions of The Philippines* (Chicago, 1910), 218–219; and Mrs. Campbell Dauncey, *An Englishwoman in the Philippines* (New York, 1906), 5, 132. The Dauncey and Fee accounts provide a good balance for each other since Fee, a young American teacher recently recruited for Philippine service, conveys a naïveté that Mrs. Dauncey, an experienced but somewhat bigoted traveler, certainly does not.

4. General Order #99, Manila, P.I., October 13, 1903, in "Records of U.S. Army Overseas Operations and Commands, 1898–1942, Entry #2070: "Div. of Phil., General and Special Orders, Circulars 1900–1920," NNMO, NA.

5. 1904 Individual Service Report, AGO #487448 (Douglas MacArthur, Appointment, Commission, and Personal File), NNMO, NA.

6. See David R. Sturtevant, *Popular Uprisings in the Philippines, 1840–1940* (Ithaca, 1976), 119, 129–131. See also undated report on Iloilo and Camp Jossman, Leonard Wood Papers, "Philippine Miscellaneous Material," LC; and "Company 'D,' 8th Infantry, Philippines" in the Charles Gerhardt Papers, USAMHI.

7. MacArthur, *Reminiscences*, 36; "The Harbor that MacArthur Built," *Philippine Free Press*, September 12, 1964, Vol. 57, 55–56; and the many accounts in the Manila newspapers of *ladrón* activity in Panay during this period, particularly, *The Manila America*, October 18, 1903, and February 5, 1904.

8. To clarify the *ladrón* activity, the *ladrónes* were referred to as *ladrónes politicos, ladrónes fanáticos,* or just plain *ladrónes.* Among those *ladrónes fanáticos* encountered by the men at Camp Jossman were the "Pulajanes," a group of religious rebels who continued harassing the Department of the Visayas for the next several years. See Sturtevant, *Popular Uprisings,* 129.

9. Ibid., 127–129.

10. Jackson to War Dept., August 10, 1908, AGO #487448, NNMO, NA. See also Elliott, *The Philippines,* 443–444.

11. Information concerning all of MacArthur's assignments during this period is to be found in his 1904 Individual Service Report, AGO #487448, NNMO, NA. See also "Records of U.S. Army Overseas Operations and Commands 1898–1942; Dept. of Luzon, Roster of Officers, 1901–1909; entry #2070, "Div. of Phil., General & Special Orders, 1902–1905," S.O. 40, Manila, February 27, 1904, NNMO, NA.

12. This account has been drawn from Fee, *A Woman's Impressions;* Dauncey, *An Englishwoman;* and Mrs. Fred Arnold's report of her stay in Manila shortly after MacArthur's, Fred Arnold Papers, USAMHI.

13. *Manila-American,* December 15 and 22, 1903.

14. For the complete report on the War Department investigation of this incident, see AGO #5551, NNMO, NA.

15. President Theodore Roosevelt to Secretary of War, March 7, 1904, in Elting E. Morison and John M. Blum, eds., *The Letters of Theodore Roosevelt* (8 vols., Cambridge, Mass., 1951–1954), IV, 744; and Root to MacArthur, December 22, 1903, in AGO #5551, NNMO, NA.

16. For a particularly grand account of Gov. Taft's forthcoming departure in late December, 1903, see *Manila-American,* October 16, 1903. Further accounts of the festivities and honors which accompanied the departure can be found frequently in that newspaper in November and December. Mention of Chaffee's appointment is to be found in *Manila-American,* January 10, 1904.

17. *Manila-Cablenews,* January 8, and February 18, 1904. The announcement of Forbes's appointment proved also to be premature, and eventually James F. Smith actually succeeded Wright. Forbes was finally appointed governor general in 1909.

18. *Manila-American,* June 11, 1904.

19. See Bell, U.S. Engineers, Spanish-American War Survey, USAMHI; and James, *Years,* I, 89–90.

20. Gleeck, "American Club Life."

21. See Wood to MacArthur, November 19, 1935, file AG 201, MacArthur, Douglas, in "Headquarters, USAF, Far East/USAF, Phil.," NNG, NA; and Bell, U.S. Engineers, Spanish-American War Survey, USAMHI. Bell, a young engineer who shared the first names (James Franklin) but not the prestige of the soon-to-be Chief of Staff of the Army, accompanied MacArthur to the Philip-

pines in 1903, and also lived in the Army-Navy Club. I am indebted to Dr. Forrest Pogue for clarifying this point for me.

22. Guy Henry to Seton Henry, Manila, October 31, 1904, in Henry Papers, USAMHI.

23. Bell, U.S. Engineers, Spanish-American War Survey, USAMHI.

24. Frank E. Vandiver, *Black Jack; The Life and Times of John J. Pershing* (2 vols., College Station, Texas, 1977), I, 424.

25. MacArthur, *Reminiscences,* 37. See also *Manila-American,* June 25, 1904; and Agoncillo, *History,* 292. Correspondence in the James G. Harbord Papers, Personal Letters, Vols. I and II, LC, confirms the close relationship Harbord had with the future Philippine leaders.

26. "Records of U.S. Army Overseas Operations and Commands 1898–1942; Dept. of Luzon," Entry #2070, "Div. of Phil., General and Specific Orders, 1902–1904," S.O. 112, Manila, May 31, 1904, NNMO, NA; *Manila-American,* June 1, 1904; AGO #487448 and AGO #532673, and MacArthur to Military Secretary, September 9, 1904, AGO #487448, NNMO, NA. The anecdote is to be found in Bell, U.S. Engineers, Spanish-American War Survey, USAMHI.

27. AGO #487448, AGO #991816, and U.S.A.—DL, Entry #2070, S.O. 59, 130, and 205, NNMO, NA.

28. Diary for the years 1901–1905, Perry L. Boyer Papers, USAMHI; and Grant to Farman, February 12, 1942, Douglas MacArthur File, Special Collection, USMA Archives.

29. *Manila-American,* June 28, 1904; Boyer Diary, entry for July 13, 1904, USAMHI; and James, *Years,* I, 90.

30. *Manila-American,* August 14, 1904.

31. Individual Service Report, 1905, AGO #487448, NNMO, NA.

32. MacArthur, *Reminiscences,* 34; and James, *Years,* I, 81–82.

33. Bell, U.S. Engineers, Spanish-American War Survey, USAMHI.

34. U.S.A.—DL, Entry #2979, S.O. 205, Manila, October 1, 1904, NNMO, NA; and Grant to Farman, February 12, 1942, Douglas MacArthur File, Special Collection, USMA Archives.

35. *Manila-American,* October 5, 1904.

36. "Memorandum for the Secretary of War," January 13, 1914, in AGO #2116873, NNMO, NA; and John J. Pershing Papers, Special Correspondence, c. 1904–1948, LC; and MacArthur to Military Secretary, January 9, 1907, AGO #1123029, f/w 1101481, NNMO, NA.

37. William H. Taft to John Hay, December 31, 1904; and Ainsworth to MacArthur, January 1, 1905, in AHF, NNMO, NA.

38. Handbury to War Dept., August 19, 1908, in AGO #487448, NNMO, NA.

39. Harts to War Dept., August 8, 1908, in AGO #487448, NNMO, NA.

40. James, *Years,* I, 91.

41. MacArthur, *Reminiscences,* 37.

42. Special Order #229, War Dept., October 3, 1905, in AHF, NNMO, NA. Unless otherwise noted, the material detailing this assignment and the subsequent "reconnaissance" tour of Asia are to be found in this file.

43. MacArthur to Chaffee, December 24, 1904, with attached memorandum of the same date. On February 4, 1904, after receiving Taft's blessing for his proposed observations, MacArthur wrote to the Secretary of War to let him "know something of the eagerness and enthusiasm with which I once investi-

gated Americo-Oriental questions," and enclosed a copy of the 1882 manuscript. MacArthur to Taft, February 4, 1904, also in AHF, NNMO, NA.

44. Beach to MacArthur, January 18, 1905, and Griscom to Hay, March 15, 1905, both in AHF, NNMO, NA.

45. MacArthur to Chaffee, March 24, 1905, AHF, NNMO, NA.

46. MacArthur to Chief, Second Division, General Staff, October 7, 1905, AHF, NNMO, NA.

47. Comment penciled onto the summary by C. H. Muir, November 22, 1905; and MacArthur to Chief, 2nd Div., War Dept., September 21, 1905, AHF, NNMO, NA.

48. MacArthur to Taft, February 4, 1905, AHF, NNMO, NA.

49. Taft to Chief of Staff, February 17, 1905; and Beach to MacArthur, February 20 and 28, 1905, AHF, NNMO, NA.

50. Charles Vevier, *The United States and China 1906–1913: A Study of Finance and Diplomacy* (New York, 1968), 16–34 and passim. See also Richard W. Van Alstyne, *The United States and East Asia* (New York, 1973), 89; James, *Years,* I, 87 and 103; Griscom to Hay, March 15, 1905, AHF, NNMO, NA.

51. Hunt, *Untold Story,* 35.

52. MacArthur to Military Secretary, September 17, 1905, AHF, NNMO, NA.

53. West to Beach, September 19, 1905, AHF, NNMO, NA.

54. Special Order #229, October 3, 1905, AHF, NNMO, NA.

55. West to Beach, November 6, 1905, and "Memorandum of Expenses . . . ," April, 1907, AHF, NNMO, NA. This memorandum is very detailed and provides much of the information used in the following paragraphs.

56. MacArthur to Beach, December 3, 1905.

57. James, *Years,* I, 93; and MacArthur, *Reminiscences,* 39–40.

58. MacArthur, *Reminiscences,* 39; and see Philip Magnus, *Kitchener: Portrait of an Imperialist* (New York, 1959), 196–239.

59. MacArthur, *Reminiscences,* 39. In 1904, Col. Francis E. Younghusband had sought out and negotiated with the "Grand Llama" in order to forestall the continuation of Russia's prewar advance into Tibet.

60. MacArthur to Chief, 2nd Div., War Dept., February 28, and March 20, 1906, AHF, NNMO, NA.

61. MacArthur, *Reminiscences,* 39.

62. Sen. Doc. #331, Pt. II, 876.

63. K. M. Panikkar, *Asia and Western Dominance* (New York, 1969), 171–174; and David Joel Steinberg, ed., *In Search of Southeast Asia* (New York, 1971), 169–196.

64. King to Root, April 10, 1906, AHF, NNMO, NA.

65. I am indebted to Colonel William F. Strobridge of the Center of Military History, Washington, D.C., who brought this diary to my attention and kindly allowed me to review his copy of the portion pertaining to the MacArthur visit. Unless otherwise noted, the following description is taken from this source.

66. MacArthur, *Reminiscences,* 40. Mrs. King does not note this incident in her diary.

67. West to Beach, April 17, 1905, Beach to West, May 17, 1905, both in AHF; and Beach to MacArthur, January 13, 1906, AGO #5551, NNMO, NA.

68. MacArthur to Taft, February 25, 1907; and Taft to MacArthur, March 5, 1907, AGO #5551, NNMO, NA.

69. War Dept. to MacArthur, March 25, 1907; MacArthur to War Dept., March 26, 1907, AGO #5551, NNMO, NA.

70. MacArthur, *Reminiscences,* 43.

71. King to AG, September 7, 1912, AGO #5551, NNMO, NA; and James, *Years,* I, 42–43.

72. MacArthur to Chief, Second Division, General Staff, War Dept., May 2, 1906, AHF, NNMO, NA.

73. Bell to Adjutant General, April 10, 1907, AG #1233880; MacArthur to Beach, May 4, 1906; and Beach to MacArthur, June 11, 1906, AHF, NNMO, NA. See also MacArthur, *Reminiscences,* 38; and James, *Years,* I, 94.

74. Speech given to the Thirteenth Annual Convention of the Wisconsin Bankers Association, Milwaukee, 1907, and forwarded by General MacArthur to the War Department that year. "Personal Name File," MacArthur, Arthur, Records of the Bureau of Insular Affairs Relating to the Philippine Islands, 1898–1935, NNFN, NA. Although it is likely that the copy of this speech that MacArthur forwarded to the War Department got no further than the file cabinet, the address is nonetheless another example of the General's advanced attitudes concerning international affairs. I am indebted to Professor Keith Nelson for pointing out this parallel between MacArthur's argument and the later Wilsonian plan.

75. MacArthur, *Reminiscences,* 39–40.

76. Ibid., 38.

Chapter Four: The Middle Years

1. Remnant of untitled poem by Douglas MacArthur, c. 1908, in "MacArthur Poetry," RG 15, MMBA.

2. Much of the summary which follows is taken from James, *Years,* I, 95–294; supplemented by Hunt, *Untold Story,* 38–112; Lee and Henschel, *MacArthur,* 24–47; and MacArthur, *Reminiscences,* 40–91. Where the interpretation differs from these sources, it is my own.

3. Winslow to McKenzie, C of E., August 7, 1908, quoted in James, *Years,* I, 96.

4. MacArthur, *Reminiscences,* 41.

5. Judson to AG, July 17, 1908, AGO #487448, NNMO, NA.

6. The poems discussed in this passage were retrieved and identified by Philip Brower, first archivist of the MacArthur Archives. Although the handwritten poetry is clearly in Douglas MacArthur's distinctive script, and the internal evidence, i.e., references to "Douglas," "Fan," and their imagined children, "Arthur," "Belle," and "Malcolm," makes the identification even more certain, Brower had the handwriting analyzed professionally. There can be little question that the poems are the work of the young officer. Postmarks on the envelopes addressed to Miss Stuart, and the stationery marked "War Department, United States Engineer Office, Milwaukee, Wisconsin," establish the place and date, RG 15, MMBA.

7. While Panama and the Philippines were not considered at this time, MacArthur was nominated to become an instructor at West Point during his year in Milwaukee, but was rejected for the post by the Academy Superintendent. James, *Years,* I, 99.

8. MacArthur, *Reminiscences,* 42

9. Mrs. Arthur MacArthur to Mr. E. H. Harriman, April 17, 1909, RG 10, MMBA.

10. Alex Millar to Mrs. Arthur MacArthur, April 28, 1909, RG 10, MMBA.

11. C. H. Bates to J. Kruttschnitt, May 5, 1909, RG 10, MMBA.

12. D. C. Buell to W. L. Park, July 27, 1909, RG 10, MMBA

13. Memorandum for the Chief of Staff, October 10, 1912, AGO #487448, NNMO, NA.

14. MacArthur, *Reminiscences*, 44.

15. James, *Years*, I, 108.

16. The literature of mourning is extensive. Particularly helpful, however, is R. J. Lifton and E. Olson, *Living and Dying* (New York, 1974); and George H. Pollock, "On Mourning, Immortality, and Utopia," in *Journal of American Psychoanalytic Association*, Vol. 23 (2) (1975), 334–362.

17. Weigley, *History*, 313–341; and Jack C. Lane, *Armed Progressive: General Leonard Wood* (San Rafael, California, and London, 1978), 148–149.

18. James, *Years*, I, 115.

19. Douglas MacArthur to Major General Leonard Wood, September 30, 1914, in Major General Leonard Wood to The Adjutant General of the Army, November 25, 1914, AGO #487448, NNMO, NA.

20. All the quotes referred to in this summary are taken from the file concerning Wood's recommendation that MacArthur be awarded the Congressional Medal of Honor, AGO #487448, NNMO, NA. For a more detailed account of the whole affair, see James, *Years*, I, 115–127.

21. MacArthur, *Reminiscences*, 49.

22. Ibid., 51.

23. Ibid., 53.

24. Ibid., 53.

25. For a discussion of MacArthur's switch to the Infantry, see James, *Years*, I, 135; and Manchester, *American Caesar*, 79.

26. The details of Douglas MacArthur's experience in World War I have been more than adequately discussed in most of the books written about the General, and it is not the purpose of this work to reiterate these incidents at any length. For further information, see particularly Hunt, *Untold Story*, 60–98; and James, *Years*, I, 139–256.

27. Once again, MacArthur's promotion seems to have been helped along by a well-timed letter from Pinkie, this time to General Pershing, who, as she reminded him, was an old friend. After reviewing Douglas's career, and asserting that he was "a most capable officer and a hard working man," she strengthened her case by referring to her intimate friendship with the Secretary of War, Newton Baker, who was "very deeply attached to Colonel MacArthur." As if this were not enough, Pinkie went on to point out that several of Douglas's juniors had already achieved brigadier general rank. Finally she appealed to his sympathy: ". . . my hope and ambition in life is to live long enough to see this son made a General Officer, and I feel I am placing my entire life, as it were, in your hands. . . ." Although there is no evidence that Pershing received this letter before he made the promotion, he was more than happy to cable his congratulations to Mrs. MacArthur in July. Mrs. MacArthur to Pershing, June 12, 1918, John J. Pershing Papers, LC. For a detailed discussion of the timing of these letters, see James, *Years*, I, 171.

28. Quoted in James, *Years*, I, 160.

29. The concept of patterns of adaptation as it is used here is most carefully and extensively explained in George E. Vaillant, *Adaptation to Life* (Boston, 1977), 29 and passim. Vaillant, in his discussion of the results of the Grant Study, a longitudinal study of Harvard undergraduates undertaken in 1937 and still ongoing, argues persuasively for a multifaceted explanation of behav-

ior. While his analysis is heavily influenced by the Eriksonian model of developmental stages, Vaillant's approach is particularly valuable in that it attempts to clarify behavioral patterns in the adult—that phase of the Eriksonian model which is least developed. The study is additionally germane to the issues of this book because it deals with men who, although of a somewhat younger cohort than the one to which Douglas MacArthur belonged, achieved success and a reasonable amount of adjustment according to the values of their society —as did MacArthur.

30. Quoted in James, *Years,* I, 217.

31. MacArthur, *Reminiscences,* 76.

32. Ibid., 79. Once again, MacArthur identified with the cowboy of his youthful fantasy, if not with his experiences.

33. Hunt, *Untold Story,* 76.

34. Henry J. Reilly, *Americans All: The Rainbow at War* (Columbus, 1936), 746–748, quoted in James, *Years,* I, 224. One senses from Reilly's remark that unfortunately there was "no stenographer present to take it down and preserve it," that MacArthur's unique rhetoric did not always have the desired effect on his audience.

35. MacArthur, *Reminiscences,* 81.

36. William Allen White, *The Autobiography of William Allen White* (New York, 1946), 572–573.

37. MacArthur to AG-AEF, April 14, 1919, quoted in James, *Years,* I, 256.

38. Manchester, *American Caesar,* 114.

39. MacArthur, *Reminiscences,* 66.

40. Quoted in James, *Years,* I, 269.

41. David Lawrence, "MacArthur and the Government," in *The Evening Star,* April 7, 1964, RG 10, MMBA.

42. The often-repeated story of the courtship of Douglas MacArthur and Louise Cromwell Brooks can be found in all the MacArthur biographies. This version, unless otherwise noted, is drawn largely from James, *Years,* I, 291–294; Manchester, *American Caesar,* 127–130; and newspaper articles found in MacArthur scrapbooks, RG 24, MMBA.

43. The discussion over this matter has, over the years, been blown completely out of proportion to its real importance. James, in his treatment of the debate, argues less than convincingly that the transfer was the result of Pershing's dissatisfaction with MacArthur's innovations at West Point. Manchester, and most of the other MacArthur writers, have preferred the more spectacular explanation, to which Louise Brooks gave credence when she told a *New York Times* reporter that "Jack wanted me to marry him. . . . I wouldn't do that—so here I am, packing my trunks." *New York Times,* February 10, 1922. Certainly, although Louise seemed to encourage the rumors of a liaison with Pershing, other suitors also vied for her attention before she met MacArthur. One of these, Colonel John G. Quekemeyer, a Pershing aide, seems to have been a serious contender for Brooks's attention between 1919 and 1921, and there is evidence to suggest that, as her marriage to MacArthur soured, Louise looked fondly back to the earlier relationship, and was deeply saddened when Quekemeyer's sudden death in 1926 put an end to whatever renewed hopes she felt. See Louise MacArthur to Pershing, n.d., Pershing Papers, LC. James, *Years,* I, 672, n. 26, dates the letter in March, 1926. Possibly, both Pershing and Quekemeyer were of interest to Louise, but this possibility might not have affected Pershing's decision. More than likely, MacArthur's assignment to the

Philippines was the result of Pershing's disapproval of all that MacArthur had come to represent—in the war, at West Point, *and* as Louise's new suitor. Whatever the real reason, MacArthur was due for overseas assignment, and was somewhat relieved to return to the Islands and escape his unsuccessful efforts at the academy.

44. MacArthur, *Reminiscences*, 91–92.

45. The description of 1 Calle Victoria is taken from pictorial coverage found in "MacArthur's Philippine Scrapbook," RG 24, MMBA.

46. Interview with Mrs. A. Bolos, daughter of Alfredo Roensch who rented the cottage to the MacArthurs, Manila, January 1978; see also diary of Leonard Wood, entry for February 26, 1924, Leonard Wood Papers, LC.

47. Betty Beale, "The Fabulous Louise Took Her Memories," in *The Sunday Star*, Washington, D.C., June 27, 1965, found in file HRC 293.1, OCMH. See also Manchester, *American Caesar*, 133.

48. Unsigned letter to "My dear President of Senate" [Manuel Quezon], January 19, 1924, Manuel Quezon Papers, PNL. No record remains of the solution to this problem. "Juan de la Cruz" is the name used to refer to the average Filipino, much as "John Doe" is used in the United States.

49. Quezon to Louise MacArthur, June 11, 1924, December 12, 1924, and June 6, 1925.

50. MacArthur to Wood, January 23, 1922, Leonard Wood Papers, LC. Before Douglas arrived in October, Wood had entertained Captain Arthur MacArthur at a dinner party that Emilio Aguinaldo attended. Diary entry for August 4, 1922, Leonard Wood Papers, LC.

51. The summary of these years is drawn from Agoncillo, *History*, 362–383; George E. Taylor, *The Philippines and the United States* (New York, 1964), 47–81; and Theodore Friend, *Between Two Empires: The Ordeal of the Philippines 1929–1946* (New Haven, 1965), 1–11. Particularly relevant to this period is Michael Onorato, "Leonard Wood and the Philippine Crisis of 1923," *Journal of the East Asiatic Studies*, Vol. 2 (March, 1967); Walter Littlefield, "What Wood Really Thought About the Philippine Problem" in "Personal Name File, Leonard Wood, Pt. 6," NNFN, NA; and "Psychology of the Filipino; Conversation with Major General Leonard Wood," (Manila, 1925), found in Military Intelligence Division files (MID), NNMO, NA. See also Lane, *Armed Progressive*, 250–276.

52. MacArthur, *Reminiscences*, 92.

53. The Leonard Wood Papers and Diary, LC, for this period are extensive, frank, and very helpful. They reveal a close personal and professional relationship with both Louise and Douglas during these years and often refer to the inadequacy of Douglas's first assignment in Manila in 1922. See particularly diary entry for October 16, 1922, in which Wood states that MacArthur "feels very naturally that the command of the city of Manila is hardly a general officer's command, as there are only a handful of troops here." See also entries for November 3 and 18, 1922.

54. Major C. A. Mitchell, "The Philippine Department," *Infantry Journal*, Vol. XXX, No. 4 (April, 1927).

55. James, *Years*, I, 301–302.

56. Louis Morton, *Strategy and Command: The First Two Years* (Washington, 1962), 22–31.

57. Pershing to Sec. War, July 7, 1923, quoted in Morton, *Strategy*, 39.

58. Guy V. Henry Memoirs, USAMHI. Henry, who served as chief of staff for the Philippine Division during this period, stated that "General Douglas

MacArthur was on duty as a brigade commander in the Philippines, and we had numerous discussions on the plan in question. He was never in accord with the plan. . . . " Leonard Wood believed that the plan was "purely defensive without much thought of offensive and a failure to recognize that the best defensive is a vigorous offensive." Diary entry for December 28, 1922, Leonard Wood Papers, LC.

59. Wood to MacArthur, January 9, 1924; MacArthur to Wood, January 10, 1924; Louise MacArthur to Mrs. Wood, January 8, 1924, in Leonard Wood Papers, LC.

60. Guy V. Henry, Jr., Papers, USAMHI, and AGO #353.8, Phil. Dept., December 20, 1924, NNMO, NA.

61. Wood Diary, entry for July 4, 1924, Leonard Wood Papers, LC.

62. The most comprehensive examination of the day-to-day cabinet conflict during this period is Onorato, "Leonard Wood," 46–74. Onorato concludes that "from July 1923 to the sudden death of Wood in August 1927, the Filipino leader [Quezon] was forced by political expediency to maintain a strong, inflexible posture toward Wood."

63. The information concerning the history and subsequent action of the Philippine Scouts during this period is drawn from the detailed reports prepared by the Army after the mutiny in 1924. The reports are extensive and often repetitive, and may be found in "Summary of Statement made by General Hagood in Reference to Disaffection Among Native Troops in the Philippine Islands," August 13, 1924, and W. E. Prosser to Major Jarvis J. Bain, September 4, 1924, in MID files #10582–59; "Memorandum for the Chief of Staff," July 30, 1924, Arthur F. Fischer to General LeRoy Eltinge, October 26, 1924, Maj. Robert A. Gilmore, PS to General Leroy Eltinge, September 27, 1924, "Memorandum for the Chief of Staff: Subject: Mutiny in the Philippine Scouts," March 19, 1925, all in War Plans Division Numerical File, 1920–1942, Records of the War Department General and Special Staffs, NNMO, NA; and "Special Plan Brown," December 28, 1923, Adm. Services Div., Oper. Branch, Special Project—War Plans "Color," 1920–1948, Records of the Adjutant General's office, 1917—also NNMO, NA. Most helpful as a summary statement is Eugene F. Ganley's discussion in Ganley to Eakin, December 12, 1969, in the William E. Carraway Papers, USAMHI. Wood's attitude toward the mutiny is recounted in Leonard Wood Diary, entries for July 12 and 14, and September 11, 1924, Leonard Wood Papers, LC.

64. James, *Years,* I, 303–305, and n. 10, 670, dates the promotion on September 23, 1924, almost immediately after the mutiny, and suggests "the change possibly being made in an effort to placate the Filipino soldiers since MacArthur was known to favor equal status for them with the white troops." Although the early date would favor this argument, MacArthur, in *Reminiscences,* 92, dates the assignment after his promotion to major general in January 1925.

65. James, *Years,* I, 303.

66. Wood to Sec. War, July 22, 1924, in MID 10582–59, NNM0, NA. In his diary entry from July 12, 1924, Wood argued that the Philippine political leaders' actions "tended to a spirit of resistance to authority and a lowering of respect for authority, which has culminated in the Scouts in the mutiny. . . . " Leonard Wood Papers, LC.

67. Report on Mutiny in the Philippine Scouts, March 19, 1925, in War Plans Division Numerical File, 1920–1942, Records of the War Department General and Special Staffs, NNMO, NA.

68. Chief of Constabulary to My dear Mr. President, September 6, 1923, Quezon Papers, PNL. Wood's awareness of this information is mentioned in Wood to Sec. War, July 22, 1924, MID 10582–59, NNMO, NA.

69. Quezon to Roxas, July 24, 1924, in Quezon Papers, PNL.

70. Leonard Wood Diary, entry for July 9, 1923, Wood Papers, LC. Both the General and his wife, Louise, apparently were disappointed in Pershing. See Wood Diary, entry for February 26, 1924, which comments: "Mrs. MacArthur was full of reminiscences of Washington days and particularly bitter concerning General Pershing and the treatment which had been meted out to General MacArthur which does seem very unjust."

71. Twice during the early months in Manila, MacArthur was considered and rejected for positions as military attaché in London and Tokyo. See James, *Years,* I, 303.

72. Wood to Weeks, May 9, 1924, Wood Papers, LC.

73. Weeks to Wood, June 13, 1924, Wood Papers, LC.

74. Mary MacArthur to General Pershing, n.d., Pershing Papers, LC.

75. James, *Years,* I, 305.

76. *New York Times,* September 23, 1924.

77. MacArthur, *Reminiscences,* 92; and James, *Years,* I, 306–331.

78. From the Articles of War, quoted in James, *Years,* I, 307.

79. MacArthur, *Reminiscences,* 93–94.

80. Ibid., 94.

81. Louise MacArthur to Pershing, n.d., Pershing Papers, LC.

82. James, *Years,* I, 320–321.

83. Lee and Henschel, *MacArthur,* 50.

84. Betty Beale, "First Mrs. Mac Speaks Up," *Washington Sunday Star,* April 19, 1964, and *Manila Evening News,* April 20, 1964.

85. Robert Considine, *It's All News to Me: A Reporter's Deposition* (New York, 1967), 342.

86. For a particularly outspoken account of Louise's stories, see Harold L. Ickes Diaries, diary entry for Sept. 25, 1943, 8196–97, Ickes Papers, LC.

87. *New York Times,* June 18, 1929.

88. This sensitivity is best exemplified by MacArthur's refusal to ever discuss this marriage or its dissolution. In his memoirs, the only mention is in a terse "in February 1922 I entered into matrimony, but it was not successful, and ended in divorce years later for mutual incompatibility," MacArthur, *Reminiscences,* 91. In addition, when asked to prepare sketches for *Who's Who,* and similar directories, he never mentioned the marriage; James, *Years,* I, 323.

89. The information concerning MacArthur's professional responsibilities is taken from "Annual Report of the Commanding General, Philippine Department," August 27, 1929, AGO General File, 1926–39, 319.12 Phil. Dept., Records of the Adjutant General's Office, 1917–, NNMO, NA. It is important to note that while the pay increases and additional benefits did improve Philippine Scout circumstances and morale, their condition never equaled that of the U.S. Army, and their numbers never reached authorized strength until shortly before the U.S. entry into World War II. My thanks to Robert Ross Smith for this information.

90. Morton, *Strategy,* 33.

91. F. W. Sladen to Gen. E. E. Booth, A. C. of S., G–4, War Dept., August 12, 1927, AGO 600.3, Phil. Dept., NNMO, NA.

92. General Staff report of survey of military establishment, November 1, 1929, WPD 3345; quoted in James, *Years,* I, 336.

93. Annual Report of the Commanding General, August 27, 1929.

94. "Report of 1929 Annual Inspection and Survey of Headquarters Philippine Department," by Colonel Louis J. Van Schaick, January 12, 1929, in WPD Corres., 1920–42, #3295, Records of the War Dept., General and Special Staffs, NNMO, NA.

95. Douglas MacArthur to Adj. Gen. Office, "Tactical Inspection of Philippine Dept. for 1929," March 22, 1929, AGO Central File 1926–39, 333.3 Phil. Dept., Records of the Adjutant General's Office, 1917–, NNMO, NA.

96. Henry L. Stimson Diaries, V, 68 (mf#1), Manuscripts and Archives, Yale University Library, New Haven, (YUL) entry for January 21, 1919, in which Stimson refers to MacArthur as "keen and intelligent." See also, MacArthur, *Reminiscences,* 96; and James, *Years,* I, 110–111.

97. Theodore Friend, *Between Two Empires,* 80. See also Henry L. Stimson and McGeorge Bundy, *On Active Service in Peace and War* (New York, 1947–48), 117–152.

98. Henry L. Stimson Diaries, XX, 170–171 (mf#4), entry for February 14, 1932, YUL. See also X, 41 (mf#2), entry for October 1, 1930, and VIII, 54 (mf#1) entry for April 3, 1928.

99. Agoncillo, *History,* 370.

100. Cablegram to Governor General Stimson, May 10, 1928, quoted in Townshend to Whal, May 11, 1928, File No. 2092–97, NNFN, NA. This debate gives some credence to the contention of General George Van Horn Moseley who, in a 1950 "historical note," recalled that "sometime after MacArthur reported as Chief of Staff, he told me of the differences he had had with Mr. Stimson when the latter was Governor General of the Philippine Islands. One of the principal difficulties was referred to Washington and MacArthur's position was fully sustained." MacArthur denied any conflict with Stimson when Moseley sent the note to him, but Moseley held to his beliefs. See "Memorandum in reference to letter from General Douglas MacArthur, dated June 11, 1950," in Moseley Papers, Vol. 16, LC. MacArthur, in his memoirs, stated "we [Stimson and MacArthur] became fast friends," MacArthur, *Reminiscences,* 96. Although Moseley's political views were somewhat eccentric by the 1950s, acquaintances still contend that on issues not directly relating to his particular fixations, his memory was sharp and his judgment sound. Interview with Edward M. Coffman, USMA, August 1977.

101. "Annual Report of the Commanding General, Philippine Dept.," August 27, 1929.

102. MacArthur to AG, report on "Taxation of the United States by the Philippine Government," September 7, 1929, AGO 012.3, Phil. Islands, NNMO, NA.

103. Stimson to MacArthur, December 22, 1928, AGO 014.12 P. I., NNMO, NA.

104. Stimson, *On Active Service,* 144–145.

105. For a discussion of the various candidates, see Friend, *Between Two Empires,* 41, and 77–79. Evidence of Gilmore's consideration was found in Roxas to Quezon, April 22, 1929, Quezon Papers, PNL. Stimson's choice of Strawn is confirmed in Henry L. Stimson Diaries, X, 39–42 (mf#2) diary entry for August 28, 1930. See also Stimson Diaries, IX, 127 (mf#2) diary entry for January 17, 1929, regarding Stimson's expectation that in the event a Filipino

was chosen it would be Quezon, YUL. MacArthur's candidacy, substantiated in the papers of Manuel Quezon, PNL, was serious, at least for the General. Interestingly, James, *Years,* I, 334, states that "no evidence was found, however, that MacArthur was considered for the governor generalship, nor that he desired it." As we shall see, this was not the case. See also, "Down the Big Road," Chap. XLV, 457–466, Hagood Collection, USAMHI.

106. Friend, *Between Two Empires,* 78.

107. Quezon to Osmeña/Roxas, April 16, 1929, Quezon Papers, PNL.

108. Quezon to Osmeña/Roxas, April 13 and 16, 1929; MacArthur to Quezon, March 29, April 30, 1929; Quezon to MacArthur, May 16, 1929; and MacArthur to Quezon, n.d., all in Quezon Papers, PNL.

109. Friend, *Between Two Empires,* 78, states that "MacArthur had his sights set higher anyway," referring to the General's subsequent appointment as chief of staff. James, who did not see the MacArthur-Quezon correspondence, comments that "even the least astute politician would not have suggested the Philippine governor generalship as a stepping-stone to the presidency." Here, I believe he is wrong. James, *Years,* I, 334. Certainly the General's interest in the presidency, as reflected in his attempts to secure the Republican nomination in both 1944 and 1948, is well documented. See particularly Carolyn Jane Mattern, "The Man on the Dark Horse: The Presidential Campaigns for General Douglas MacArthur, 1944 and 1948" (Ph.D. dissertation, University of Wisconsin–Madison, 1976).

110. *New York Times,* April 20 and 21, 1929.

111. For a summary of the debate over MacArthur's appointment, see James, *Years,* I, 340–347; Hunt, *Untold,* 125; and "Historical Note," Vol. 16, Moseley Papers, LC.

112. MacArthur, *Reminiscences,* 97–98.

113. Ibid., 96.

114. Ibid., 36. For a discussion of the press coverage of the MacArthur divorce, see Manchester, *American Caesar,* 141.

115. The information concerning Isabel Cooper which follows is drawn from personal interviews which I conducted with her cousin, Mercedes Sotelo, in Manila, Jan., Feb., 1978, and correspondence with her brother, Allen Cooper, March 4, 1978. In addition, there is a brief description of her career in the *Philippine Bulletin,* December 26, 1976. See also Oliver Pilat, *Drew Pearson, An Unauthorized Biography* (New York, 1973), 141–146. Pilat refers to Cooper as "Helen Robinson" but offers no explanation for his choice. Manchester, *American Caesar,* 144–145, assumes that the Pilat account refers to Cooper, and the interviews and correspondence mentioned above confirm this fact. Pilat and other writers have accepted the age (46) on Cooper's death certificate in 1960, and therefore assumed that she was 16 at the time of her relationship with the General. Considering her fame in Manila, however, it is likely that she was at least a few years older, and may later have moved her birth date forward for professional purposes.

116. MacArthur's uncertainty about how best to deal with Isabel in the States is suggested by his request, in July 1930, for assignment to II Corps Area in New York. As James, *Years,* I, 342, suggests: "Since his mother then lived in Washington and his former wife resided in New York, . . . MacArthur's request is intriguing, especially some of its phrasing: 'I have never before made special application for station [!] and I earnestly solicit favorable consideration. The most impelling personal reasons dictate the request.' " Although

James remains intrigued by the request, it is possible that MacArthur had decided that it would be easier to keep Isabel under wraps in New York City than Washington. Certainly, MacArthur's comments suggested that his concern for the transfer was a serious one.

117. The letters MacArthur wrote to Isabel during their separation are the subject of much debate. Most certainly, according to Sotelo and Cooper, correspondence did occur. Photostatic copies of these letters were kept by Drew Pearson's lawyer, Morris Ernst, and were later deposited with the Ernst papers at the Humanities Research Center, University of Texas at Austin. Due to this author's inability to visit Austin, information regarding these letters was supplied to me by the Research Librarian at the Humanities Research Center, and by Robert Sherrod, journalist and MacArthur scholar. See also Dan Schwartz, "Passionate Letters Reveal the Sensational Love Affair of 50-Year-Old Gen. Douglas MacArthur—& a 16-Year-Old Filipino Girl," in *The National Enquirer,* September 21, 1976, and "Enquirer Avoids Legal Action; Publication of MacArthur Letters Ordered to Cease," in *The Daily Texan,* December 3, 1976. For obvious reasons, my discussion of the letters paraphrases their contents. (For a more complete explanation of the Pearson involvement in this matter, see chapter five.)

118. Ronald Hyam, *Britain's Imperial Century, 1815–1914* (London, 1976), 135. Hyam's discussion of this phenomena (135–148) argues that "there were emotional opportunities and sexual satisfactions available overseas greater than could be had in inhibited Britain; and for those who denied themselves such possibilities as there were, empire-building provided a sublimating alternative."

119. Ibid., 141. Hyam states that "the empire was an exceedingly masculine affair, based on a somewhat cynical view of women, and a particular rejection of the Regency and Victorian female."

Chapter Five: The Last Years Before the War

1. MacArthur to Quezon, June 1, 1935, RG 17, MMBA.

2. James, *Years,* I, 345.

3. Weigley, *History,* 402; much of the following analysis of MacArthur's years as Chief of Staff is drawn from Weigley, *History,* 402–415; and James, *Years,* I, 351–475.

4. During the 1929 debate over the appointment of the chief of staff, Hurley had initially believed that "a man who couldn't hold his women shouldn't be Chief of Staff," but was eventually convinced by President Hoover. Quoted in James, *Years,* I, 344. MacArthur and Hurley later developed a sound relationship which continued throughout World War II. See Hurley-MacArthur correspondence, RG 10, MMBA.

5. At the time of the World Disarmament Conference in early 1932, MacArthur told Pierrepont Moffat, Stimson's chief adviser on armament, that "our ultimate aim should be to obtain an agreement on the part of all nations that they would give no government support in any form to aviation." Henry Stimson Diary, XXII, 66 (mf#4), entry for June 3, 1932.

6. O'Laughlin to Pershing, April 1, 1934, Pershing Papers, LC.

7. *New York Times,* June 3, 1931, quoted in James, *Years,* I, 376–377.

8. Donald J. Lisio, "A Blunder Becomes Catastrophe: Hoover, the Legion, and the Bonus Army," *Wisconsin Magazine of History,* 51 (Autumn, 1967),

37–50; the account in these paragraphs is drawn from this article. See also John W. Killigrew, "The Army and the Bonus Incident," *Military Affairs,* XXV (Summer, 1962), 55–62; and James, *Years,* I, 382–414. For an Army version of part of the story, see General Order No. 6, Fort Myer, Virginia, August 9, 1932, RG 15, MMBA.

9. Quoted in James, *Years,* I, 403.

10. *New York Times,* July 29, 1932, quoted in James, *Years,* I, 404. See also Dwight D. Eisenhower, *At Ease: Stories I Tell to Friends* (New York, 1967), 216.

11. James, *Years,* I, 409.

12. Statements which support the MacArthur position may be found in the O'Laughlin-Pershing Papers, LC. MacArthur's own sensitivity is amply reflected in his later account of the episode in *Reminiscences,* 101–106, in which he maintained, in the face of years of contradictory evidence, that "not more than one in ten of those who stayed was a veteran. By this time Waters had been deposed and the Communists had gained control" (103).

13. Much of the story concerning Isabel in Washington is taken from Pilat, *Drew Pearson,* 141–146. See also Manchester, *American Caesar,* 144–145, 156, for a somewhat confused account of the story. Correspondence in the Morris Ernst Collection, Humanities Research Center, University of Texas at Austin, suggests that the relationship between MacArthur and Cooper remained steady at least until late 1932. The information concerning Isabel's education and the fellow student's role in the affair was recounted by Allen Cooper, letter to author, March 4, 1978.

14. Manchester, *American Caesar,* 156.

15. Robert G. Sherrill, "Thirty-Six Years on the Merry-Go-Round—Drew Pearson on War, Love, Graft, Politics, Revolution and the Hiding Places of Power," *The Nation* (July 7, 1969), 15. For evidence suggesting that the Pearson-MacArthur conflict was not entirely over, see Memo for Record, 22 Dec., 1945, OPD, Sec. VI, Cases 194, NNMM, NA.

16. See Diary of Harold L. Ickes, entry for May 24, 1942, 6638, Ickes Papers, LC.

17. Certificate of Death, #7053, issued on June 29, 1960, Dept. of Public Health, State of California. I am indebted to Mr. Robert Sherrod for a copy of this certificate. The information concerning her last years was related in Cooper to author, March 4, 1978.

18. The often-told story of Roosevelt's assessment of MacArthur as "one of the two most dangerous men in the country," can be found in Rexford G. Tugwell, *The Democratic Roosevelt* (Garden City, N.Y., 1957), 348–351.

19. Evidence that Roosevelt understood MacArthur's pleasure in this extended tenure is found in Roosevelt to Dern, October 2, 1935, OF 25, FDRL.

20. MacArthur, *Reminiscences,* 111. For a suggestion that there were other conflicts with Roosevelt during this period, see Ickes Diary, entry for July 21, 1933, 201, Ickes Papers, LC.

21. For the best discussion of the development of Commonwealth legislation, see Friend, *Between Two Empires,* 95–148. Also helpful is Agoncillo, *History,* 388–399.

22. Friend, *Between Two Empires,* 138.

23. MacArthur, *Reminiscences,* 112; Quezon, *The Good Fight,* 153–155; Lee and Henschel in *MacArthur,* 61, state that MacArthur was more cautious. When Quezon asked if the Islands could be defended, MacArthur supposedly said, "I don't think so . . . but . . . they can be protected . . . if you have the necessary money. . . ." [ellipses his]. All the other evidence seems to support MacAr-

thur's more positive view, and it is possible that Lee and Henschel were involved in an after-the-fact justification. Dwight Eisenhower, who was serving in the War Department during this period and later accompanied MacArthur to Manila to become a member of the Military Advisory Group, recounted the episode in detail in an undated "Draft" wherein he attributes the General's positive response to a belief "that there existed, or could be developed among Filipinos a fervid spirit of nationalism, ready to express itself in a unified and continuous effort to preserve the independence they were shortly to obtain; [and] that military preparation in the Philippine Islands need seek no more ambitious objective than a passive defense of territory." See "Draft," 4 in Dwight D. Eisenhower, Papers as President of the United States, 1953–1961 (Whitman File), Personal Diary, DDEL. I am indebted to Richard H. Immerman for making copies of this material available to me.

24. MacArthur to Quezon, June 1, 1935, RG 17, MMBA.

25. Quezon's letter to Dern, November 19, 1934, may be found in AGO #093.5 Philippine Islands, NNMA, NA. The amended laws are listed in *U.S. Statutes at Large*, XLIV, 565 (1927), and XLIX, 218 (1936). Payment figures and arrangements were agreed upon after MacArthur made sure that they would equal those of the Governor General of the Philippines. See Memorandum for the Chief of Staff, November 12, 1934, RG 18, MMBA. See also Quezon to MacArthur, December 31, 1935, RG 10, MMBA: "Memorandum of the Terms of Agreement . . .," 1935, RG 1, MMBA; "The Vargas-Saulo Interviews" (second interview), 29, and (fourth interview), 67; and Domingo C. Abadilla, "The Manila Hotel Story," September 29, 1975, Vargas Foundation; and Quezon to MacArthur, October 25, 1935, Quezon Papers, PNL. The peso-dollar calculation is based on the rate of exchange during the 1930s, which was regulated by the U. S. government and did not fluctuate.

26. MacArthur to Quezon, December 27, 1934, RG 18, MMBA.

27. MacArthur to Quezon, December 27, 1934, and Quezon to MacArthur, n.d., RG 18, MMBA. See also James, *Years*, I, 485.

28. MacArthur to Quezon, June 1, 1935, in response to Quezon to MacArthur, May 21, 1935, both in RG 17, MMBA.

29. MacArthur to Roosevelt, September 9, 1935, RG 17, MMBA, in which the General quotes Revised Statutes 1222 and 1223, which clearly forbid officers of the Army to accept civil office.

30. Roosevelt to MacArthur, September 19, 1935, PSF 102, FDRL.

31. Michael P. Onorato, ed., *Origins of the Philippine Republic; Extracts from the Diaries and Records of Francis Burton Harrison* (Ithaca, N.Y., 1974), 18. Although D. Clayton James argues that MacArthur's chances for the appointment were hurt by a subsequent conflict with Murphy and ended before his departure for the Islands, the Harrison diaries suggest that this was not the case. See James, *Years*, I, 490; and Onorato, *Origins*, entry for October 21 and 22, 1935, 5–6.

32. O'Laughlin to MacArthur, November 14, 1936, O'Laughlin Papers, LC.

33. MacArthur, *Reminiscences*, 112.

34. Adding credence to this argument is the fact that after his retirement from the Army in 1937, the General once again pursued the appointment. See MacArthur to Early, July 14, 1939, OF 400, FDRL, and a discussion of this attempt later in this chapter.

35. Dern to Roosevelt, n.d., and Roosevelt to Sec. War., July 18, 1935, PSF "War Dept. 1933–41," FDRL.

36. Conley to MacArthur, September 18, 1935, RG 1, MMBA.

37. Johnson to The President, April 30, 1935, and Roosevelt to Johnson, May 2, 1935, OF 25t, FDRL.

38. Johnson to Lahand, September 4, 1935 and Roosevelt to Johnson, September 9, 1935, OF 25t, FDRL. Roosevelt's decision is also confirmed in an unsigned memo dated August 31, 1935, which states that "Confidentially, a day or so after MacArthur leaves Washington, the President expects to telegraph Secretary Dern saying that he has decided to appoint————[*sic*] as Chief of Staff." OF 25t, FDRL.

39. Eisenhower, *At Ease*, 223.

40. D. Clayton James attributes Roosevelt's action to his determination that Simonds not receive the appointment as chief of staff. Simonds, who had only four years to serve early in 1935, was too close to retirement to get the appointment by October. Since, however, the decision was always Roosevelt's to make, it seems hardly necessary for him to have been so devious after extending MacArthur's tenure. See James, *Years*, I, 493–494.

41. The festivities on board the *Hoover* were recounted in a song written by Major James B. Ord, MacArthur's assistant chief of staff, entitled "Whoopee on the Hoover," RG 15, MMBA. The lyrics, which included several verses, suggest that the mood was gala and the refreshments plentiful—"With headaches in the morning and some other aches at night,/But we never sprung a leak because the ship was very tight,/Which was funny for a boat with such a name."

42. The information concerning Jean Faircloth comes from Janet Flanner, "General and Mrs. Douglas MacArthur," *Ladies' Home Journal* (June, 1942), 15, 59; and several unattributed newspaper clippings, c. 1942, in MacArthur Scrapbooks, RG 24, MMBA.

43. See Report of Death, Dec. 23, 1935, Dept. of Police, Manila, P. I. in "Personal Name File," MacArthur, Douglas, NNFN, NA. The report attributed the death to "general thrombosis, chronic myocarditis" and stated that Mrs. MacArthur left "no estate to be inventoried."

44. MacArthur, *Reminiscences*, 113.

45. MacArthur to O'Laughlin, December 9 and 18, 1935, O'Laughlin Papers, LC. See also Eisenhower, *At Ease*, 224.

46. For a discussion of the internalization of the values of a dead loved one, see Pollock, "On Mourning." As late as September 1936, MacArthur was still refusing invitations because "I am still preserving full mourning for my Mother; . . . due to the pressure of events have been unable to return her body for burial; . . . I will not be available until this is accomplished." MacArthur to T. J. Davis, AG 201, Douglas MacArthur, Headquarters, USAF, Far East/ USAF, Philippines, NNG, NA.

47. L. Siguion Reyna, "Preliminary Study on the Problem of our National Defense," May, 1935, Quezon Papers, PNL.

48. This statement and the following information are taken from MacArthur, *Report on National Defense*, passim.

49. Louis Morton, *The Fall of the Philippines* (Washington, D.C., 1953), 13, confirms this point when he states: "certainly, the Philippine Government did not anticipate that the United States would stand idly by if the security of the Philippines was threatened."

50. Morton, *Strategy*, 43–44.

51. Stimson Diary, XXVII, 131 (mf#5) entry for March 20, 1935, states: "I told him [Quezon] that the defense of the Islands from Japan would be

purely a naval defense and that the American garrison and any garrison which he could raise would be merely a pawn to fall into the hands of Japan and force the naval issue, perhaps in an unfavorable way."

52. Even as late as December 1934, after the passage of the Tydings-McDuffie Act, MacArthur denied its full implication. In a handwritten note attached to a plan for withdrawal of military property in the Philippines, he commented: "Any action along this line would seem to be premature at present. Take it easy and do not force developments in this matter. We may be there ten years—we may even be there indefinitely. Any studies like this might create a false impression of our attitude." Kilbourne to Sec., Gen. Staff, December 14, 1934, File #3251-22, WPD, NNMO, NA.

53. *The Philippine Forum,* Vol. II, #4 (March, 1937), Vol. II, #5 (April, 1937), and Vol. I, #6 (May, 1936); and *Manila Bulletin,* Oct. 8, 1938, in Vargas Scrapbooks, VF.

54. Friend, *Between Two Empires,* 87–88.

55. Speech by Quezon taken from radiogram received January 21, 1937, by the Sec. War, PPF 1984, FDRL.

56. MacArthur's attacks on the New Deal can be found in letters to two of his conservative friends, George Van Horn Moseley and John Callan O'Laughlin. See particularly MacArthur to Moseley, October 7, 1936, March 1, 1937, and March 9, 1938, Vol. 19, Moseley Papers, LC; and MacArthur to O'Laughlin, February 13, and December 12, 1936, O'Laughlin Papers, LC.

57. Dern to MacArthur, June 11, 1936, MacArthur 201, Headquarters, USAF, Far East/USAF Philippines, NNG, NA; and in MacArthur to O'Laughlin, December 12, 1936, O'Laughlin Papers, LC.

58. O'Laughlin to MacArthur, August 7, 1936, O'Laughlin Papers, LC.

59. Craig to MacArthur, August 5, 1936, AGO 093.5 Phil. Islands, NNMO, NA.

60. Hull to Woodring, Sept. 18, 1936, AGO 093.5 Phil. Islands, NNMO, NA. It may be worth noting that this letter was attached to the copy of Craig's earlier warning to MacArthur of August 5.

61. The quotations from Sayre are found in Sayre to Roosevelt, February 13, 1937, PSF 64, FDRL. Information concerning the 1937 trip is taken from War Dept. Bureau of Insular Affairs Memorandum, February 13 through March 23, 1937, "Manuel Quezon Missions, 1934–1937," NNFN, NA; MacArthur to Jones, January 11, 1937, AG 201, Douglas MacArthur, Headquarters, USAF, Far East/USAF Philippines, NNG, NA; "Memorandum for Mrs. Helm, February 24, 1937, OF 400, FDRL; see also James, *Years,* I, 510–513; Friend, *Between Two Empires,* 157; and MacArthur, *Reminiscences,* 116–118.

62. Janet Flanner, "General and Mrs. Douglas MacArthur." Much of the information in the following paragraphs is drawn from this source. Mrs. MacArthur was buried at Arlington National Cemetery because her husband, General Arthur MacArthur, had been reinterred there in 1926. James, *Years,* I, 495.

63. Lee and Henschel, *MacArthur,* 68.

64. For the most convincing account of Jean MacArthur's devotion to her husband, and of both to their son, see Huff, *My Fifteen Years,* passim. A personal reflection of this devotion may be found in Jeannie to Dearest Sir Boss, January 26, 1945, RG 10, MMBA.

65. The problems in the training of the Philippine Army are discussed at length in many of the reports from the Islands during this period. See particu-

larly Diary of Major William J. Priestley, Morton Collection, USAMHI; Jones
Diary and Subject Documents, Philippine File, OCMH; Commonwealth of the
Philippines Army Headquarters Bulletin No. 35, March 13, 1940, "Publica-
tions, P. I. Army," Office of Territories, NNFN, NA; "Philippine Islands,
6200-Personnel-General," April 15, 1936, War Dept. General and Special
Staff, NNMO, NA; Dwight David Eisenhower, Papers as President of the
United States, 1953–1961 (Whitman File), Personal Diary, Introduction and
entries through July 20, 1937, DDEL; and James, *Years,* I, 513–515.

66. Dwight David Eisenhower, Papers as President of the United States,
1953–1961 (Whitman File), Personal Diary, Entry for February 15, 1936,
DDEL; and James, *Years,* I, 514–515.

67. Early to Sec. War, August 5, 1937, PSF 9, FDRL.

68. Cal O'Laughlin, as usual, was privy to most of the rumors and kept
everyone, including General Pershing, aware of the developments. Pershing,
who in later years had somewhat readjusted his earlier critical attitude toward
MacArthur, nonetheless took a certain delight in this new situation. He told
O'Laughlin that "It is not surprising that MacArthur is to be recalled. He has
certainly carried things with a high hand over there. His rather boastful claims
as to the soundness and efficiency of the organization proposed for the Philippine army were bound to attract unfavorable attention. Then, of course, his
appointment as Field Marshal of a State and an army, neither of which has, as
yet, an independent existence, was more or less ridiculous." Pershing to O'-
Laughlin, June 10, 1937, Pershing Papers, LC. See also O'Laughlin to MacArthur, Oct. 22, 1937, O'Laughlin Papers, LC.

69. James, *Years,* I, 523.

70. Craig to Early, August 3, 1937, PSF 102, FDRL. This document, which
contains statements on the matter by the Judge Advocate General's Office,
found that while MacArthur's orders of 1935 could be rescinded, nothing
could be done to stop him from continuing as Military Adviser in a private
capacity if he chose to retire from the Army. The Judge Advocate did, however,
point out that without United States support for the office, the remaining staff
members would have to be placed under the control of the Philippine Department.

71. "Memorandum for the Chief of Staff, Subject: Military Adviser to the
Commonwealth Government of the Philippine Islands," January 19, 1938,
AGO #093.5, Phil. Islands, NNMO, NA.

72. MacArthur to Craig, Sept. 16, 1937, PPF 4914, FDRL.

73. Craig to MacArthur, Oct. 11, 1937, RG 10, MMBA.

74. James, *Years,* I, 524–525.

75. MacArthur to Quezon, June 1, 1935, RG 17, MMBA.

76. Eisenhower, *At Ease,* 225–226.

77. Evidence of the growing dissension in the Military Advisory Group was
reflected in 1942 when Eisenhower, now back in Washington, noted: "Today,
in a most flamboyant radio [speech], MacArthur recommends successor in case
of 'my [MacArthur's] death.' He picked Sutherland, showing that he still likes
his boot lickers." Dwight David Eisenhower, Papers as President of the United
States, 1953–1961 (Whitman File), Personal Diary, entry for January 23, 1942,
DDEL. Charles A. Willoughby and John Chamberlain, *MacArthur, 1941–1951*
(New York, 1954), 35; Eisenhower, *At Ease,* 226–228.

78. The last years of MacArthur's tenure in the Philippines before U.S.
entry into World War II have been written about extensively by all the MacAr-

thur biographers, as well as World War II scholars and students of Philippine-American relations. The summary which follows is drawn largely from Morton, *Fall of the Philippines*, 8–360; Friend, *Between Two Empires*, 190–195; John Jacob Beck, *MacArthur and Wainwright: Sacrifice of the Philippines* (Albuquerque, 1974), 1–144; and, of course, James, *Years*, I, 525–619, and II, 3–104. New information discovered in my research and any differences in interpretation will be noted specifically.

79. Quezon to Sec. of National Defense Sison, n.d. (c. 1939), Quezon Papers, PNL.

80. Quezon speech, Rizal Stadium, Manila, November 15, 1939, quoted in James, *Years*, I, 537.

81. Friend, *Between Two Empires*, 195. In the pages (190–195) which precede this passage, Friend lays out the best discussion of the Philippine situation in this period to be found anywhere.

82. Stimson to the Chief of Staff, May 21, 1941; Marshall to Grunert, May 29, 1941, AGO #093.5, Phil. Islands, NNMO, NA.

83. MacArthur to Quezon, October 12, 1940, RG 1, MMBA.

84. Quezon's request was overheard by Evett Hester, a Commonwealth official and quoted in Friend, *Between Two Empires*, 193–194. See also Sayre to Mr. President [Roosevelt], January 11, 1940, PSF 74, FDRL; and "Memorandum of conversation between High Commissioner Sayre and President Quezon regarding Philippine national defense," February 28, 1940, P.I. 1933–1943 File, Ickes Papers, LC.

85. MacArthur to Early, July 14, 1939, OF 400 and OF 4771, FDRL.

86. MacArthur to Early, March 21, 1941, OF 400, FDRL.

87. Watson to MacArthur, April 15, 1941, OF 400, FDRL. See also MacArthur to Early, May 11, 1941, Early Papers, Box 10, FDRL.

88. Hunt, *Untold Story*, 204–205; and James, *Years*, I, 585.

89. Marshall to MacArthur, June 20, 1941, OCS 20850–15, quoted in James, *Years*, I, 586.

90. Adams to MacArthur, July 26, 1941, RG 2, MMBA; and Marshall to MacArthur, July, 1941, OF 400, FDRL.

91. Quezon to MacArthur, July 27, 1941, RG 10, MMBA.

92. James, *Years*, I, 592–593.

93. MacArthur to O'Laughlin, October 6, 1941, O'Laughlin Papers, LC.

94. Morton, *Strategy*, 90–91.

95. James, *Years*, I, 609.

96. Since the International Date Line lies between Hawaii and the Philippines, the attacks on both posts, although separated by only a few hours, occurred on two different calendar dates.

97. The conflicting accounts of the USAFFE decisions on the morning of December 8 have been the subject of thirty-five years of debate. The best treatment of the details of that day is in Morton, *Fall of the Philippines*, 77–97, wherein the author states that "faced with these conflicting accounts, the historian can be sure only of five facts: (1) That an attack against Formosa was proposed; (2) that such an attack was deferred in favor of a photo reconnaissance mission requested either by Brereton or Sutherland; (3) that about 1100 on 8 December a strike against Formosa, to take place that day, was finally authorized; (4) that the heavy bombers were back on Clark Field after 1130 on the morning of 8 December; and (5) that MacArthur planned an attack against Formosa for the morning of 9 December." See also pages 83–84.

98. The strategic and tactical developments leading to the final surrender are well beyond the scope of this study. For a clearer picture of this period, see Morton, *Fall*, passim; and James, *Years*, II, 3–154.

99. Nearly everyone who met MacArthur, particularly after 1935, remarked about his habit of pacing the length of his quarters as he carried on long discursive monologues. For an interesting discussion of this "locomotor restlessness," see Erik H. Erikson, *Gandhi's Truth* (New York, 1969), 108.

100. Morton, *Fall of the Philippines*, passim; Beck, *MacArthur and Wainwright*, 11–131; and "Diary, General Douglas MacArthur Commanding General United States Army Forces in the Far East," RG 2, MMBA.

101. Marshall to MacArthur, December 31, 1941, "Quezon File," Army-Operations, OPD Executive Files, 1940–45, NNMM, NA.

102. Quezon, who had suffered from tuberculosis for many years, was weakened at this time by the stress of the situation and the hours spent in the dark and dusty Malinta Tunnel. Eventually, in August 1944, he succumbed to the disease. The USAFFE response referred to here is MacArthur to Marshall, January 1, 1942, AGO #381, Dec. 41, Far East Situation, NNMM, NA.

103. "By the President of the Philippines, Executive Order #1," Fort Mills, Corregidor, Jan. 3, 1942, in Sutherland Papers, NNMM, NA. For a complete discussion of this document, its discovery, and its meaning, see Carol M. Petillo, "Douglas MacArthur and Manuel Quezon: A Note on an Imperial Bond," *Pacific Historical Review*, XLVIII, No. 1 (Feb., 1979), 107–117.

104. The best discussion of the puppet government in the Philippines during World War II is David Joel Steinberg, *Philippine Collaboration in World War II* (Ann Arbor, Mich., 1967).

105. For a record of Sayre's role during this period, see Francis Bowes Sayre, *Glad Adventure* (New York, 1957), 230–351; and "Philippine Islands, Reports 1938–1942," Sayre Papers, LC.

106. For other examples of Quezon's continuing argument regarding neutralization and the United States failure to keep its commitment to the Philippines, see Quezon to Vargas, December 30, 1941, Vargas Scrapbooks, Vol. OP57, VF; and Quezon to MacArthur, January 28, 1942, RG 10, MMBA. The quote is in Quezon to MacArthur, February 7, 1942, Sutherland Papers, NNMM, NA.

107. MacArthur to Marshall, February 8, 1942, in "Quezon File," Army-Operations, OPD Executive Files, 1940–45, NNMM, NA. All of the messages discussed in the following paragraphs may be found in this file.

108. Roosevelt to MacArthur, February 9, 1942, "Quezon File," NNMM, NA.

109. James K. Eyre, Jr., *The Roosevelt-MacArthur Conflict* (Chambersburg, Pa., 1950), 40–41.

110. MacArthur to Roosevelt, February 11, 1942, RG 4, MMBA.

111. Marshall to MacArthur, February 4, 1942, "Quezon File," NNMM, NA. See also Beck, *MacArthur and Wainwright*, 90–91.

112. MacArthur to Chase National Bank, February 15, 1942, Radio No. 285, PSF 64, FDRL; and MacArthur to the Adj. Gen., February 15, 1942, Files of Division of Territories and Island Possessions, "9–7–4 Banking," NNFN, NA.

113. Deane to Brown, February 17, 1942, "9–7–4 Banking," NNFN, NA; "Memo for Record," February 20, 1942, OPD 004.2, NNMO, NA; Radio No. 1063, 2120142 to CG, USAFFE, mentioned in "Memo for Record," February 20, 1942, OPD 004.2, NNMO, NA. Records which seem to corroborate this transfer may also be found in miscellaneous bank statements from 1946 in

"Old Tax Papers," RG 10, MMBA. While this exchange was being processed, MacArthur was given the equivalent in Filipino pesos "in the event that orders issued to the Chase National Bank . . . are not carried out." On February 25, the pesos were returned to Manuel Roxas, at the time in charge of the Philippine Treasury. See receipt attached to Executive Order #1, February 25, 1942, and MacArthur to Quezon, February 27, 1942, Sutherland Papers, NNMM, NA. For a complete explanation of the development of the process by which Philippine funds were disbursed in the U.S., see "Memorandum for the Under Secretary," November 25, 1942, and attached documents, "General Files, 9–7–43, Money Phil. Funds Reports," NNFN, NA.

114. Army Regulations 600–10, Par. 2e (9) (War Department, Washington, D.C., Dec. 6, 1938), NNMO, NA. The best explanation of the implications of this regulation is to be found in *The Officer's Guide* (8th ed., Harrisburg, Pa., 1942), 381–382. See also Articles 95 and 96, "The Articles of War," in *A Manual for Courts-Martial, U.S. Army* (Washington, D.C., 1928), 224; and *The Code of the Laws of the United States of America,* 1934 (Washington, D.C., 1935), 18 U.S.C. 91, and 10 U.S.C. 1565, 1567, 1568. In 1943, a wire sent by MacArthur to AGWAR, seems to suggest that indeed he believed himself justified in accepting the "award" because it "did not . . . include the period of hostilities." MacArthur to AGWAR, May 13, 1943, WD402, Sutherland Papers, NNMM, NA. Of course, this explanation is technically incorrect, since hostilities began in the Philippines on December 8, 1941, while Executive Order #1 covered the period through December 30, 1941.

115. Although no papers have been found for Sidney Huff, I carefully examined the available papers of MacArthur, Quezon, and Richard Marshall after finding Executive Order #1 in the recently opened Sutherland Papers, where Richard Sutherland had either intentionally or negligently left it. A letter of thanks mentioning but not describing this executive order is in Quezon to MacArthur, February 20, 1942, RG 10, MMBA. Otherwise, none of the papers examined revealed further information. Needless to say, the published works of the men involved offered no insight into the exchange. In an effort to determine why this document had not been published with other Philippine executive orders from this period, I visited the Malacanang Library in Manila, repository of Philippine government documents, and was told by the archivist in charge that no executive orders had been issued between December 1941, when Quezon left Manila, and May 1942, when he arrived in Washington. It is true that many of the earlier executive orders issued by the Commonwealth government during the period from 1936 to 1941 were not published and most of the official records had been destroyed during the Japanese occupation. Consequently, it is small wonder that the records pertaining to this order were lost or destroyed and never missed by the postwar Philippine government.

116. James, *Years,* II, 90–91.

117. Steinberg, *Philippine Collaboration,* 4. While I am indebted to Peter Stanley for pointing out the applicability of the concept of *utang na loob* to this situation, the best discussion of this complex value in this context is in Steinberg, *Philippine Collaboration,* 1–17, 101, and passim. See also Mary R. Hollensteiner, "Reciprocity in Lowland Philippines," *Philippine Studies,* IX, 3 (July, 1961), 387–413; and Charles Kaut, "Utang na loob: A System of Contractual Obligations among Tagalogs," *Southwest Journal of Anthropology,* XVII, 3 (1961), 256–272.

118. Steinberg, *Philippine Collaboration,* 28.

119. Dwight David Eisenhower, Papers as President of the United States, 1953–1961 (Whitman File), Personal Diary, entries for January 19, February 3, and February 8, 1942, DDEL.

120. Executive Order No. 3–W, attached to Manuel L. Quezon to Major General Dwight David Eisenhower, June 20, 1942, and Memorandum for Record, June 20, 1942, "Manuel Quezon" folder, Dwight David Eisenhower, Pre-Presidential Papers, 1916–1952, DDEL. Since Eisenhower declined the award, no amount was entered onto the Executive Order. I am indebted to Vicente Pacis for making this set of documents available to me.

121. See Commandant, Sixteenth Naval District to Commander, Motor Torpedo Boat Squadron Three, Fort Mills, PI, March 10, 1942, RG 15, MMBA.

122. MacArthur, *Reminiscences*, 154–155.

Chapter Six: The Return

1. The strategic and tactical developments occurring during the days between MacArthur's departure on March 11, and Wainwright's surrender in May are well beyond the scope of this work and have been detailed thoroughly in many sources. Foremost of these are Morton, *Fall of the Philippines*, 360–584; James, *Years*, II, 3–154; and Beck, *MacArthur and Wainwright*, 171–230.

2. James, *Years*, II, 141–151.

3. Ibid., 109.

4. Again, it is not the object of this work to enter into any detailed overall discussion of World War II in the Pacific. The bibliography for this period is very large and more than adequate. For the purposes of this study, I have relied on Robert Ross Smith, *Triumph in the Philippines* (Washington, 1963), entire; M. Hamlin Cannon, *Leyte: The Return to the Philippines* (Washington, 1954), entire; and, of course, James, *Years*, II, entire.

5. The story of Douglas MacArthur's dramatic appeal to Roosevelt at Pearl Harbor regarding the return to the Philippines has been repeated often, frequently placing more importance on the impact of MacArthur's argument on the ultimate strategic decision than is true. Although the decision to approach Japan through the Philippines was reached early in the debate, the recapture of the entire archipelago was not approved until October 3. For the most complete and accurate account, see Smith, *Triumph in the Philippines*, 3–17. For an interesting suggestion that MacArthur and Roosevelt made "an informal deal" at Pearl Harbor whereby FDR would support MacArthur's position vis-à-vis the Philippines in exchange for reports of battlefield successes in the Pacific which would aid the President's position in the forthcoming election, see James, *Years*, II, 534.

6. James, *Years*, II, 506–511.

7. See, for example, MacArthur to AGWAR, Q4461, 3 November 1943; Sutherland to MacArthur, 356 Twelfth, Phil. Gov't. 1–100; Quezon to MacArthur, 843 Twenty-Third, Phil. Gov't. 1–100; MacArthur to AGWAR, 26 November 43, Phil. Gov't. 1–100; Quezon to MacArthur, War 24762 18th April 1944, all in Sutherland Papers, NNMM, NA; MacArthur to Quezon, January 27, 1944, Quezon Papers, PNL. For policy decisions in regard to the Philippine propaganda and psychological warfare mapped out in 1942, see Michael L. Stiver to General Douglas MacArthur, December 30, 1942, and attachments, WD 314, Sutherland Papers, NNMM, NA.

8. Quezon to MacArthur, March 4, 1943, Sutherland Papers, NNMM, NA.

9. Quezon to MacArthur, "For Confesor," 4368 Nineteenth February 44, Quezon 94, Sutherland Papers, NNMM, NA.

10. MacArthur to Mrs. Quezon, 29 July 1946, RG 26, MMBA.

11. The problem of Philippine collaboration is discussed best in Steinberg, *Philippine Collaboration,* entire; and Friend, *Between Two Empires,* 211–228 and passim. For MacArthur's view on collaboration, see MacArthur, *Reminiscences,* 272–274. See also James, *Years,* II, 91–94, 504–507, and 519–520. For a detailed but somewhat biased view, see Hernando J. Abaya, *Betrayal in the Philippines* (New York, 1946), entire.

12. James, *Years,* II, 515–520 and 581–583.

13. For the most complete discussion of MacArthur's presidential efforts, see Mattern, "The Man on the Dark Horse," entire; and James, *Years,* II, 403–440.

14. MacArthur, *Reminiscences,* 216–217.

15. For detailed studies of this massive undertaking, see Cannon, *Leyte,* entire; Smith, *Triumph in the Philippines,* 73–139; and James, *Years,* II, 521–565.

16. Quoted in James, *Years,* II, 554.

17. For an amusing and explanatory account of this first of many "wading episodes" at Red Beach, see James, *Years,* II, 555.

18. MacArthur, *Reminiscences,* 252–253.

19. James, *Years,* II, 548. The narrative contained in this description of the Philippine liberation is taken from Smith, *Triumph in the Philippines,* 73–357; and James, *Years,* II, 521–669.

20. Smith, *Triumph in the Philippines,* 249.

21. James, *Years,* II, 636. See also Smith, *Triumph in the Philippines,* 240–244.

22. James, *Years,* II, 644; and Smith, *Triumph in the Philippines,* 306–307.

23. MacArthur to Mrs. Douglas MacArthur, 18 February 1945, RG 26, Folder #7, MMBA. This message, in radio language, has been edited for clarity.

24. James, *Years,* II, 590; and Manchester, *American Caesar,* 398–399.

25. Friend, *Between Two Empires,* 266.

26. For accounts of this emotional speech, see James, *Years,* II, 646–648; Steinberg, *Philippine Collaboration,* 114; and MacArthur, *Reminiscences,* 290–291.

27. Steinberg, *Philippine Collaboration,* 106.

28. Ibid., 108.

29. James, *Years,* I, 345.

30. Steinberg, *Philippine Collaboration,* 40–42.

31. Ibid., 73–75, 107.

32. For examples of the Quezon-MacArthur correspondence regarding Roxas, see MacArthur to Wainwright, April 18, 1942, AG 347; Wainwright to CG USAFFE, 249 Nineteenth TOR 125 OP; Wainwright to CG USAFFE, 241 Eighteenth; MacArthur to Quezon, 4/14/43, Phil. Gov't. File 1–100; MacArthur to AGWAR, 8 March 1944; MacArthur to AGWAR, 14 April 1944; and MacArthur to AGWAR, 1 August 44; all in Sutherland Papers, NNMM, NA.

33. Quezon to MacArthur, March 4, 1943, Sutherland Papers, NNMM, NA.

34. *Victory News,* April 18, 1945, 1, quoted in Steinberg, *Philippine Collaboration,* 115. For the eyewitness account of the details of Roxas's capture and subsequent release, see Dale Pontius, "MacArthur and the Filipinos," *Asia and the Americas,* XLVI (1946), 436–440, 509–512. Roxas's promotion to brigadier general in the U.S. Army occurred during the war.

35. MacArthur, *Reminiscences*, 273–274.

36. MacArthur to Hilldring, 2 September 1944, WD 821, Sutherland Papers, NNMM, NA.

37. Memorandum to General Watson from John J. McCloy, 28 September 1944, Sutherland Papers, NNMM, NA. Attachments to this document refer to the conflict with Ickes and assert that the War Department's position was opposed to that of the Department of Interior. A handwritten note on the McCloy memorandum indicates that Roosevelt agreed with Stimson.

38. MacArthur to AGWAR, 7 February 1945, WD 925, Sutherland Papers, NNMM, NA.

39. For discussions of how the acceptance of the Bell Trade Act of 1946 complicated the early national period in the Philippines, see George E. Taylor, *The Philippines and the United States: Problems of Partnership* (New York, 1964), 114–232; and Steven R. Shalom, "Philippine Acceptance of the Bell Trade Act of 1946: A Study of Manipulatory Democracy," *Pacific Historical Review*, XLIX (Aug., 1980), 499–517.

40. For a discussion of Hukbalahap input into the postwar political situation, see Shalom, "Philippine Acceptance"; and James, *Years*, II, 507.

41. In 1946, MacArthur's old nemesis, Drew Pearson, related these rumors in his "Washington Merry-Go-Round" column of March 8; MacArthur's response appeared in the April 3, 1946, issue of the *Manila Times*, 5. I am indebted to Professor Steven R. Shalom for calling this statement to my attention. Despite extensive efforts, neither D. Clayton James nor I have been able to prove or disprove the assertions concerning MacArthur's Philippine holdings. See James, *Years*, II, 892, n. 13.

42. George C. Kenney, *General Kenney Reports: A Personal History of the Pacific War* (New York, 1949), 533–534, quoted in Manchester, *American Caesar*, 435.

43. James, *Years*, II, 724.

44. For the complete directive appointing MacArthur supreme commander, see James, *Years*, II, 776–777.

45. Diary of Harold Ickes (microfilm edition, reel #7), entry dated August 26, 1945, 9949, LC.

46. MacArthur's statement to Robert Sherwood, quoted in James, *Years*, II, 783–784. Friend, *Between Two Empires*, 253, emphasizes the irony of MacArthur's liberal position in Japan when he points out that "thus the initial American years in conquered Japan conferred more benefits than did the final stages of the American presence in the Philippines."

47. It is interesting to note that although MacArthur maintained a warm correspondence with Manuel Roxas until his death in April 1948, the General showed a real reluctance to return for the Independence Day celebrations. Finally agreeing to make the trip, he left almost immediately after the ceremony to return to his duties in Japan. See MacArthur to Roxas, 30 April, 1946, RG 26, MMBA; as well as miscellaneous exchanges from this period in the Roxas Papers, PNL.

48. Friend, *Between Two Empires*, 261–262.

Epilogue

1. MacArthur, *Reminiscences*, 476. For an interesting explanation of Kennedy's decision to send MacArthur to the Philippines in 1961, see the transcript of interview with Clyde D. Eddleman, Interview #4, 48, Oral History Collection, USAMHI.

2. Information regarding the 1961 visit to the Philippines may be found in clippings from several Manila newspapers in "Scrapbook of 1961 Trip," RG 24, MMBA.

3. " 'I have Returned'—General MacArthur," in *The Manila Chronicle,* July 4, 1961, 30, in "Scrapbook of 1961 Trip," RG 24, MMBA.

4. Teodoro F. Valencia, "Over a Cup of Coffee," in *Manila Times,* June 28, 1961, in "Scrapbook of 1961 Trip," RG 24, MMBA.

5. Ignacio P. Lacsina, "MacArthur Viewed In Different Light," *The Forum,* uncaptioned clipping in "Scrapbook of 1961 Trip," RG 24, MMBA.

6. Stephen B. Oates, "The Academy of Saints Rejects the Lincoln Application," in *The New York Times,* February 12, 1977, 21.

Bibliography

Primary Sources

Archives

Dwight David Eisenhower Library, Abilene, Kansas.

Library of Congress, Washington, D.C.
   Papers of: Tasker H. Bliss, James G. Harbord, Harold I. Ickes, George Van Horn Moseley, John Callan O'Laughlin, John J. Pershing, Francis B. Sayre, Leonard Wood.
   MS Diaries of: Harold I. Ickes and Leonard Wood.

MacArthur Memorial Bureau of Archives, Norfolk, Virginia.
   RG 1: Records of the United States Military Adviser to the Philippine Commonwealth, 1935–1941.
   RG 2: Records of Headquarters, United States Army Forces in the Far East (USAFFE), 1941–1942.
   RG 3: Records of General Headquarters, Southwest Pacific Area (SWPA), 1942–1945.
   RG 4: Records of General Headquarters, United States Army Forces, Pacific (USAFPAC), 1942–1945.
   RG 10: General of the Army Douglas MacArthur's Private Correspondence, 1932–1964.
   RG 15: Documents Donated by the General Public.
   RG 17: Records of the Department of the Philippines, 1934–1935.
   RG 18: Records of the Chief of Staff, United States Army, 1929.
   RG 20: Records of General Arthur MacArthur, 1880–1912.
   RG 24: MacArthur Scrapbooks.

National Archives, Washington, D.C.
   Navy and Old Army Branch
      RG 94: Office of the Adjutant General Central Files 1926–39.
      RG 107: SecWar Classified File, Puerto Rico and Philippine Islands.
      RG 165: War Dept. General and Special Staff.
      RG 225: Joint Board Files.
      RG 395: Records of U.S. Army Overseas Operations and Commands, 1898–1942.

RG 407: Office of the Adjutant General Central Decimal Files, Project Files 1917–1925.
Modern Military Branch
  RG 59: General Records of the Department of State.
  RG 200: Papers of Richard K. Sutherland.
  RG 218: U.S. Joint Chiefs of Staff.
  RG 319: Army-Operations, OPD Executive Files, 1940–1945.
Natural Resources Branch
  RG 126: Office of Territories, including the Former Division of Territories and Island Possessions.
  RG 350: Records of the Bureau of Insular Affairs.
General Archives Branch, Suitland, Maryland
  RG 332: Headquarters, USAF, Far East/USAF Philippines.
New Mexico State University Library, Las Cruces, New Mexico.
  Collection of General Hugh Milton, Tapes of MacArthur Birthday Parties, 1950–1960.
Office of the Chief of Military History, United States Army, Washington, D.C.
  General Historical Files.
Philippine National Library, Manila, P.I.
  Papers of: Sergio Osmeña, Manuel L. Quezon, Manuel Roxas
Franklin D. Roosevelt Library, Hyde Park, N.Y.
  Papers of: Wayne Coy, Stephen T. Early, Harry L. Hopkins, Henry M. Morgenthau, Jr., Franklin D. Roosevelt, particularly the Official File (OF), President's Personal File (PPF), President's Secretary's File (PSF), and the War Department Confidential File (CF).
  Records of the National Committee of the Democratic Party, 1928–1948.
United States Army Military History Institute, Carlisle Barracks, Pa.
  Oral History Transcripts of: Edward M. Almond, William H. Arnold, Donald V. Bennett, Lucius Clay, Mark Clark, James F. Collins, Michael S. Davison, George H. Decker, Clyde D. Eddleman, Paul L. Freeman, Andrew Goodpaster, Barksdale Hamlett, Kenneth J. Hodson, William M. Hoge, Hamilton Howze, John E. Hull, Hugh M. Milton, Frank Pace, Jr., Matthew B. Ridgeway, Arthur G. Trudeau, Robert J. Wood.
  Papers of: Edward M. Almond, Lorenzo Alvarado, Lewis C. Beebe, Charles L. Bolte, Perry L. Boyer, William H. Braddock, William C. Braly, William Carey Brown, William E. Carraway, Stephen J. Chamberlain, Marion Patton Echols, John P. Finley, Charles Gerhardt, Johnson Hagood, Halstead-Maus Family, Guy V. Henry, Jr., Edward L. Hooper, Richard Johnson, Charles S. Lawrence, Joseph Marmon, Richard J. Marshall, Frank Parker, William & Grace Paulding, Clinton A. Pierce, Sladen Family, Charles P. Summerall, Charles A. Willoughby.
  Special Collections: Army War College Files, The William and James Belote Collection on Corregidor, The Louis Morton Collection, The Santo Tomas Prison Camp Papers, The Spanish-American War Survey, The Mark M. Wohlfeld Collection on Bataan and Corregidor.
United States Military Academy, Archives and Special Collections, West Point, N.Y.
  Historical File: Correspondence.
  Douglas MacArthur File, 1942.
  Records of the United States Military Academy.
University of Texas at Austin, Humanities Research Center.

University of the Philippines, Quezon City, P.I.
  Papers of Carlos P. Romulo.
Vargas Foundation, Manila, P.I.
  Papers, scrapbooks, diary, and interview transcript of Jorge B. Vargas.
Yale University Library, New Haven, Conn.
  Diary of Henry Lewis Stimson, microfilm edition.

Oral Interviews

Bolas, A. Personal interview, Manila, P.I., January 1978.

Hester, Evett. Personal interview, Manila, P.I., January 1978.

Parsons, Mr. & Mrs. Charles E. Personal interview, Manila, P.I., February 1978.

Romulo, General Carolos P. Personal interview, Manila, P.I., February 1978.

Sotelo, Mercedes. Personal interviews, Quezon City, P.I., January and February 1978.

Personal Correspondence

Cooper, Allen. One letter, March 4, 1978, to the author.

Public Documents and Government Publications

Annual Report of the Governor General, Philippine Islands, 1905–1935. Washington, D.C.

Annual Report of the United States High Commissioner to the Philippine Islands to the President and Congress of the United States, 1935–1942. Washington, D.C.

The Code of the Laws of the United States of America, 1934.

Correspondence Relating to the War With Spain. Washington, D.C., 1902.

A Manual for Courts-Martial, U.S. Army. Washington, D.C., 1928.

MacArthur, Douglas. *Report on National Defense in the Philippines.* Manila, 1936.

U.S. Congress, Senate Committee on the Philippines. *Hearings Before the Committee on the Philippines of the U.S. Senate, Affairs in the Philippine Islands.* 57th Congress, 1st Session, Doc. #331, 1902.

U.S. *Statutes at Large.* Vols. XLIV and XLIX.

Secondary Sources

Articles in Periodicals

Bertoff, Rowland Tappan. "Taft and MacArthur, 1900: A Study in Civil-Military Relations," *World Politics,* 5 (1953), 166–213.

Cain, A. C., Fast, I., and Erickson, M. E. "Children's Disturbed Reactions to the Death of a Sibling," *American Journal of Orthopsychiatry,* 34 (1964), 741–752.

Coffman, Edward M. "Army Life on the Frontier, 1865–1898," *Military Affairs,* 20 (Winter, 1956), 196–197.

——. "Batson of the Philippine Scouts," *Parameters,* Vol. VII, No. 3 (1977), 68–72.

Dunn, Arthur Wallace. "Government in the Philippines, 1898–1902: A Review of the Successive Steps in the Evolution from Military to Civil Administration," *American Monthly Review of Reviews*, Vol. 26 (November, 1902), 594–597.

Flanner, Janet. "General and Mrs. Douglas MacArthur," *Ladies Home Journal*, (June, 1942).

Gleeck, Lewis E., Jr. "American Club Life in Old Manila," *Bulletin of American Historical Collection*, Vol. III, No. 4 (October, 1975).

Hollensteiner, Mary R. "Reciprocity in Lowland Philippines," *Philippine Studies*, Vol IX, No. 3 (July, 1961), 387–413.

Kaut, Charles. "Utang na loob: A System of Contractual Obligations Among Tagalogs," *Southwest Journal of Anthropology*, Vol. XVII, No. 3 (1961), 256–272.

Killigrew, John W. "The Army and the Bonus Incident," *Military Affairs*, XXV (Summer, 1962), 55–62.

Lasch, Christopher. "Anti-Imperialists, the Philippines, and the Inequality of Man," *Journal of Southern History*, 24 (August, 1958), 319–331.

Lisio, Donald J. "A Blunder Becomes Catastrophe: Hoover, the Legion, and the Bonus Army," *Wisconsin Magazine of History*, 51 (Autumn, 1967), 37–50.

Mann, Cutter. "Some Ancestral Lines of General Douglas MacArthur," *The New York Genealogical and Biographical Record*, LXXIII (July, 1942), 167–172.

Minger, Ralph Eldin. "Taft, MacArthur, and the Establishment of Civil Government in the Philippines," *The Ohio Historical Quarterly*, Vol. 70 (October, 1961), 308–331.

Mitchell, Major C. A. "The Philippine Department," *Infantry Journal*, Vol. XXX, No. 4 (April, 1927), 341–346.

Moore, Robert L. "Justification Without Joy: Psychohistorical Reflections on John Wesley's Childhood and Conversion," *History of Childhood Quarterly: The Journal of Psychohistory*, II, nr. 1 (Summer, 1974), 31–52.

Morton, Louis. "The Bibliography of a Defeat: The Search for Records on the Loss of the Philippines," *The American Archivist*, (July, 1953), 195–212.

Onorato, Michael. "Leonard Wood and the Philippine Crisis of 1923," *Journal of East Asiatic Studies*, Vol. 2 (March, 1967), 1–74.

Petillo, Carol M. "Douglas MacArthur and Manuel Quezon: A Note on an Imperial Bond," *Pacific Historical Review*, XLVIII, No. 1 (February, 1979), 107–117.

Pollock, George H. "Childhood Parent and Sibling Loss in Adult Patients," *Archives General Psychiatry*, 7 (1962), 295–305.

——. "On Mourning, Immortality, and Utopia," *Journal of American Psychoanalytic Association*, Vol. 23(2) (1975), 334–362.

Pontius, Dale. "MacArthur and the Filipinos," *Asia and the Americas*, (October and November, 1946), 436–440 and 509–512.

Schumacher, John N. "Recent Historical Writing on the Philippines Abroad," *Philippine Studies*, Vol. 9, No. 1 (January, 1961), 97–127, and Vol. 11, No. 4 (October, 1963), 557–572.

Shalom, Steven R. "Philippine Acceptance of the Bell Trade Act of 1946: A Study of Manipulatory Democracy," *Pacific Historical Review*, Vol. XLIX, No. 3 (August, 1980), 499–517.

Sherrill, Robert G. "Thirty-Six Years on the Merry-Go-Round—Drew Pearson on War, Love, Graft, Politics, Revolution and the Hiding Places of Power," *The Nation,* (July 7, 1969).

Taft, Charles P. "Charlie-Baby Taft in the Philippines, 1900–1903," *Bulletin of American Historical Collection,* Vol. II, No. 3 (July, 1974).

Bibliographies

Hellman, Florence S. *General Douglas MacArthur: A List of References.* Washington, D.C.: Library of Congress, 1942.

Higham, Robin (ed.). *Guide to the Sources of U.S. Military History.* Hamden, Conn.: Archon Books, 1975.

Munden, Kenneth (comp.). *Records of the Bureau of Insular Affairs Relating to the Philippine Islands, 1898–1935: A List of Selected Files.* Washington, D.C.: The National Archives, 1942.

Onorato, Michael P. (ed.). *Philippine Bibliography (1899–1946).* Santa Barbara, CA: ABC Clio, 1968.

Books

Abaya, Hernando J. *Betrayal in the Philippines.* New York: A. A. Wyn, 1946.

Adams, Brooks. *The Law of Civilization and Decay: An Essay on History.* New York: Macmillan & Co., 1895.

Adams, Henry. *The Education of Henry Adams.* Boston: Houghton Mifflin Co., 1918 and 1946.

Agoncillo, Teodoro A., and Guerrero, Milagros C. *History of the Filipino People.* 5th ed. Quezon City, PI: R.P. Garcia Publishing Co., 1977.

Baclagon, Uldarico S. *Military History of the Philippines.* 2nd ed., revised. Manila, PI: St. Mary's Publishing Co., 1975.

———. *Philippine Campaigns.* Manila, PI: Graphic House, 1952.

Beck, John Jacob. *MacArthur and Wainwright; Sacrifice of the Philippines.* Albuquerque, NM: University of New Mexico Press, 1974.

Bernstein, David. *The Philippine Story.* New York: Farrar, Straus & Co., 1947.

Borg, Dorothy. *The United States and the Far Eastern Crisis of 1933–1938.* Cambridge: Harvard University Press, 1964.

Cannon, M. Hamlin. *Leyte: The Return to the Philippines.* Washington, D.C.: Office of the Chief of Military History, 1954.

Cline, Ray S. *Washington Command Post: The Operations Division.* Washington, D.C.: Office of the Chief of Military History, 1951.

Coffman, Edward M. *The Hilt of the Sword: The Career of Peyton C. March.* Madison: University of Wisconsin Press, 1966.

———. *The War to End All Wars.* New York: Oxford University Press, 1968.

Coles, Robert. *Erik H. Erikson: The Growth of His Work.* Boston: Little, Brown & Co., 1970.

Considine, Robert B. *It's All News to Me: A Reporter's Deposition.* New York: Meredith Press, 1967.

———. *MacArthur the Magnificent.* London: Hutchinson Co., 1942.

Cosmas, Graham A. *An Army for Empire: The United States Army in the Spanish-American War.* Columbia, MO: University of Missouri Press, 1971.

Cullum, George W. *Biographical Register of the Officers and Graduates of the United States Military Academy.* Boston: Houghton, Mifflin & Co., 1891, and supplements to date.

Dauncey, Mrs. Campbell. *An Englishwoman in the Philippines.* New York: E. P. Dutton & Co., 1906.

de la Costa, H., S. J. *Readings in Philippine History.* Manila-Cebu-Makati, PI: Bookmark Publishers, 1965.

deMause, Lloyd (ed.). *The History of Childhood.* New York: Harper & Row, Publishers, 1974.

de Trobriand, Philippe Régis. *Military Life in Dakota: The Journal of Philippe Régis de Trobriand.* Translated and edited by Lucile M. Kane. St. Paul, Minn.: Alvord Memorial Commission, 1951.

Eisenhower, Dwight David. *At Ease: Stories I Tell to Friends.* Garden City, NY: Doubleday & Co., 1967.

Elliott, Charles B. *The Philippines to the End of the Military Regime.* Indianapolis, Ind.: The Bobbs-Merrill Company, 1916.

Erikson, Erik H. *Childhood and Society.* 2nd ed., revised and enlarged. New York: W. W. Norton & Co., 1963.

——. *Dimensions of a New Identity: The 1973 Jefferson Lectures in the Humanities.* New York: W. W. Norton & Co., 1974.

——. *Gandhi's Truth: On the Origins of Militant Nonviolence.* New York: W. W. Norton & Co., 1969.

——. *Identity: Youth and Crisis.* New York: W. W. Norton & Co., 1968.

——. *Insight and Responsibility.* New York: W. W. Norton & Co., 1964.

——. *Young Man Luther, A Study in Psychoanalysis and History.* New York: W. W. Norton & Co., 1968.

Eyre, James K. Jr. *The Roosevelt-MacArthur Conflict.* Chambersburg, PA: The Craft Press, 1950.

Fee, Mary H. *A Woman's Impressions of the Philippines.* Chicago: A. C. McClurg & Co., 1910.

Fernandez, Alejandro M. *The Philippines and the United States: The Forging of New Relations.* Quezon City: NSDF-UP Integrated Research Program, 1977.

Fodor, Nandor, and Gaynor, Frank (eds.). *Freud: Dictionary of Psychoanalysis.* Greenwich, Conn.: Fawcett Publications, Inc., 1958.

Forbes, W. Cameron. *The Philippine Islands.* Two volumes. Boston: Houghton, Mifflin Co., 1928.

Fredricks, Edgar J. *MacArthur: His Mission and Meaning.* Philadelphia: Whitmore Publishing Co., 1968.

Freud, Sigmund. *An Outline of Psycho-Analysis.* Edited and translated by James Strachey. New York: W. W. Norton & Co., 1949.

Friend, Theodore. *Between Two Empires: The Ordeal of the Philippines 1929–1946.* New Haven: Yale University Press, 1965.

Funston, Frederick. *Memories of Two Wars: Cuban and Philippine Experiences.* New York: C. Scribner's Sons, 1911.

Ganoe, William A. *History of the United States Army.* New York: Appleton-Century, 1936.

Gates, John Morgan. *Schoolbooks and Krags: The United States Army in the Philippines, 1898–1902.* Westport, Conn.: The Greenwood Press, Inc., 1973.

George, Alexander L., and George, Juliette L. *Woodrow Wilson and Colonel House: A Personality Study.* New York: Dover Publications, Inc., 1956.

Gleeck, Lewis E., Jr. *The Manila Americans (1901–1964).* Manila, PI: Carmelo & Bauermann, Inc., 1977.

Grunder, Garel A., and Livezey, William E. *The Philippines and the United States.* Norman, Okla.: Oklahoma University Press, 1951.

Gunther, John. *The Riddle of MacArthur: Japan, Korea and the Far East.* New York: Harper & Brothers, 1951.

Hagedorn, Herman. *Leonard Wood.* Two volumes. New York: Harper & Brothers, 1931.

Hall, Calvin S. *A Primer of Freudian Psychology.* New York: New American Library, 1954.

Hayden, Joseph R. *The Philippines: A Study in National Development.* New York: The Macmillan Co., 1942.

Hersey, John. *Men on Bataan.* New York: Alfred Knopf, 1943.

Higgins, Trumbull. *Korea and the Fall of MacArthur: A Precis in Limited War.* New York: Oxford University Press, 1960.

Huff, Sidney, and Morris, Joe Alex. *My Fifteen Years with General MacArthur.* New York: Curtis Publishing Co., 1951.

Hunt, Frazier. *MacArthur and the War Against Japan.* New York: Charles Scribner's Sons, 1944.

——. *The Untold Story of Douglas MacArthur.* New York: Devin-Adair Co., 1954.

Hyam, Ronald. *Britain's Imperial Century, 1815–1914: A Study of Empire and Expansion.* London: B. T. Batsford, 1976.

Ickes, Harold L. *The Autobiography of a Curmudgeon.* New York: Reynal & Hitchcock, 1943.

——. *The Secret Diary of Harold L. Ickes.* Three volumes. New York: Simon & Schuster, 1953–54.

Ind, Allison. *Bataan, The Judgment Seat.* New York: Macmillan Co., 1944.

James, D. Clayton. *The Years of MacArthur.* Two volumes. Boston: Houghton-Mifflin Co., 1970–1975.

Jones, Ernest. *The Life and Work of Sigmund Freud.* Edited and abridged by Lionel Trilling and Steven Marcus. New York: Basic Books, Inc., 1961.

Kelley, Frank & Ryan, Cornelius. *MacArthur, Man of Action.* Garden City, New York: Doubleday, Doran, 1950.

Kelly, George A. *A Theory of Personality: The Psychology of Personal Constructs.* New York: W. W. Norton & Co., Inc., 1963.

Kett, Joseph F. *Rites of Passage: Adolescence in America 1790 to the Present.* New York: Basic Books, Inc., 1977.

Kirk, Grayson. *Philippine Independence.* New York: Farrar, 1936.

Kluckhohn, Clyde, and Murray, Henry A., with Schneider, David M. *Personality in Nature, Society, and Culture.* 2nd edition, revised and enlarged. New York: Alfred A. Knopf, 1971.

Kren, George M., and Rappoport, Leon H. (eds.). *Varieties of Psychohistory.* New York: Springer Publishing Co., 1976.

La Feber, Walter. *The New Empire: An Interpretation of American Expansion, 1860–1898.* Ithaca: Cornell University Press, 1963.

Lane, Jack C. *Armed Progressive: General Leonard Wood.* San Rafael and London: Presidio Press, 1978.

Larkin, John A. *The Pampangans: Colonial Society in a Philippine Province.* Berkeley, CA: University of California Press, 1972.

Lauzun, Gerard. *Sigmund Freud: The Man and His Theories.* Greenwich, Conn.: Fawcett Publications, Inc. 1962.

Lebeaux, Richard. *Young Man Thoreau.* Amherst, Mass.: University of Massachusetts Press, 1977.

Lee, Clark, and Henschel, Richard. *Douglas MacArthur.* New York: Henry Holt and Co., 1952.

LeRoy, James A. *The Americans in the Philippines: A History of the Conquest and the First Years of Occupation, With an Introductory Account of the Spanish Rule.* Two volumes. Boston: Houghton, Mifflin Co., 1914.

Lifton, Robert Jay, and Olson, Eric (eds.). *Exploration in Psychohistory: The Wellfleet Papers.* New York: Simon & Schuster, 1974.

——. *Living and Dying.* New York: Praeger Publishing Co., 1974.

Long, Gavin. *MacArthur As Military Commander.* London: Batsford, 1969.

MacArthur, Douglas. *Reminiscences.* New York: Fawcett World Library and Time, Inc., 1965.

——. *A Soldier Speaks: Public Papers and Speeches of Douglas MacArthur.* New York: Praeger Publishing Co., 1965.

McLane, Charles B. *Soviet Strategies in Southeast Asia: An Exploration of Eastern Policy under Lenin and Stalin.* Princeton: Princeton University Press, 1966.

Maier, Henry W. *Three Theories of Child Development.* New York: Harper & Row, Publishers, 1965.

Magnus, Philip. *Kitchener: Portrait of an Imperialist.* New York: E. P. Dutton & Co., Inc., 1959.

Malcolm, George A. *American Colonial Careerist: Half a Century of Official Life: Personal Experience in the Philippines and Puerto Rico.* Boston: Christopher Publishing House, 1957.

Manchester, William. *American Caesar, Douglas MacArthur 1880–1964.* Boston: Little, Brown & Co., 1978.

Manuel, Frank E. *A Portrait of Isaac Newton.* Cambridge: Belknap Press of Harvard University Press, 1968.

Marquardt, Frederic S. *Before Bataan and After.* New York: Bobbs-Merrill Co., 1943.

Maslow, Abraham H. *The Farther Reaches of Human Nature.* New York: The Viking Press, 1971.

——. *Toward a Psychology of Being.* 2nd edition. New York: Van Nostrand Reinhold Co., 1968.

Mazlish, Bruce (ed.). *Psychoanalysis and History.* New York: Grosset & Dunlap, 1963.

Meyer, Milton Walter. *A Diplomatic History of the Philippines.* Honolulu: University of Hawaii Press, 1965.

Miller, Francis Trevelyan. *General Douglas MacArthur, Fighter for Freedom.* Philadelphia: Winston, 1942.

Millis, Walter. *The Martial Spirit: A Study of Our War With Spain.* Boston: Houghton-Mifflin Co., 1931.

Minger, Ralph Eldin. *William Howard Taft and United States Foreign Policy: The Apprenticeship Years.* Chicago: The University of Illinois Press, 1975.

Morison, Elting E., and Blum, John M. *The Letters of Theodore Roosevelt.* Eight volumes. Cambridge: Harvard University Press, 1951–1954.

Morton, Louis. *The Fall of the Philippines.* Washington, D.C.: Office of the Chief of Military History, 1953.

———. *Strategy and Command: The First Two Years.* Washington, D.C.: Office of the Chief of Military History, 1962.

The Officer's Guide. 8th edition. Harrisburg, PA: The Military Service Publishing Co., 1942.

Onorato, Michael P. (ed. and annotator). *Origins of the Philippine Republic: Extracts from the Diaries and Records of Francis Burton Harrison.* Ithaca: Cornell University Dept. of Asian Studies, 1974.

Pacis, Vicente Albano. *President Sergio Osmeña, A Fully-Documented Biography.* Two volumes: Manila, PI: Philippine Constitution Association; Araneta University Research Foundation; President Sergio Osmeña Memorial Foundation, 1971.

Panikkar, K. M. *Asia and Western Dominance.* New York: Macmillan Co., 1969.

Pervin, Lawrence. *Personality: Theory, Assessment, and Research.* 2nd edition. New York: John Wiley & Sons, Inc., 1975.

Pilat, Oliver. *Drew Pearson: An Unauthorized Biography.* New York: Harper & Row (Harper's Magazine Press), 1973.

Pratt, Julius. *America's Colonial Experiment.* New York: Prentice-Hall, 1950.

Pringle, Henry F. *The Life and Times of William Howard Taft.* Two volumes. New York: Farrar & Rinehart, Inc., 1939.

Quezon, Manuel L. *The Good Fight.* New York: D. Appleton Century Co., 1946.

Retizos, Isidro L., and Soriano, D. H. *Philippines Who's Who.* Quezon City, PI: Capital Publishing, 1957.

Roe, Francis M. A. *Army Letters from an Officer's Wife (1871–1888).* New York: D. Appleton & Co., 1909.

Romulo, Carlos P. *I Saw the Fall of the Philippines.* New York: Doubleday and Co., Inc., 1942.

Ross, Dorothy. *G. Stanley Hall: The Psychologist as Prophet.* Chicago: The University of Chicago Press, 1972.

Rovere, Richard H., and Schlesinger, Arthur M. *The General and the President and the Future of American Foreign Policy.* New York: Farrar, Straus & Young, 1951.

Ruitenbeek, Hendrik M. (ed.). *Varieties of Personality Theory.* New York: E. P. Dutton & Co., Inc., 1964.

Sayre, Francis Bowes. *Glad Adventure.* New York: Macmillan Co., 1957.

Sexton, William T. *Soldiers in the Sun.* Harrisburg, PA: Military Service Publishing Co., 1939.

Sherwood, Robert E. *Roosevelt and Hopkins: An Intimate History.* New York: Harper & Row, Publishers, 1950.

Smith, Robert Ross. *Triumph in the Philippines.* Washington, D.C.: Office of the Chief of Military History, 1963.

Spanier, John W. *The Truman-MacArthur Controversy and the Korean War.* New York: W. W. Norton & Co., Inc., 1965.

Steinberg, David Joel (ed.). *In Search of Southeast Asia.* New York: Praeger Publishers, 1971.

——. *Philippine Collaboration in World War II.* Ann Arbor: University of Michigan Press, 1967.

Stimson, Henry L., and Bundy, McGeorge. *On Active Service in Peace and War.* New York: Harper and Bros., 1947.

Sturtevant, David R. *Popular Uprisings in the Philippines, 1840–1940.* Ithaca: Cornell University Press, 1976.

Taft, Mrs. William Howard. *Recollections of Full Years.* New York: Dodd, Mead & Co., 1914.

Taylor, George E. *The Philippines and the United States: Problems of Partnership.* New York: Frederick A. Praeger, 1964.

Thomas, David Yancey. *A History of Military Government in Newly Acquired Territory of the United States.* New York: Columbia University Press, 1904.

Thorne, Christopher. *Allies of a Kind: The United States, Britain, and the War Against Japan, 1941–1945.* Oxford, New York, Toronto, Melbourne: Oxford University Press, 1978.

Toland, John. *But Not in Shame.* New York: Random House, 1961.

Tugwell, Rexford G. *The Democratic Roosevelt.* Garden City, NY: Doubleday and Co., Inc., 1957.

Vaillant, George E. *Adaptation to Life.* Boston: Little, Brown & Co., Inc., 1977.

Van Alstyne, Richard W. *The United States and East Asia.* New York: W. W. Norton & Co., Inc., 1973.

Vandiver, Frank E. *Black Jack: The Life and Times of John J. Pershing.* Two volumes. College Station, TX: Texas A&M University Press, 1977.

Vevier, Charles. *The United States and China 1906–1913.* New York: Greenwood Press, 1968.

Wainwright, Jonathan. *General Wainwright's Story.* New York: Doubleday & Co., 1946.

Waldrop, Frank C. (ed.). *MacArthur on War.* New York: Duell, Sloan and Pearce, 1942.

Weigley, Russell F. *History of the United States Army.* New York: The Macmillan Company, 1967.

Weissblatt, Franz J. (ed.). *Who's Who in the Philippines.* Manila, PI: McCullough Printing Co., 1937.

White, Robert W. *Lives in Progress: a Study of the Natural Growth of Personality.* New York: The Dryden Press, 1952.

White, William Allen. *The Autobiography of William Allen White.* New York: The Macmillan Company, 1946.

Whitney, Courtney. *MacArthur: His Rendezvous in History.* New York: Knopf, 1955.

Williams, William Appleman. *The Roots of the Modern American Empire.* New York: Random House, 1969.

Bibliography

Willoughby, Charles A., and Chamberlain, John. *MacArthur, 1941–1951.* New York: McGraw-Hill, 1954.

Witmer, Helen L., and Kotinsky, Ruth. *New Perspective for Research.* Washington, D.C.: Dept. of Health, Education and Welfare, 1956.

Wittner, Lawrence S. (ed.). *MacArthur.* Englewood Cliffs, NJ: Prentice-Hall, Inc., 1971.

Wolff, Leon. *Little Brown Brother: How the Americans Conquered the Philippines in 1898–1902.* Makati, PI: Erewhon Press, 1960.

Worcester, Dean C. *The Philippines Past and Present.* Two volumes. New York: The Macmillan Company, 1914.

Newspapers and Journals:

Army & Navy Journal, 1924; *Manila American,* 1903–1904; *Manila Cablenews,* 1903–1904; *Manila Evening News,* 1964; *The New York Times,* 1922, 1929; *The Philippine-American Advocate,* 1937–1938; *The Philippine-American News Digest,* 1940; *The Philippine Bulletin,* 1976; *Philippine Commonwealth,* 1934–1936; *Philippine Forum,* 1935–1937; *Philippine Free Press,* 1964; *The Philippine Magazine,* 1939–1940; *The Philippine Messenger,* 1935–1936; *Philippines,* 1940–1941; *Philippines Enterprise,* 1934–1936; *The Washington Post,* 1964; *The Washington Star,* 1964.

Unpublished Material

Brown, Richard Carl. "Social Attitudes of American Generals 1898–1940." Doctoral dissertation, University of Wisconsin, 1951.

Carpenter, Suzanne Gronemeyer. "Toward the Development of Philippine National Security Capability, 1920–1940: With Special Reference to the Commonwealth Period, 1935–1940." Doctoral dissertation, New York University, 1976.

Killigrew, John W. "The Impact of the Great Depression on the Army, 1929–1936." Doctoral dissertation, Indiana University, 1960.

Mattern, Carolyn Jane. "The Man on the Dark Horse: The Presidential Campaigns for General Douglas MacArthur, 1944 and 1948." Doctoral dissertation, University of Wisconsin-Madison, 1976.

Robb, Stephen. "Fifty Years of Farewell: Douglas MacArthur's Commemorative and Deliberative Speaking." Doctoral dissertation, Indiana University, 1967.

Woolard, James Richard. "The Philippine Scouts: The Development of America's Colonial Army." Doctoral dissertation, Ohio State University, 1975.

Index